行经千折水

SAILING THROUGH
THOUSANDS OF
TWISTS AND TURNS

文化遗产系列
Cultural Heritage Series

中国大运河博物馆◎编
Compiled by the
China Grand Canal Museum

丝绸之路上的
麦积奇观

Maiji Miraculous
Heritage along the Silk Road

上海书画出版社

行经千折水

丝绸之路上的麦积奇观

MAIJI MIRACULOUS HERITAGE ALONG THE SILK ROAD
SAILING THROUGH THOUSANDS OF TWISTS AND TURNS

2024
12.12
—
2025
03.16

文化遗产系列

主办单位
中国大运河博物馆
麦积山石窟艺术研究所

中国大运河博物馆
CHINA GRAND CANAL MUSEUM

麦积山石窟 | Maijishan Grottoes

展览地址
中国大运河博物馆
5号厅

目录
Contents

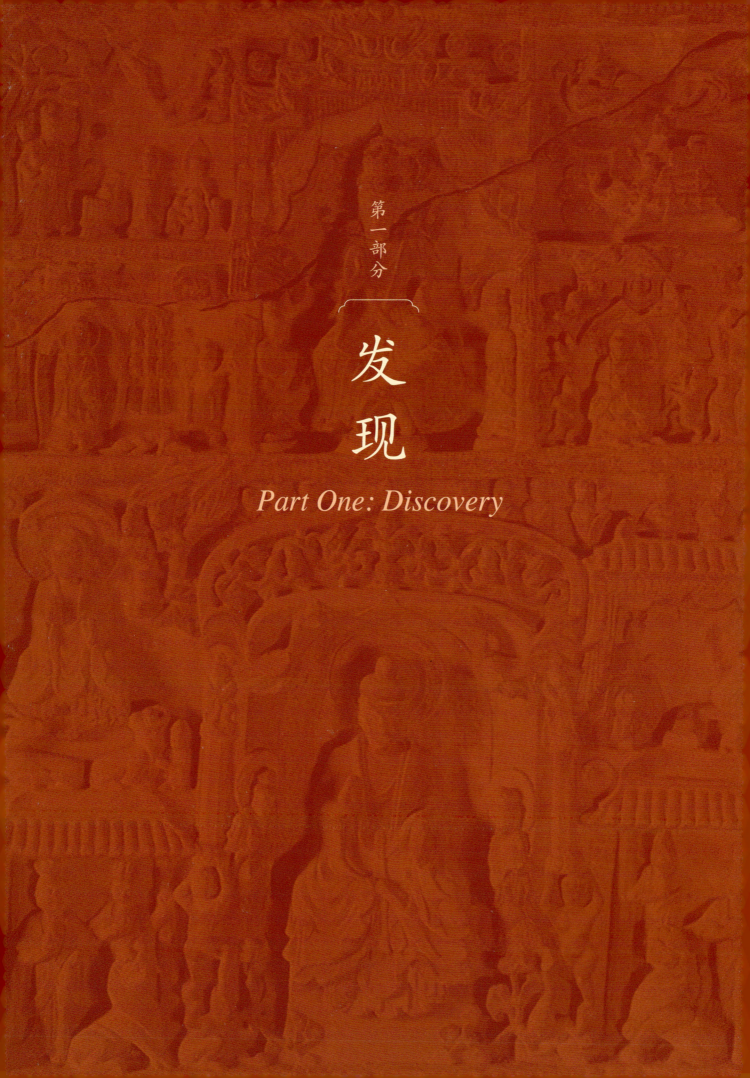

第一部分

发现

Part One: Discovery

麦积山现存洞窟 221 座，泥塑石雕 10632 身，壁画 979.54 平方米，营建之妙，令人叹为观止：自后秦开窟，经"六国共修"，于山峰河流环抱之地，赤红孤峰之上，凿山为窟，铸就崖阁，以无限想象力塑泥绘画，终成"麦积奇观"。麦积山在中国石窟寺中保有时代序列最完整的泥质造像体系、最早的大型经变壁画，这些洞窟、造像、壁画历经千年时空的变迁和世间的沧桑，依然展现着中国文化的独特魅力，静谧磅礴，撼人心弦。

Maijishan Grottoes currently houses 221 caves, 10,632 clay sculptures and stone carvings, and 979.54 square meters of murals, all of which boast breathtaking and masterful construction. Since the cave excavations during the Later Qin Dynasty and through the joint contributions of the "Six States", caves have been carved into the mountain, and cliff pavilions built, atop the isolated red peak surrounded by hills and rivers. Using boundless imagination, clay sculptures and paintings were created, culminating in the "Marvel of Maijishan". Maijishan is renowned for having the most complete chronological sequence of clay statuary in China and the earliest large-scale sutra illustration murals among the Chinese grotto temples. Despite thousands of years of temporal and spatial changes and worldly vicissitudes, these caves, statues, and murals continue to exhibit the unique charm of Chinese culture and radiate a profound human brilliance.

泥塑弟子立像

1

西魏
高 120 厘米　宽 29 厘米　厚 21 厘米　重 34 千克
第 102 窟
麦积山石窟艺术研究所藏

泥塑弟子立像线描图
Line Drawing of Clay Sculpture of Standing Disciple

　　弟子面型方圆，眉宇舒朗高耸，长眉细目，高鼻，嘴角内敛。面容俊秀，长颈圆肩，身躯饱满，体型匀称清秀。着袒右肩袈裟，袈裟在胸前交叉自双臂处自然下垂，衣纹线条简洁流畅，表现出少年弟子形象。

　　微眯的双眼，微笑的嘴角，眉宇间透露出的喜悦神情，都被艺术工匠们刻画得惟妙惟肖，是一件形神兼备的西魏艺术佳作，20 世纪 90 年代从 102 窟移入文物库房保存。

　　102 窟为平面方形四角攒尖窟，现存造像五身：正壁佛及左右二胁侍菩萨、左壁维摩诘及右侧弟子。右壁文殊菩萨及左侧弟子现已搬入库房保存，此即为左侧弟子像。（张萍、谈叶闻）

Clay Sculpture of Standing Disciple

Western Wei Dynasty
Height：120 cm, Width: 29 cm, Thickness: 21 cm, Weight: 34 kg
Cave 102
Art Institute of Maijishan Cave-Temple Complex

第 102 窟主佛
Main Buddha in Cave 102

The disciple has a roundish face with a broad and lofty forehead, long eyebrows, thin eyes, a high nose, and inward-turned corners of the mouth, creating a handsome appearance. He features a long neck, round shoulders, a full body, and a well-proportioned and delicate figure. He wears a kasaya that exposes the right shoulder, crossing at the chest and naturally drooping from the arms. The clothing lines are simple and smooth, presenting the image of a young disciple.

The slightly narrowed eyes, smiling corners of the mouth, and joyful expression in his forehead are all vividly depicted by the craftsmen. This piece is an excellent work of art, capturing both spirit and form, from the Western Wei Dynasty. In the 1990s, it was relocated from Cave 102 and stored in the cultural relics warehouse.

Cave 102 is a flat square cave with four corners gathered to a point roof, currently housing five statues: a Buddha on the main wall with two attendant Bodhisattvas on his left and right, Vimalakirti on the left wall, and the disciple on the right. The Manjusri Bodhisattva on the right wall and the disciple on the left have now been relocated to the warehouse for preservation. This is the statue of the disciple on the left. (By Zhang Ping & Tan Yewen)

中央勘察团绘
『石窟编号简图』
3

1953 年
长 172 厘米　宽 90 厘米
麦积山石窟艺术研究所藏

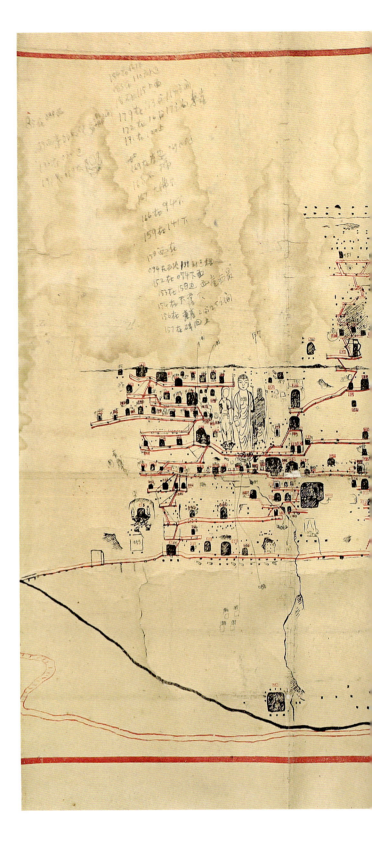

　　中央勘察团于 1953 年 8 月 20 日绘制此图，
当时的麦积山文物保管所（现麦积山石窟艺术研
究所）曾经在此图基础上重新进行测量编号，图
上所改文字均为当时所记，是 1953 年编号之原
始记录。后由程新民转交中央美术学院美术史系。
1963 年 6、7 月，美术史系在麦积山进行洞窟测
绘时，移交麦积山文物保管所作为档案资料收存。

　　此图完整记录了麦积山石窟崖面上东西洞窟
的分布及编号完整记录，洞窟外观形制及位置均
有标注，栈道的走向、有些洞窟的位置，用红色
标注，是重新编号改动过的，在图上方用文字的
形式对洞窟位置加以说明，下方说明此图的绘制
信息等内容，是麦积山石窟珍贵的原始资料。

（张萍）

"Simplified Map of Grotto Numbers" drawn by the Central Survey Team

1953
Length: 172 cm, Width: 90 cm
Art Institute of Maijishan Cave-Temple Complex

The Central Survey Team drew this map on August 20, 1953. The Maijishan Cultural Relics Preservation Institute at that time(the Maijishan Grottoes now) re-measured and numbered the caves based on this drawing, and all text changes were recorded at that time, serving as the original records of the 1953 numbering. Cheng Xinmin later transferred it to the Department of Art History at the Central

中央勘察团绘
「麦积山全景图」

2

1952 年
长 181 厘米　宽 93.5 厘米
麦积山石窟艺术研究所藏

　　1952 年 10 月，西北文化部麦积山石窟勘察组
在麦积山石窟勘察时绘制写景图，赠予瑞应寺留存。
　　此图绘制了麦积石窟山体形状、周围环境（植
被、道路走向）、栈道、洞窟分布及残损状况等内
容，是麦积山石窟 20 世纪 50 年代的原貌图。此
图为了解加固工程前的状况及考古方面，提供了
珍贵的资料。（张萍）

"Panoramic View of Maijishan" drawn by the Central Survey Team

1952
Length: 181 cm, Width: 93.5 cm
Art Institute of Maijishan Cave-Temple Complex

In October 1952, the Maijishan Grottoes Survey Team of the Northwest Ministry of Culture conducted a survey of the Maijishan Grottoes. During this survey, they created a scenic drawing, which was presented to Ruiying Temple for preservation.

This drawing depicts the mountain shape of the Maijishan Grottoes, the surrounding environment (including vegetation and road directions), plank roads, the distribution of caves, and the condition of damage. It provides an original view of the Maijishan Grottoes in the 1950s, offering valuable information about the site's condition before reinforcement projects and for archaeological research. (By Zhang Ping)

西北文化部麦積石窟勘察組繪製圖

一九五二年十月

據寺瑞應寺保存

中央勘察团绘『石窟编号简图』

3

1953 年
长 172 厘米　宽 90 厘米
麦积山石窟艺术研究所藏

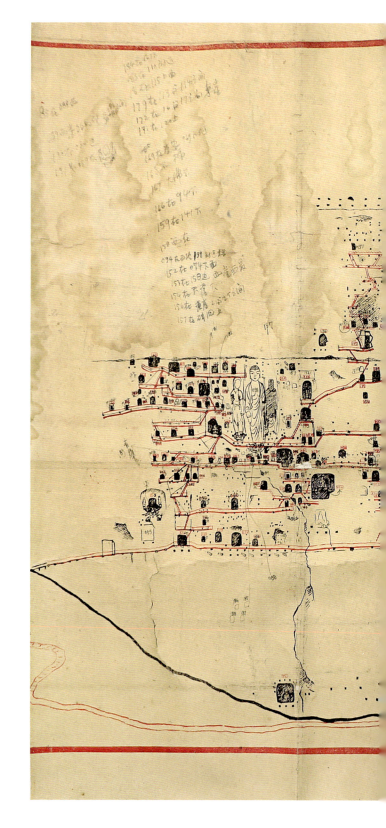

　　中央勘察团于 1953 年 8 月 20 日绘制此图，当时的麦积山文物保管所（现麦积山石窟艺术研究所）曾经在此图基础上重新进行测量编号，图上所改文字均为当时所记，是 1953 年编号之原始记录。后由程新民转交中央美术学院美术史系。1963 年 6、7 月，美术史系在麦积山进行洞窟测绘时，移交麦积山文物保管所作为档案资料收存。

　　此图完整记录了麦积山石窟崖面上东西洞窟的分布及编号完整记录，洞窟外观形制及位置均有标注，栈道的走向、有些洞窟的位置，用红色标注，是重新编号改动过的，在图上方用文字的形式对洞窟位置加以说明，下方说明此图的绘制信息等内容，是麦积山石窟珍贵的原始资料。

（张萍）

"Simplified Map of Grotto Numbers" drawn by the Central Survey Team

1953

Length: 172 cm, Width: 90 cm

Art Institute of Maijishan Cave-Temple Complex

The Central Survey Team drew this map on August 20, 1953. The Maijishan Cultural Relics Preservation Institute at that time(the Maijishan Grottoes now) re-measured and numbered the caves based on this drawing, and all text changes were recorded at that time, serving as the original records of the 1953 numbering. Cheng Xinmin later transferred it to the Department of Art History at the Central

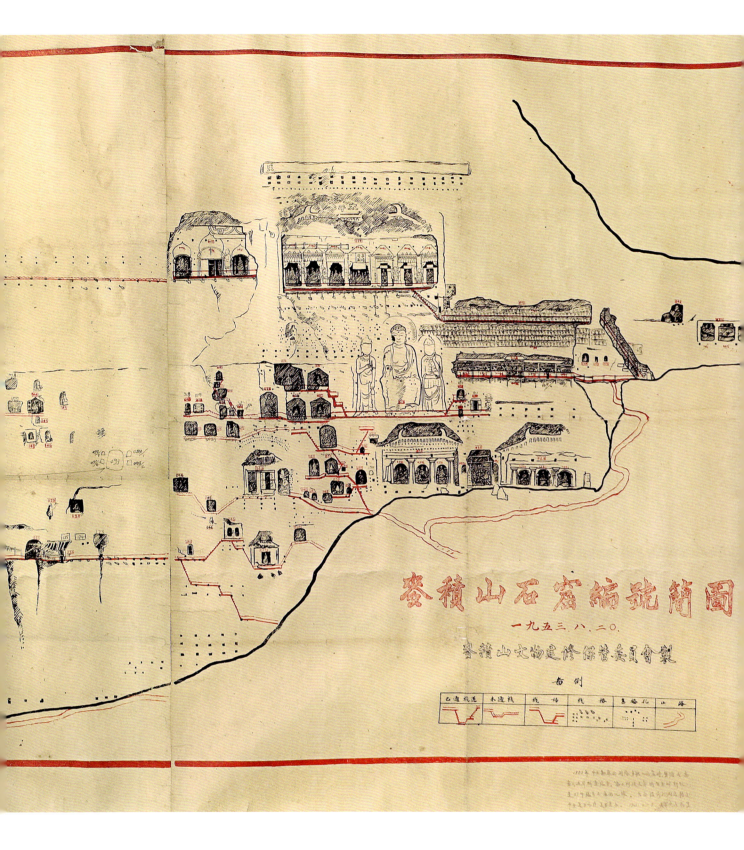

麦積山石窟編號簡圖

一九五三.八.二〇.

麦積山文物建修保管委員會製

圖例

已遊棧道	木遊棧	棧桥	棧 梯	鳥峪孔	山路

Academy of Fine Arts. In June and July 1963, when the Department of Art History was surveying and mapping caves in Maijishan, it was subsequently transferred to the Maijishan Cultural Relics Preservation Institute for archival storage.

　　This drawing comprehensively records the distribution and numbering of the caves on the eastern and western cliff surfaces of the Maijishan Grottoes. The exterior shapes and locations of the caves are marked, with the direction of the plank roads and some cave locations highlighted in red to indicate renumbering and changes. The upper corner contains textual explanations of the cave locations, while the lower corner provides details about the creation of the drawing. This is a valuable original document of the Maijishan Grottoes. (By Zhang Ping)

麦积山石窟洞窟分布图
Distribution of the Caves of the Maijishan Grottoes

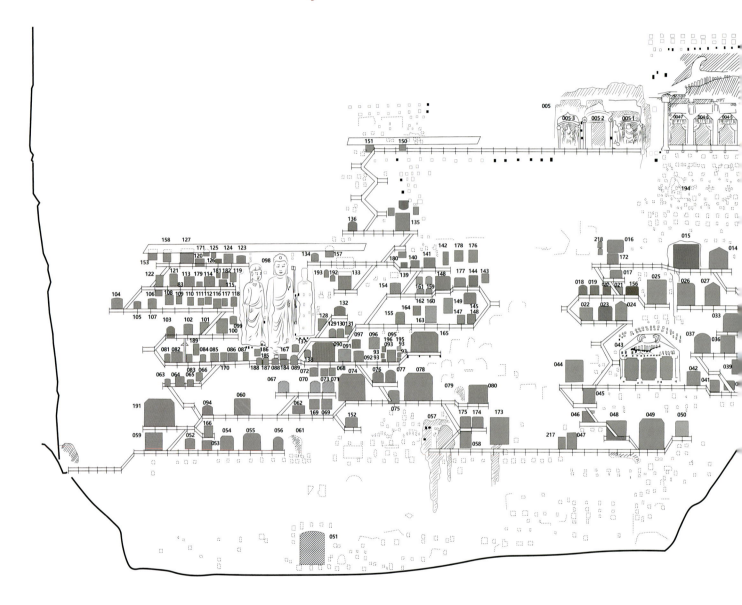

不明　　　隋唐宋明期　　北周時期　　西魏時期　　北魏時期　　西秦時期

后秦时期　北魏时期　西魏时期　北周时期　隋唐宋时期　不明

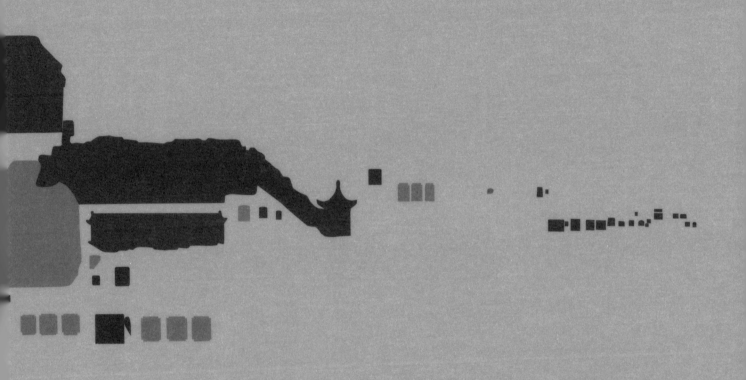

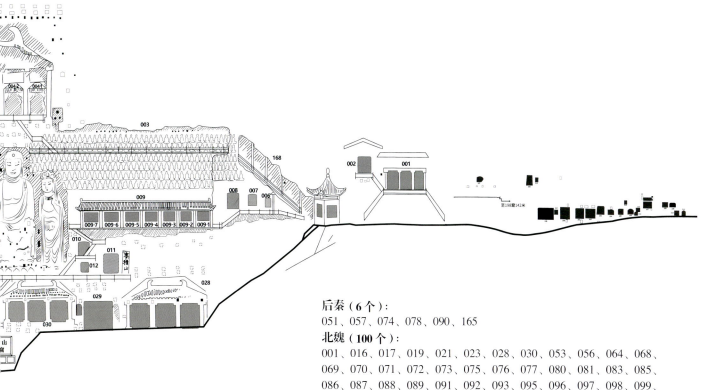

后秦（6个）：
051、057、074、078、090、165
北魏（100个）：
001、016、017、019、021、023、028、030、053、056、064、068、
069、070、071、072、073、075、076、077、080、081、083、085、
086、087、088、089、091、092、093、095、096、097、098、099、
100、101、103、107、108、110、111、112、114、115、116、117、
119、121、122、125、126、127、128、129、130、131、132、133、
135、138、139、140、142、143、144、145、147、148、149、152、
153、154、155、156、158、159、160、161、162、163、164、167、
169、170、175、176、177、178、179、181、182、195、196、217、
218、219、220、221
西魏（15个）：
020、041、043、044、054、060、102、105、120、123、124、146、
172、191、197
北周（68个）：
002、003、004、006、007、009、011、012、015、018、022、026、
027、029、031、032、034、035、036、038、039、042、045、046、
047、048、052、055、062、063、065、067、082、084、094、104、
109、113、118、134、136、137、141、157、166、168、171、189、
194、198、199、200、201、202、203、204、205、206、207、208、
209、210、211、212、213、214、215、216
隋唐宋（15个）：
005、008、010、013、014、024、025、033、037、040、049、050、
058、059、106
不明（17个）：
061、066、079、150、151、173、174、180、183、184、185、186、
187、188、190、192、193

（以上数据由麦积山石窟艺术研究所提供，数据更新至2024年7月）

洞窟
Caves

　　绝壁之上，密如蜂巢的洞窟，是来自营造不绝的"刀刻斧凿"，是浓缩非凡智慧的"超级工程"。漫长的岁月中，因地震山崩，麦积山崖面中部坍塌，洞窟的分布遂划作西崖和东崖两个区域，最早的窟龛大都分布在西崖，而东崖较晚。

On the steep cliffs, there are caves like a beehive, which are created continuously through the generations. This is also a "super project" that has concentrated great wisdom. Over the course of the long years, due to earthquakes and landslides, the middle part of the cliff collapsed, dividing the distribution of grottoes into two zones: the western cliff and the eastern cliff. The earliest grottoes are mostly distributed on the western cliff, while those on the eastern cliff are relatively later.

4 『麦积山开除常住地粮碑』拓片

明
拓片高 222 厘米　宽 94 厘米
原碑出自第 168 窟
麦积山石窟艺术研究所藏

明崇祯十五年（1642）立《麦积山开除常住地粮碑》，碑首方形，正中呈竖向排列阴刻双钩篆书"大明"二字。碑面左右线刻二方连续忍冬纹图案。姚隆运撰书，其中记载："麦积山为秦地林泉之冠，其古迹系历代敕建者，有碑碣可考。自姚秦至今一千三百余年，香火不绝。林壑幽峭，松桧阴森，有瀑布泻出苍崖之间，天然奇景也。"

首行刻碑题。碑文楷书十八行，满行三十字，保存完好，字迹清晰。碑文记述麦积山瑞应寺僧有常驻田三百二十亩，但土地贫瘠，坡陡阴寒，只适合种燕麦、荞麦等产量较低的农作物，所收粮食不能自给。所剩无几的寺僧，多半食野菜充

饥。周边山民想占田，妄告增粮二石九斗五升，寺僧输官司后逃走人数过半，加之兵荒，又"牛种无出"，土地全部荒芜，佃户填沟，催租者敲门不休，致使寺院草长丈许。巡道范学颜驻麦积山寺，闻知寺僧生活困难，免去常住地粮，并由州守毛凤冠开除详文，乃谕乡里，不得混催比缴。

《麦积山开除常住地粮碑》现存于 168 窟，碑高 1.24 米、宽 0.77 米、厚 0.22 米。碑座高 0.30 米、宽 0.95 米、厚 0.58 米。168 窟位于东崖，是在崖壁上凿出的从地面通往第 3 窟的斜长廊，坡度 45°，共凿出 24 级石台阶，每级台阶高度为 0.35 米。（张萍、谈叶闻）

麥積山開除常住地糧碑

按廣輿記稱麥積山秦地林泉之冠其古
姚秦至今一千三百餘年香火不絕林壑之
間天然奇景也杜南李師中俱有題咏忠可順
產靈芝聖燈貝光照耀林谷春回暑際霄可順五
寒山僧多拾野菜資生杜詩云野寺殘僧少
二十畝皆脊薄獨此寺重困之後牛種占山田
住僧不前逃寺不入糧額資生杜詩云野
輸者不前逃寺不入糧額
祖者尚打寺門不休致寺僧乗色淬一夫良可惜也幸
巡道范公祖征寇駐寺見法堂前草色淬一夫
州守毛父母神明慈諒追呼不免議開種者欣然仍頭
慨然曰手回幾何追呼不免議開種者
極剴切懇至纖悉慮其稅畝不足以悍國儲宜勤
僧打已安生矣蠲念三世諸佛老現混得其稅畝
祖暨安生矣
范公祖行已安生
范公不朽炳炳如是三世愚妄人辛酉鄉進士毛公
范公講學顏山西萬泉縣人辛酉鄉進士毛公
崇禎十五年九月十五日庚午舉人姚隆運撰

Rubbing of the "Stele of Removing Grain Tax for Permanent Residences in Maijishan"

Ming Dynasty
the Rubbing: Height: 222 cm, width: 94 cm
Originally from Cave 168
Art Institute of Maijishan Cave-Temple Complex

In 1642, the 15th year of Chongzhen in the Ming Dynasty, the Stele of Removing Grain Tax for the Permanent Residences in Maijishan was erected. The top of the stele is square, featuring the characters " 大明 " (Great Ming) engraved vertically in seal script with double outlines. The left and right sides are adorned with two continuous honeysuckle patterns in a linear style. It's written by Yao Longyun which records: "Maijishan is the crown of forests and springs in the Qin region. Its ancient sites were built by imperial decrees in successive dynasties, as evidenced by steles and inscriptions. Since Yao's Qin (Later Qin) until now, for more than 1,300 years, the stream of Pilgrims have never ceased. The forests and valleys are secluded and steep, and the pine and cypress trees are somber, with a waterfall pouring out between the blue cliffs. It is such a natural wonder."

The first line of the stele is engraved with the title. The inscription, rendered in regular script, consists of eighteen lines, each with thirty characters. It is well preserved, with clear text. The inscription details the following: The monks of the Ruiying Temple at Maijishan held 320 mu of permanent fields. Unfortunately, the land was flat and barren, characterized by steep slopes and cold shade, making it suitable only for low-yield crops such as oats and buckwheat. The harvested grain was insufficient for sustenance.

Consequently, the remaining monks mainly subsisted on wild vegetables to alleviate hunger. Local mountain people attempted to seize the fields, falsely reporting an increase of 29.5 dou of grain. After the monks lost the lawsuit, more than half fled. The situation was worsened by the chaos of war and the "meager harvest due to lack of cattle and seeds", leaving all land barren. The tenants had perished and filled the ravines, and persistent rent collectors continually visited. Consequently, wild grass grew as high as ten feet within the temple grounds. Fan Xueyan, the patrol inspector, upon learning of the monks' hardship, exempted the permanent residences from the grain tax. Additionally, Mao Fengguan, the prefect, issued a detailed document and instructed villages and towns to avoid confusion in the collection and urging of payments.

The Stele of Removing Grain Tax for the Permanent Residences in Maijishan is currently housed in Cave 168. The stele measures 1.24 meters in height, 0.77 meters in width, and 0.22 meters in thicknesses. Its base is 0.30 meters high, 0.95 meters wide, and 0.58 meters thick. Cave 168 is located on the eastern cliff and features an inclined long corridor chiseled into the cliff wall, leading from the ground to Cave 3. The corridor has a 45-degree slope, with 24 chiseled stone steps, each 0.35 meters high. (By Zhang Ping and Tan Yewen).

铭文：

大明麦积山开除常住地粮碑

按广舆记称麦积山为秦地林泉之冠。其古迹系历代敕建者，有碑碣可考，自姚秦至今一千三百余年，香火不绝，林壑幽峭，松桧阴森，有瀑布泻出苍崖之间，天然奇景也。杜甫、李师中俱有题咏志，云：何谷不兰苣？何渊无蛟龙？麦积屡产灵芝，圣灯贝光照耀林谷，洵一方名胜，可与五岳竞高矣。旧设常住田三百二十亩，皆脊薄山岗，阴寒陡碉（涧），春回暑际，霜落秋前，所出不过燕麦小荞等。寥寥山僧，多拾野菜资生。杜诗云"野寺残僧少"，山田碗确，故僧突不黔耳，各处常住地原不入粮额，独此寺香火田乡愚侵占不遂，妄告增粮二石九斗五升，僧输不前，逃窜过半，兼兵荒重困之后牛种无出，地全荒芜，佃户已填沟壑。而催租者尚打寺门不休，致法堂前草深一丈，良可惜也！幸巡道范老公祖征

寇驻寺，见寺僧菜色未苏，问及香火之资，僧人能信泣诉前因，公慨然曰：寺田几何！追呼不免，此地方官之羞也。即准诉察免。又幸值州守毛父母神明慈谅，具有佛种者，欣然愿藉是作一大因缘事，申请开除详文，极剀切恳至，蒙批荒粮如议，开豁仍谕里老，不得混催此缴，繇是名刹中兴，僧行安生矣，窃念山地数亩，得其税不足以裨国储，贻其害遂足以累山灵。

范公祖暨毛父母，信是三世诸佛，现宰官身护法者乎，理宜勒石，以志二公之德□不朽，如再有乡愚妄许及里老混催诈骗者，本寺僧禀官重治法不贷。

范公讳学颜，山西万泉县人，辛酉乡进士，毛公讳凤冠，四川富顺县人，丁卯乡进士。

崇祯十五年九月十五日庚午举人姚隆运撰。

（沈玉璋）

Ming Dynasty Stele of Removing Grain Tax
for the Permanent Residences in Maijishan

According to Guang Yu Ji (Records of the Extensive Territory), Maijishan is the crown of forests and springs in the Qin region. Its ancient sites were built by imperial decrees in successive dynasties, as evidenced by steles and inscriptions. Since Yao's Qin (Later Qin) until now, for more than 1,300 years, the stream of Pilgrims have never ceased. The forests and valleys are secluded and steep, and the pine and cypress trees are somber, with a waterfall pouring out between the blue cliffs. It is such a natural wonder. Both Du Fu and Li Shizhong penned poems about it, noting: "Which valley lacks orchids and endives? Which abyss is without dragons?" Maijishan has repeatedly produced ganoderma lucidum. Sacred lights illuminate the forests and valleys, making it a notable scenic spot vying in grandeur with the Five Sacred Mountains. Previously, the temple had 320 mu of permanent fields on infertile mountain ridges and in cold, steep valleys. From spring to autumn, the land yielded only oats and small buckwheat. Few monks remained, subsisting mostly on wild vegetables. A poem by Du Fu states: "There are few remnant monks in the wild temple." The barren mountain fields left the monks impoverished. These permanent fields did not originally contribute to grain quotas. However, this temple's incense fields were encroached upon by villagers who falsely reported a 29.5 dou grain increase when they failed to occupy the land. Unable to pay, more than half the monks fled. After war and famine, with no cattle or seeds, the land was completely barren, and the tenants had perished and filled the ravines. Rent collectors persistently knocked on the temple gate. In front of the Dharma Hall, grass grew ten feet tall. It is truly a pity! Fortunately, Lord Fan, the patrol inspector, while suppressing

bandits, noticed the monks' emaciated state. Upon hearing their plight from monk Nengxin, he declared: "How many temple fields are there? If they cannot avoid taxation, it shames local officials." He immediately approved tax exemption. Prefect Lord Mao, kind-hearted and understanding, happily took this as a great karmic event. He applied for the removal of the detailed document with sincerity. It was approved that the barren land be exempted from grain tax. He also instructed village elders not to confuse or urge payment. Thus, the famous temple was revived, and monks lived in peace. I reflect that taxing a few mu of mountain land contributes little to the national treasury, yet the harm caused burdens the mountain spirits.

Lord Fan and Lord Mao were truly akin to the Buddhas of the three generations, manifesting in the forms of officials while upholding the Dharma. It would be reasonable to engrave their eternal virtue on stone. Should there be any future instances of ignorant villagers making false report or village elders confusing and pressuring for fraudulent payments, the monks of this temple shall report to the officials, who shall mete out severe and unsparing punishment.

Lord Fan, formerly named Fan Xueyan, was from Wanquan County, Shanxi Province, and was a Jinshi (a successful candidate in the highest imperial examinations) of the year of Xinyou. Lord Mao, formerly named Mao Fengguan, was from Fushun County, Sichuan Province, and was also a Jinshi in the year of Dingmao. This text was composed by Yao Longyun, a juren (provincial graduate) on 15th September in the year of Gengwu, the 15th year of Chongzhen reign. (By Shen Yuzhang)

5 佛传故事碑

孙纪元临摹
北魏
高149厘米　宽80厘米　厚11厘米
第133窟
麦积山石窟艺术研究所藏

　　10号造像碑（俗称佛传故事造像碑）位于133窟东侧后室前中央，花岗岩质，长方形碑，圆拱碑头，通碑从上到下、从左到右，均采用了三段构图的方式，在14个分格内雕刻12段佛传故事或经变，共一百多位身份不同的人物，全碑以释迦在忉利天发愿为中心，从燃灯授记到娑罗林中涅槃，形象生动地再现了佛祖的一生，为我国早期石刻连环画。

　　碑上段正中"释迦多宝二佛并坐说法"，左侧上下分两栏，上部"阿育王施土""树下思惟"，下部"佛入涅槃"，右侧"深山剃度"。中间部分正中是"交脚弥勒说法"，左右两侧上下两个分栏，左上部"乘象入胎"，下部"降魔成道"；右上侧"腋下诞生""九龙灌顶"，下部"燃灯授记""借花献佛"。下段正中是场面宏大，人物众多的"王

舍城说法"，左右两侧上下各两个分栏，左上部"维摩辩法"，下部两门柱两力士。右侧上部"初转法轮"等内容。

　　整个画面布局精巧，将人物、动物、山石、树木巧妙组合，以诠释从久远的过去世到现在世和未来世的佛陀故事。将佛传故事和说法图结合在一起，构图细密完整，历史叙事流畅，刻画细腻生动，主题明确突出，故事情节与雕刻形式自然和谐，具有很高的艺术价值。

　　原碑中间断为两截，1966年黏接在一起，采取的具体技术是拼接对位——相应位置打锚杆——环氧树脂粘结等技术流程。

　　第133窟内保存有18通北朝时期的造像碑，除10号造像碑外，其他的造像碑多以千佛雕刻为主。（张萍、谈叶闻）

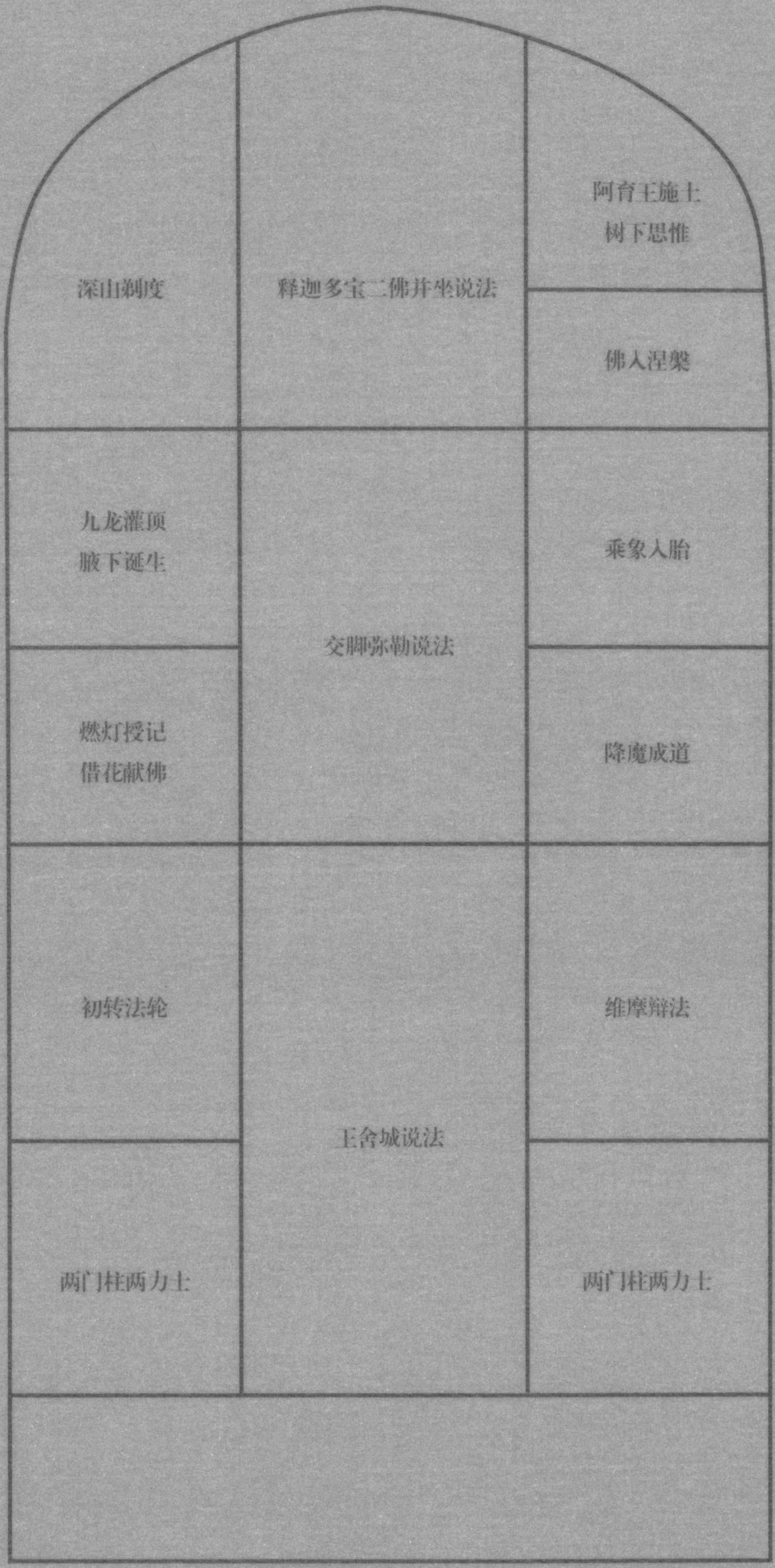

阿育王施士
树下思惟

深山剃度

释迦多宝二佛并坐说法

佛入涅槃

九龙灌顶
腋下诞生

乘象入胎

交脚弥勒说法

燃灯授记
借花献佛

降魔成道

初转法轮

维摩辩法

王舍城说法

两门柱两力士

两门柱两力士

壁转故事画雕刻内容

Stele of Buddha's Life Story

Copy by Sun Jiyuan
Northern Wei Dynasty
Height: 149 cm, Width: 80 cm, Thickness: 11 cm
Cave 133
Art Institute of Maijishan Cave-Temple Complex

Statue Stele 10 (commonly known as the statue stele of Buddha's Life Story), located in the center in front of the back chamber on the east side of Cave 133, is made of granite and is a rectangular stele with a round arched top. The entire stele, from top to bottom and from left to right, utilizes a three-segment composition method, with twelve sections depicting Buddha's life stories or sutra illustrations carved into 14 compartments, including more than 100 figures of different identities. The stele centers on Sakyamuni making a vow in the Trayastrimsa Heaven, vividly reproducing the life of the Buddha from Dipamkara's prediction to nirvana in the Sala Forest. This work is considered an early example of stone-carved comic strip art in China.

In the upper section of the stele, the central image depicts "Sakyamuni and Prabhutaratna sitting side by side preaching". The left side is divided into two columns: the upper part features "King Asoka bestowing earth" and "Contemplating under the tree", while the lower part shows "Buddha entering nirvana". The right side illustrates "Taking tonsure in the deep mountains". In the center of the middle section, "Maitreya preaching with crossed legs" is prominently displayed. Each side includes two columns: the upper left features "Entering the womb on an elephant" and the lower left depicts "Overcoming demons and attaining enlightenment". On the upper right side, the inscriptions read "Birth from the armpit" and "Nine dragons pouring water on the head", while the lower right includes "Dipamkara Buddha's prediction" and "Presenting flowers to the Buddha". In the lower section, the center scene portrays the grand scene of "Preaching in Rajagrha City," populated with numerous figures. Each side has two columns: The upper left features "Vimalakirti's debate on Dharma", and the lower left shows two door pillars and two Warriors. The upper right side portrays images such as "First turning of the Dharma wheel".

The entire composition is exquisitely laid out, cleverly combining figures, animals, hills, rocks, and trees to interpret the Buddha's stories spanning the distant past, the present, and the future. By seamlessly integrating the Buddha's life stories and preaching scenes, the stele's composition is meticulous and complete, the historical narrative flows smoothly, the depictions are delicate and vivid, the theme is clear and prominent, and the story plot and carving form are naturally harmonious - all of which contribute to the stele's exceptionally high artistic value.

The original stele was broken into two pieces in the middle. In 1966, the fragments were rejoined using a specific technical process. This involved aligning the corresponding sections, driving anchor rods into the matching positions, and bonding the pieces together with epoxy resin.

Cave 133 houses 18 statue steles from the Northern Dynasties period. Except for Statue Stele 10, the majority of the other statue steles are primarily carved with depictions of the Thousand Buddhas. (By Zhang Ping and Tan Yewen)

第 133 窟 第 11、12、13 号造像碑
Statue Stele 11, 12, 13 of Cave 133

6 泥塑佛头像

孙靖临摹
北魏
高 92 厘米　宽 56 厘米　厚 45 厘米
第 74 窟
麦积山石窟艺术研究所藏

　　麦积山北魏早期造像表现出的外来因素更为复杂，这与当时秦州地区所处的特殊地理、历史和地域文化背景有密切关系：秦州由于独特的地理位置，在两晋十六国时期成为各个割据势力频繁争夺之地，先后有前凉、前赵、后赵、前秦、后秦、西秦、仇池、大夏等政权参与混战之中，其中仅前、后秦统治时期政局略为稳定。而这阶段佛教在秦州的传播也十分活跃，主要有常年活跃于秦凉、岷蜀、长安之间的高僧竺法护、帛远、玄高、昙弘、昙绍等，其中又以禅僧居多，禅修过程中观像是很重要的一环，他们先后活动或生活过的长安、凉州、益州均为重要的佛教文化中心，故可知麦积山石窟造像粉本极有可能来自上述地区，其中长安地区的影响最为明显，体现出较多中西融合特征。

　　第 74 窟就是这一时期的洞窟。开凿于后秦、北魏、明重修，是麦积山现存最早的洞窟之一。佛头像为水波纹高肉髻，面形方颐，突眉杏眼，鼻梁高直，鼻翼鼓起，双唇较厚，嘴角上翘，具有典型的西域和北方游牧民族人种特征。其造型概括，鼻孔未塑出，是麦积山石窟早期造像的代表作之一，具有古朴雄健、浑厚沉稳之感。（张萍）

第 74 窟实景图
Real Image of Cave 74

Clay sculpture of Buddha head

Copy by Sun Jing
Northern Wei Dynasty
Height: 92 cm, Width: 56 cm, Thickness: 45 cm
Cave 74
Art Institute of Maijishan Cave-Temple Complex

The early Northern Wei dynasty statues at Maijishan exhibit more complex foreign elements, which are closely related to the special geographical, historical and regional cultural background of the Qinzhou area at that time. Due to Qinzhou's unique geographical location, it became a place frequently contested by various separatist forces during the Sixteen Kingdoms period of the Jin Dynasty. Successive regimes such as Former Liang, Former Zhao, Later Zhao, Former Qin, Later Qin, Western Qin, Chouchi, and Great Xia participated in the chaotic battles. Among them, only the reigns of Former Qin and Later Qin saw a relatively stable political situation. During this stage, the spread of Buddhism in Qinzhou was also very active. The prominent Buddhist monks who were constantly active between Qinzhou,

Liangzhou, Yizhou and Chang'an included Zhu Fahu, Bo Yuan, Xuan Gao, Tan Hong, Tan Shao, and others. Most of them were Zen monks, for whom observing images was a crucial part of their meditation practice. The locations where they successively carried out activities or lived, such as Chang'an, Liangzhou, and Yizhou, were all important Buddhist cultural centers. Therefore, it is likely that the models for the statues in the Maijishan Grottoes came from these regions, with the influence of the Chang'an area being the most prominent, reflecting a great integration of Chinese and Western elements.

Cave 74 dates from this period. It was carved during the Later Qin Dynasty and renovated in the Northern Wei Dynasty and the Ming Dynasty. It is one of the earliest existing caves at

Maijishan. The Buddha head features a high wavy hair bun and a square face with a broad chin. His eyebrows are prominent, and the eyes are almond-shaped. The bridge of his nose is tall and straight, with flared nostrils. His lips are relatively thick and the corners of his mouth are upturned, displaying typical ethnic characteristics of people from the Western Regions and northern nomadic ethnic groups. Notably, the nostrils are not sculpted, which is characteristic of early statues at the Maijishan Grottoes. This piece conveys a sense of simplicity, vigor, and stability. (By Zhang Ping)

第 74 窟 西侧 坐佛
Cave 74, West Side, Seated Buddha

第 76 窟剖面图
Profile of Cave 76

7
泥塑菩萨像

孙靖临摹
北魏
高 97 厘米　宽 45 厘米　厚 19 厘米
第 76 窟
麦积山石窟艺术研究所藏

第 76 窟位于第 74 龛左上方，是一个约 1 米见方的小窟，因正壁佛座前墨书题记而为学界所关注。

左壁菩萨像，头戴三面花冠，面形方圆，细颈宽肩，颈戴桃形宽项圈，身躯扁平修长，上身袒露，斜披络腋，披帛带绕双臂飘扬下垂。臂饰钏，手腕戴镯，左臂自然下垂、左手执帛带；右臂屈肘上举、右手置胸前轻握莲蕾。下着长裙，紧裹双腿，跣足立于半圆形台座上。身后浮塑莲瓣形背光，残留有绿、红色彩绘。

值得注意的是，这已不纯是北魏早期胁侍菩萨一手抚于胸前、一手伸直下垂的刻板僵硬的姿态，还增加了动作的变化，尤其胯部稍稍向侧方的扭动，丰富了形体轮廓的曲线。（王通玲、谈叶闻）

Clay Sculpture of Bodhisattva

Copy by Sun Jing
Northern Wei Dynasty
Height: 97 cm, Width: 45 cm, Thickness: 19 cm
Cave 76
Art Institute of Maijishan Cave-Temple Complex

Cave 76, located above and to the left of Cave 74, is a small cave about 1 square meters. It has attracted the attention of the academic community due to the ink inscription found in front of the Buddha seated on the main wall.

The Bodhisattva statue on the left wall wears a triple-corolla crown and has a round and square face, with a slender neck and broad shoulders. Around his neck is a wide, peach-shaped necklace. His body is flat and slender, with an exposed upper body and a shawl draped obliquely over one shoulder. A silk scarf flutters and hangs down around his arms. He wears bracelets on his arms and wrists. His left arm hangs naturally, with his left hand holding the silk scarf, while his right arm is bent at the elbow and raised, lightly holding a lotus bud in front of the chest. He wears a long skirt that tightly wraps around his legs, and his bare feet stand on a semicircular pedestal. Behind him is a floating halo shaped like lotus petals, with remnants of green and red paint.

It is worth noting that this statue no longer represents the rigid and stereotyped posture of the early Northern Wei Dynasty attendant Bodhisattva, characterized by one hand on the chest and the other hanging straight down. Instead, it introduces a variation in movement, particularly with a slight twist of the hips to the side, which enriches the curves of his body's outline. (By Wang Tongling and Tan Yewen)

第 76 窟全景图
Panoramic view of Cave 76

8 《供养飞天》壁画

李西民临摹
隋
长 141 厘米　宽 89 厘米
第 76 窟
麦积山石窟艺术研究所藏

供养飞天是佛教艺术中通过歌舞、香花等方式供养诸佛菩萨的上界侍从，这些上界侍从被称为飞天，属于天龙八部之一。最初的形象见于古印度的佛塔和壁画中，通常描绘为半人半鸟或长有翅膀的形象，飞翔在佛陀象征物如菩提树、佛塔等上方，奉献花环供养。飞天的职责包括奏乐、歌舞和散花，通过这些活动来供养佛祖，象征佛国天宫的庄严和美丽。

第 76 窟是北魏具有代表性的洞窟，其中顶部饰以飞天，环绕整个窟顶，是麦积山石窟现存最完整的一幅藻井飞天壁画，画面中十身如行云流水般的飞天（现存七身）围绕莲花心旋转飞舞，组成一朵盛开的莲花，手持供盘的飞天凌空飞扬的披巾与漫天飘动的莲花组合成一幅曼妙的充满旋律的动感画面。

飞天头束高髻，戴宝珠花冠，五官清晰，绘有胡须，上身袒露，颈戴项圈，肩披飘扬的蓝色或绿色帛带，臂戴钏、腕戴环，手托供盘，下着飞飘长裙，跣足，四周有蓝白二色莲花及流云衬托。身躯呈"U"状，体态轻盈，飞舞灵动，描线清晰，色彩鲜艳如新，属于北魏中期以后的风格，但图中花心部分露出底层画迹，说明表层明丽如新的壁画是重绘的作品。（张萍）

Mural of *Apsaras Attendants*

Copy by Li Ximin
Sui Dynasty
Length: 141 cm, Width: 89 cm
Cave 76
Art Institute of Maijishan Cave-Temple Complex

In Buddhist art, apsaras attendants are celestial beings from the upper realm who pay homage to Buddhas and Bodhisattvas through singing, dancing, and presenting fragrant flowers. These attendants, known as apsaras, are part of the Eight Categories of Supernatural Beings (Tianlong Babu). The earliest representations can be found in ancient Indian stupas and murals, where they are typically depicted as half-human and half-bird or with wings, flying above the symbolic objects of the Buddha, such as the Bodhi tree and stupas, while presenting flower garlands as offerings. The duties of apsaras attendants include playing music, singing, dancing, and scattering flowers, all of which serve to honor the Buddha and symbolize the solemnity and beauty of the celestial palaces in the Buddhist realm.

Cave 76 is a representative cave of the Northern Wei Dynasty, featuring apsaras attendants that adorn the entire ceiling. It is the most complete caisson apsaras mural currently existing in the Maijishan Grottoes. In the mural, ten apsaras attendants (seven of which remain today) gracefully fly around the lotus heart, forming a blooming lotus. The scarves of the flying apsaras, who hold offering trays, combine with the lotus flowers floating in the air to create a dynamic and melodious scene.

The flying apsaras attendants are depicted with high buns adorned with pearl flower crowns, featuring clear facial features and painted beards. Their upper bodies are exposed, and they wear necklaces around their necks, with blue or green silk scarves draped over their shoulders, fluttering in the air. They have bracelets on their arms and rings on their wrists, and they hold offering trays in their hands. Their long skirts billow as they fly, and they are barefoot, surrounded by blue and white lotus flowers and flowing clouds in the background. Their bodies are shaped like a "U", conveying a light and nimble posture as they soar gracefully. The outlines of the drawing are clear, and the colors are bright and vibrant, characteristic of the style after the middle period of the Northern Wei Dynasty. However, the flower heart section of the mural reveals traces of an underlying painting, suggesting that the bright and new-looking surface mural is the result of a later repainting. (By Zhang Ping)

9 泥塑佛坐佛

Clay Sculpture of Seated Buddha

孙靖临摹
北魏
高 80 厘米　宽 47 厘米　厚 30 厘米
第 114 窟
麦积山石窟艺术研究所藏

Copy by Sun Jing
Northern Wei Dynasty
Height: 80 cm, Width: 47 cm, Thickness: 30 cm
Cave 114
Art Institute of Maijishan Cave-Temple Complex

114 窟为麦积山石窟北魏平顶方形窟，是较小的一个洞窟。三壁面开龛，龛外有胁侍菩萨。三壁面有"光化、雍熙、治平、熙宁、嘉定"等纪年墨书题记，为麦积山石窟的分期断代提供了珍贵资料。

此造像位于左壁前部的圆券形龛内，为磨光高肉髻，面型长方，前额较宽，面额略瘦，弯眉细目，鼻隆且直，与眉相连。目光深邃，双耳下垂。神态庄严肃穆，双肩圆润，通肩袈裟，衣角自左臂下垂，下摆分为三瓣。双手结禅定印置于腹部。结跏趺坐于工字型须弥座之上。衣纹运用大量的阴刻线和圆弧曲线来表现，转折自如，形如流水一般，显现轻薄服饰的质感，有"曹衣出水"之状，富于装饰趣味。造型简洁明快、端庄秀美，为麦积山北魏代表作之一。（张萍）

Cave 114 is a flat-topped square cave of the Northern Wei Dynasty in the Maijishan Grottoes, which is relatively small. Niches are opened on the three walls, and there are attendant Bodhisattvas outside the niches. There are ink inscriptions with dated records such as "Guanghua, Yongxi, Zhiping, Xining, and Jiading" on the three walls, providing precious materials for the periodization and dating of the Maijishan Grottoes.

This sculpture is situated in the front part of the left wall, within an arched niche. It features a polished high bun hairstyle, a rectangular face, a broad forehead, and a slightly lean visage. The eyebrows are gracefully curved, and the eyes are slender, with a prominent, straight nose that connects to the brows. The figure's gaze is deep, and the earlobes hang low. Exuding a solemn and dignified presence, the figure has rounded shoulders and wears a robe draped over both shoulders. The robe's hem falls beneath the left arm, with the lower section divided into three parts. The hands are placed in a meditation gesture over the abdomen. The figure is seated in a lotus position atop an I-shaped Sumeru throne. The garment's drapery is skillfully rendered with numerous incised lines and curved arcs, creating a fluid, water-like effect. This technique captures the texture of the light, delicate fabric, reminiscent of the "Cao's clothes emerging from water" style, and is rich in decorative charm. The sculpture's design is simple yet elegant, dignified, and graceful, marking it as one of the representative works of the Northern Wei period at Maijishan. (By Zhang Ping)

10 泥塑菩萨像

Clay Sculpture of Bodhisattva

孙靖临摹
北魏
高 97 厘米　宽 45 厘米　厚 19 厘米
第 115 窟
麦积山石窟艺术研究所藏

Copy by Sun Jing
Northern Wei Dynasty
Height: 97 cm, Width: 45 cm, Thickness: 19 cm
Cave 115
Art Institute of Maijishan Cave-Temple Complex

　　第 115 窟为麦积山石窟北魏平面方形窟，规模虽小，却保存着麦积山石窟中所见最早、唯一有确切纪年的开窟题记："唯大代景明三年九月十五日……"北魏景明三年是公元 502 年，正值北魏中期向晚期的过渡阶段。

　　菩萨位于 115 窟左壁，面形长方，双目平视，高鼻无孔。头戴宝冠，发纹以阴刻线表现。宝缯自双耳后下垂于两侧，发辫分三绺披于肩头。颈饰宽项圈，袒胸露臂，斜披络腋，肩搭披帛，左手下垂提净瓶，右手置胸前执莲蕾。下着长裙，双腿分开，跣足立于莲台上。菩萨背光中彩绘莲花纹和忍冬纹。姿态优美典雅，是北魏中期的代表作品之一。（王通玲、谈叶闻）

Cave 115 is a planar square cave dating back to the Northern Wei Dynasty within the Maijishan Grottoes. Although relatively small in scale, it preserves the earliest and only cave-opening inscription with a definite date found in the Maijishan Grottoes. The inscription reads: "On the 15th day of the ninth month in the third year of Jingming of the Great Dynasty (Northern Wei Dynasty)...". The third year of Jingming in the Northern Wei Dynasty corresponds to the year 502 AD, which marks the transitional stage from the middle to the late period of the Northern Wei Dynasty.

The Bodhisattva is located on the left wall of Cave 115, characterized by a rectangular face, with two eyes gazing straight ahead and a high nose devoid of nostrils. Adorned with a precious crown, the hair is depicted using incised lines, with ribbons cascading down on both sides from behind the ears. The hair is styled with three braids that drape elegantly over the shoulders. The figure wears a wide necklace around the neck, exposing the chest and arms. A shawl is draped obliquely over one shoulder, complemented by a silk scarf. The left hand hangs down, holding a pure vase, while the right hand is positioned in front of the chest, grasping a lotus bud. The Bodhisattva is dressed in a long skirt, with legs apart, standing barefoot on a lotus pedestal. The halo behind the Bodhisattva is adorned with painted lotus and honeysuckle patterns. With its graceful and elegant posture, this sculpture is considered one of the representative works of the middle period of the Northern Wei Dynasty. (By Wang Tongling and Tan Yewen)

第 115 窟实景图
Real Image of Cave 115

11 | 泥塑菩萨立像

段一鸣临摹
北魏
高 81 厘米　宽 44 厘米　厚 15 厘米
第 69 窟
麦积山石窟艺术研究所藏

　　第 69 窟右侧菩萨像，头戴宝冠，发髻较高，宝缯垂肩，面形丰满圆润。左手于胸前持莲蕾，右手屈于腹前提净瓶，披帛交叉于胸前并垂直于腿部，神情恬静，造像及服饰具有汉民族文化特征，体现了 6 世纪初麦积山石窟造像新旧变化过渡的风格。

　　第 69 窟与第 169 窟是一对紧邻的双龛，两龛之间浮塑双龙交尾，将两龛连成一体，为麦积山仅有的一例。（王通玲、谈叶闻）

第 69 窟泥塑菩萨立像线描图
Line Drawing of Clay Sculpture of Standing Bodhisattva of Cave 69

Clay Sculpture of Standing Bodhisattva

Copy by Duan Yiming
Northern Wei Dynasty
Height: 81 cm, Width: 44 cm, Thickness: 15 cm
Cave 69
Art Institute of Maijishan Cave-Temple Complex

The Bodhisattva statue, located on the right side of Cave 69, is adorned with a precious crown and features a relatively high hair bun. Precious silk drapes down over the shoulders, and the statue's face is plump and rounded. In the left hand, the Bodhisattva holds a lotus bud in front of the chest, while his right hand is bent, holding a pure vase at the abdomen. A silk scarf crosses in front of the chest and hangs vertically down the legs. The statue exudes a serene expression, and both the figure and its attire reflect the cultural characteristics of the Han people. This sculpture exemplifies the transitional style of the early 6th century in the Maijishan Grottoes, marking a shift from older to newer artistic styles.

Caves 69 and 169 form a pair of adjacent double niches. Between them lies a relief sculpture depicting two dragons intertwined at their tails, effectively connecting the two niches into a cohesive unit. This unique feature represents the only example of its kind within the Maijishan Grottoes. (By Wang Tongling and Tan Yewen)

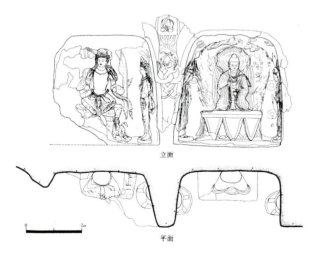

立面

平面

第 69、169 窟实测图
Surveyed Drawings of Cave 69 and Cave 169

第 69 窟右壁菩萨
Bodhisattva on the right wall of Cave 69

12 影塑坐佛

Clay-Molded Sculpture of Seated Buddha

北魏
高 26.2 厘米　宽 14.7 厘米　厚 5.7 厘米　重 1.071 千克
第 164 窟
麦积山石窟艺术研究所藏

Northern Wei Dynasty
Height: 26.2 cm, Width: 14.7 cm, Thickness: 5.7 cm, Weight: 1.071 kg
Cave 164
Art Institute of Maijishan Cave-Temple Complex

　　佛磨光高肉髻，面型方圆，眉毛弯曲，眼角细长，眼睑突鼓，双目平视；嘴阔内敛，微微上翘；鼻隆耳大，短颈，端肩平腹。内着僧祇支，外披偏袒右肩式袈裟。双手结禅定印置于腹前。呈跏趺坐状。流畅的阴刻线疏密有致、刚劲有力，丝毫没有繁杂零乱，体现了服饰的轻柔贴体。神情恬静娴雅、潇洒大度，体态古朴雄健，颇具西域造像特征。通体施彩，鲜艳如新。局部虽有磨蚀痕迹，更显示出古朴与庄重之感，为麦积山北魏早期代表作。

　　20 世纪 80 年代麦积山石窟山体加固维修工程期间由第 164 窟移入文物库房保存。（张萍）

　　The Buddha features a highly polished usnisa and a square-round face, characterized by curved eyebrows and elongated eye corners. His eyelids are slightly protruding, and his gaze is directed straight ahead. His mouth is wide yet restrained, with a subtle upturn, complemented by a prominent nose and large ears. He has a short neck, straight shoulders, and a flat abdomen. Dressed in a sanghati underneath and a draped kasaya that exposes his right shoulder, the Buddha's hands are positioned in the meditation mudra at the abdomen, sitting in a dignified half-lotus posture. The intaglio lines are smooth, well-spaced, and vigorous, devoid of complexity or disorder, highlighting the soft and form-fitting nature of the clothing. His expression is serene and elegant, exuding a natural and magnanimous demeanor. His posture is simple yet robust, reflecting distinct characteristics of statues from the Western Regions. The entire figure is painted in vibrant colors, appearing fresh and new. Despite some signs of abrasion in certain parts, this adds to the ancient and solemn aura of the piece, marking it as a representative work of the early Northern Wei Dynasty in the Maijishan Grottoes.

　　During the mountain reinforcement and maintenance project of the Maijishan Grottoes in the 1980s, the statue was relocated from Cave 164 and stored in the cultural relics warehouse. (By Zhang Ping)

第 164 窟影塑菩萨立像线描图
Line drawing of Shallow relief of Bodhisattva (standing) of Cave 164

影塑菩萨像

13

Clay-Molded Sculpture of Bodhisattva

北魏后期
高 22.5 厘米　宽 22.1 厘米　厚 4.29 厘米　重 305 克
第 164 窟
麦积山石窟艺术研究所藏

Late Later Northern Wei Dynasty
Height: 22.5 cm, Width: 22.1 cm, Thickness: 4.29 cm, Weight: 305 g
Cave 164
Art Institute of Maijishan Cave-Temple Complex

　　菩萨头戴花冠，有头光。面型长方，长眉细目，悬鼻小嘴，面目清俊秀丽。长发分两侧披于双肩，发边有宝缯。颈戴桃形项圈，下着翻边贴身羊肠大裙，披巾自双肩穿肘向后飞扬。躯体微微左倾，左手贴于左腿外侧。右臂屈肘、手提巾贴于腹前，双腿薄衣紧贴，衣褶疏密有致，双足立于莲台之上。阴刻线条流畅自如，隐约透出纤细的躯体，有清新秀丽、超凡脱俗、温婉可亲之感。

（张萍）

　　The Bodhisattva is adorned with a flower crown and a halo. The rectangular face features long eyebrows, narrow eyes, a hanging nose and a small mouth, presenting a handsome and refined appearance. Long hair is parted on both sides and cascades over the shoulders, embellished with precious silk ribbons. The Bodhisattva wears a peach-shaped necklace around the neck and a close-fitting, flared lamb intestine skirt. A scarf flows backward from the shoulders through the elbows. The figure leans slightly to the left, with the left hand resting on the outside of the left leg. The right arm is bent at the elbow, holding a scarf against the abdomen, while the legs are covered by thin clothing. The folds of the garment are well-defined and harmonious, with both feet positioned on a lotus pedestal. The intaglio lines are smooth and fluid, subtly revealing the slender form of the Bodhisattva. This depiction conveys a sense of freshness, beauty, transcendence, and a gentle, amiable presence. (By Zhang Ping)

14 泥塑佛头像

Clay Sculpture of Buddha Head

北魏晚期
通高 31.7 厘米　宽 11.9 厘米　厚 10.3 厘米
佛头高 22.2 厘米　重 2.004 千克
第 17 窟
麦积山石窟艺术研究所藏

Late Northern Wei Dynasty
Total height: 31.7 cm, Width: 11.9 cm, Thickness: 10.3 cm
Buddha head height: 22.2 cm, Weight: 2.004 kg
Cave 17
Art Institute of Maijishan Cave-Temple Complex

　　佛柱状磨光高肉髻，宽额，发际线平整。面型长方，弯眉，长细目，眼睑薄，双目微睁。鼻高且直，两翼宽厚，鼻梁直通额际；薄唇内敛微微上翘，略呈三角状，脸颊瘦削，双耳紧贴于两侧后颊。下颌上翘。长颈。面目清秀俊朗，流露出恬静之微笑，具有北朝"秀骨清像"之风，局部有磨蚀的痕迹。

　　20 世纪 80 年代麦积山石窟山体加固工程期间由 17 窟移入文物库房保存。从造像头部特征看，该头像与第 17 窟造像不同，故不属于该窟，应是其他洞窟残损后移入第 17 窟保存的。但其制作工艺精美，是麦积山北朝艺术之佳作。

（张萍）

　　The Buddha features a columnar, highly polished usnisa, complemented by a wide forehead and a neat hairline. His face is rectangular, characterized by curved eyebrows and long, narrow eyes with thin eyelids that are slightly open. The nose is high and straight, with broad, thick wings, and the bridge extends directly to the forehead. His thin lips are restrained, slightly upturned, and take on a triangular shape. The cheeks are slender, and the ears are closely attached to the back of the cheeks on both sides. The lower jaw is upturned, and he possesses a long neck. The Buddha's handsome and clear visage is adorned with a serene smile, embodying the typical style of the "elegant bones and clear features" of the Northern Dynasties. Some areas exhibit signs of abrasion, adding to the historical character of the piece.

　　During the mountain reinforcement project of the Maijishan Grottoes in the 1980s, the statue was relocated from Cave 17 and stored in the cultural relics warehouse. Analyzing the features of the statue's head reveals that it differs from the statues found in Cave 17, indicating that it does not belong to this cave. It is likely that this head was relocated to Cave 17 for preservation after being damaged in another cave. Nonetheless, its exquisite craftsmanship highlights it an outstanding example of the Northern Dynasties statue at Maijishan. (By Zhang Ping)

Clay-Molded Sculpture of Seated Buddha

15 影塑佛坐像

北魏晚期
高 26.3 厘米　宽 13.7 厘米　厚 7 厘米　重 700 克
第 17 窟
麦积山石窟艺术研究所藏

Late Northern Wei Dynasty
Height: 26.3 cm, Width: 13.7 cm, Thickness: 7 cm, Weight: 700 g
Cave 17
Art Institute of Maijishan Cave-Temple Complex

　　北魏影塑坐佛，高浮雕。磨光高肉髻，面型长方，脸颊稍瘦；弯眉细目；鼻梁直通额际，小嘴微微上翘，面容俊秀，额间有白毫。双耳紧贴于后颊，长颈端肩，平胸鼓腹。内着僧祇袄，外披偏右袒袈裟。袈裟衣摆搭于左臂自然下垂，右手屈肘外翻贴于胸前，左手抚于腹部。衣纹上阴刻线刚劲有力、简洁，弧形曲线的应用使服饰褶皱反转自如，层次清晰，透露出肌体轮廓；着褒衣博带式汉装，服饰有厚重之感。神情肃穆慈祥，体态端庄挺拔，具有北朝典型"秀骨清像"之特征，有彩绘残留。雕塑手法娴熟，技艺精湛。为麦积山北魏时期影塑代表之作。（张萍）

　　This Clay-molded Sculpture of Seated Buddha from the Northern Wei Dynasty features a highly polished usnisa and a rectangular face with slightly thin cheeks. The Buddha has curved eyebrows and narrow eyes, with a straight bridge of nose to the forehead. His small mouth is slightly upturned, contributing to his handsome appearance, and a urna is present between his eyebrows. The ears are closely attached to the back of the cheeks, complemented by a long neck, straight shoulders, a flat chest, and a bulging abdomen. He is dressed in a sanghati underneath and a kasaya draped over the right side. The hem of the kasaya naturally hangs over the left arm, while the right hand is bent at the elbow, turned outward, and placed against the chest. The left hand rests on the abdomen. The intaglio lines on the clothing are vigorous and concise, with the use of curved lines allowing the folds to flow freely, revealing the body's outline with clear layers. The Buddha wears loose robe with a wide sash in Han style, giving the attire a sense of heaviness. His expression is solemn yet kind, and his posture is dignified and upright, embodying the typical features of "elegant bones and clear features". Remnants of colored paintings are still visible, showcasing the sculptor's proficiency and superb craftsmanship. This piece is a representative clay molding work from the Northern Wei Dynasty at Maijishan. (By Zhang Ping)

16 影塑菩萨

北魏
高 14.5 厘米　宽 8.7 厘米　厚 3.5 厘米　重 173 克
第 142 窟
麦积山石窟艺术研究所藏

第 142 窟影塑菩萨线描图
Line Drawing of Bodhisattva of Cave 142

　　142 窟是麦积山造像内容最丰富的代表性洞窟之一，建于北魏晚期，在窟正、左、右壁均分上下五六层列置影塑，上二层壁面泥皮皆已剥落，下数四层保存较好。造像多、内容丰富、形态各异是此窟最大的特点，其中影塑最具特色。特别是正壁右侧的女供养人，挈领着幼儿，极富生活气息。

　　此影塑菩萨呈跪拜姿。束扇形发冠，面型长方，长眉细目，嘴角内敛，面带微笑。着宽边交领衣物，双手合十，有北朝"秀骨清像"之风。

　　20 世纪 80 年代麦积山石窟山体加固工程期间从 142 窟移入文物库房保存。（张萍、谈叶闻）

Clay-Molded Sculpture of Bodhisattva

Northern Wei Dynasty
Height: 14.5 cm, Width: 8.7 cm, Thickness: 3.5 cm, Weight: 173 g
Cave 142
Art Institute of Maijishan Cave-Temple Complex

Cave 142 is one of the representative caves at Maijishan, renowned for its rich array of statues, constructed during the late Northern Wei Dynasty. The cave features clay-molded sculptures arranged in five or six layers on the front, left, and right walls. The upper two layers of plaster have peeled away, while the lower four layers are relatively well preserved. The cave is characterized by a large number of diverse statues, showcasing a variety of forms and themes. Among these, the clay-molded sculptures stand out as the most distinctive feature. Notably, the female patron depicted on the right side of the front wall, leading a young child, exudes a vibrant sense of life and vitality.

This clay-molded Bodhisattva is depicted in a kneeling posture, adorned with a fan-shaped hair crown. The figure has a rectangular face, long eyebrows, and narrow eyes, with the corners of her mouth gently restrained, conveying a subtle smile. She is dressed in a wide-collared garment, with her hands clasped together in a gesture of reverence. The sculpture exemplifies the Northern Dynasties' style of "elegant bones and clear features". During the mountain reinforcement project of the Maijishan Grottoes in the 1980s, the sculpture was relocated from Cave 142 and stored in the cultural relics warehouse. (By Zhang Ping and Tan Yewen)

第 142 窟全景图
Panoramic view of Cave 142

第 142 窟母子供养人像
Mother and Child Patron Figures in Cave 142

第 142 窟影塑坐佛线描图
Line Drawing of Seated Buddha of Cave 142

17

影塑坐佛

Clay-Molded Sculpture of Seated Buddha

北魏
高 26.2 厘米　宽 16.1 厘米　厚 6.3 厘米
第 142 窟
麦积山石窟艺术研究所藏

Northern Wei Dynasty
Height: 26.2 cm, Width: 16.1 cm, Thickness: 6.3 cm
Cave 142
Art Institute of Maijishan Cave-Temple Complex

　　佛结柱状高发髻，面型长方，低首下视，长眉细目，嘴角内敛，微微上翘。长颈削肩，内着僧祇衼，外披通肩低领袈裟。左手屈肘抚于腹前，右手贴于胸前。呈结跏趺坐状，衣角穿左肘下垂又搭于左臂。坐于"工"字形佛座之上。袈裟衣摆成三瓣呈"M"状，下垂于佛座前，成悬裳座。整体着色，袈裟阴刻线衣纹清晰可见，宽边弧形转角曲线圆滑，如行云流水。塑像身躯修长，体态端庄，典型的"秀骨清像"造像风格，是北朝艺术佳作。

　　20 世纪 50 年代麦积山石窟山体加固维修工程前由第 142 窟移入文物库房保存，2000 年被定为国家一级文物。（张萍）

　　The Buddha features a columnar high chignon and a rectangular face, gazing downward with a lowered head. His long eyebrows and narrow eyes complement the restrained, slightly upturned corners of his mouth. He possesses a long neck and sloping shoulders, dressed in a sanghati underneath and a full-length low-necked kasaya on top. His left hand is bent at the elbow and rests on his abdomen, while his right hand is placed against his chest. He is seated in the lotus position, with the hem of his kasaya passing through his left elbow, hanging down, and draped over the left arm. The Buddha sits upon an I-shaped seat. The hem of his kasaya is in three flaps, forming an "M" shape that hangs down in front of the seat, creating a hanging skirt effect. The entire sculpture is colored, with the intaglio lines of the kasaya clearly visible. The wide-edged curved corners and smooth curves resemble flowing clouds and water. The sculpture depicts a slender body and dignified posture, exemplifying the typical "elegant bones and clear features" style, making it an artistic masterpiece of the Northern Dynasties.

　　Before the mountain reinforcement and maintenance project of the Maijishan Grottoes in the 1950s, the sculpture was relocated from Cave 142 to the cultural relics warehouse for preservation. In 2000, it was designated as a National Grade I Cultural Relic. (By Zhang Ping)

泥塑螺髻梵王头像

18

Clay Sculpture of Brahma Head with a Spiral Hair Bun

北魏晚期
高 31.8 厘米　宽 19.5 厘米　厚 17.2 厘米　重 4.03 千克
第 154 窟
麦积山石窟艺术研究所藏

Late Northern Wei Dynasty
Height: 31.8 cm, Width: 19.5 cm, Thickness: 17.2 cm, Weight: 4.03 kg
Cave 154
Art Institute of Maijishan Cave-Temple Complex

　　梵王螺髻高耸，发际线清晰规整，面型长方、细长眉，双目弯如新月，鼻高且直，薄唇嘴角内敛且微微上翘，两耳平贴于后颊，细长颈，眉清目秀的面容和含蓄的微笑，体现出古代匠师技艺之高超，是一件清新儒雅、北魏秀骨清像之艺术佳作。

　　20 世纪 80 年代麦积山石窟山体加固工程期间从 164 窟移入文物库房保存。

　　螺髻梵王指发髻像螺壳的色界初禅天的大梵天王，亦泛指此界诸天之王。（张萍）

　　The Brahma features a high spiral hair bun with a clear and well-defined hairline. He has a rectangular face adorned with long, slender eyebrows. His eyes are elegantly curved like crescent moons, complemented by a high and straight nose. The thin lips are subtly restrained at the corners, slightly upturned, while his ears lie flat against the back of the cheeks. With a long and slender neck, his handsome visage is enhanced by a reserved smile, showcasing the exceptional craftmanship of ancient artisans. This sculpture exemplifies a fresh, refined elegance, embodying the artistic style of "elegant bones and clear features" characteristic of the Northern Wei Dynasty.

　　During the mountain reinforcement project of the Maijishan Grottoes in the 1980s, the statue was relocated from Cave 164 to the cultural relics warehouse for preservation.

　　The Brahma with a spiral hair bun refers to the great Brahma king of the first Dhyana heaven in the Form Realm, characterized by a hair bun resembling a snail shell. This term also generally encompasses the kings of all heavens within this realm. (By Zhang Ping)

第 154 窟散置造像
Scattered Statues in Cave 154

19 泥塑菩萨头像

Clay Sculpture of Bodhisattva Head

北魏晚期
高 35.8 厘米　宽 16.4 厘米　厚 13.5 厘米　重 4.79 千克
第 154 窟
麦积山石窟艺术研究所藏

Late Northern Wei Dynasty
Height: 35.8 cm, Width: 16.4 cm, Thickness: 13.5 cm, Weight: 4.79 kg
Cave 154
Art Institute of Maijishan Cave-Temple Complex

20世纪50年代散落在第154窟的其中一件菩萨头像残件。菩萨束高髻，戴宝珠花冠，发际线平且规整。面型长方，宽额，弯眉细目，双目微睁，鼻隆耳大，双唇较薄，唇线清晰，圆润，嘴角内敛，下颌微翘，长颈。雕塑工匠在造像艺术上注重以形写神、形神兼备的手法，体现出亲切温和的面容，透出一副安详俊秀之美。这是麦积山石窟北魏时期具有代表性的造像之一。（张萍、谈叶闻）

This is one of the remaining head pieces of a Bodhisattva that was scattered in Cave 154 during the 1950s. The Bodhisattva features a high bun adorned with a flower crown with precious beads, characterized by a flat and regular hairline. The face is rectangular with a wide forehead, curved eyebrows, and narrow eyes that are slightly open. The Bodhisattva has a high nose, large ears, and relatively thin lips with clear, round lines. The corners of the mouth are restrained, and the lower jaw is slightly upturned, complemented by a long neck. The sculptors emphasized the technique of expressing spirit through form, achieving a harmonious balance of both in their artistry. This piece reflects a kind and gentle expression, revealing a serene and handsome beauty. It stands as one of the representative statues of the Northern Wei Dynasty within the Maijishan Grottoes. (By Zhang Ping and Tan Yewen)

第 121 窟泥塑弟子坐像线描图
Line Drawing of Seated Disciple of Cave 121

20 泥塑弟子坐像

北魏晚期
高 39 厘米　宽 15.4 厘米　厚 10 厘米　重 3.294 千克
第 121 窟
麦积山石窟艺术研究所藏

麦积山石窟的北魏晚期造像，不断呈现出活泼的形式和生动的表现。各窟内多流行三佛的主题，并配置菩萨、弟子、比丘、比丘尼和力士或天王等造像，第 121 窟是很有代表性的洞窟。正壁龛内两侧壁上部还有影塑佛弟子各一排五身，合为十大弟子之数，弟子们均着厚重宽大的袈裟，一一作不同相貌和神情，有的在聚精会神地聆听，有的因突然了悟而欣喜，有的则似乎正在慷慨激昂地争辩。现存八身，左五右三，另有一身现藏于文物库房，即为此像。

弟子结跏趺坐于高佛座之上，头和身躯微前倾，弯眉细目，嘴角内敛，短颈端肩，左臂屈肘上举，右臂置于腹前。内着僧祇枝，外着通肩圆领袈裟，袈裟衣摆分三瓣垂于佛座前，衣饰线条简洁，多采用弧形转角曲线，似行云流水，体现宽博厚重、端庄沉稳之感。（谈叶闻）

Clay Sculpture of Seated Disciple

Late Northern Wei Dynasty
Height: 39 cm, Width: 15.4 cm, Thickness: 10 cm, Weight: 3.294 kg
Cave 121
Art Institute of Maijishan Cave-Temple Complex

The late Northern Wei Dynasty statues in Maijishan Grottoes continuously present lively forms and vivid expressions. In most caves, the theme of the Three Buddhas is popular, accompanied by the statues of Bodhisattvas, disciples, bhikkhus, bhikkhunis, and Warriors or heavenly kings. Cave 121 is a highly representative example. On the upper parts of the two side walls inside the niche on the front wall, there is also a row of five clay-molded Buddha's disciples on each side, totaling Ten Great Disciples. They are all wearing thick and wide kasayas, each with a distinct appearance and expression. Some are listening attentively, some are delighted because of a sudden realization, and some seem to be arguing passionately. Eight statues remain, five on the left and three on the right. Another statue is currently stored in the cultural relics warehouse, which is this statue.

The disciple is seated in the lotus position atop a high Buddha throne, with his head and body slightly inclined forward. He has curved eyebrows, narrow eyes, and restrained corners of the mouth. His neck is short, and his shoulders are straight. The left arm is bent at the elbow and raised upward, while the right arm rests in front of the abdomen. The disciple wears a sanghati inner garment and a full-length, round-necked kasaya outer robe. The hem of the kasaya falls in three flaps, hanging down in front of the Buddha seat. The clothing lines are simple, primarily utilizing curved corner curves that evoke a sense of flowing clouds and water, reflecting a quality of breadth, thickness, dignity, and stability. (By Tan Yewen)

第 121 窟西崖佛弟子
Cave 121, Western Cliff, Buddha's disciples

21 第121窟整体复原窟

121窟位于西崖上层的西端，开凿于北魏晚期，宋重修。是麦积山石窟北魏代表性洞窟。

洞窟形制为覆斗藻井平面方形窟。高2.55米、宽2.36米、深2.15米，窟内正壁和左、右壁各开一龛，龛内各塑一佛，为三世佛组合。现左右两壁龛内被改塑为菩萨像，原作衣裾仍保留，正壁佛像也在宋代被重修。正壁龛内两侧上部还有影塑佛弟子各一排五身，合为十大弟子之数，各高约0.3米。此窟前壁门两侧各塑一力士像，头为宋代重塑。左力士袒上身，下着裙，披巾于腹部穿圆、交叉，左手持金刚杵而立，右手提风带，右力士着宽袖上衣，下着长裙，垂手而立，身穿护身铠甲，显出刚健雄武的气魄。

佛上半身为宋代重塑，下身衣裙搭于座前呈三瓣式下垂，结跏趺坐于方台上，弟子穿袈裟，下着裙。尤以主佛龛外左右两侧两组造型最为突出，是麦积山石窟北魏造像之精品。其中左侧一组上身微微前倾，而且肘、肩和头部完全靠拢在一起，相互依偎，窃窃私语，他们仿佛领悟了佛国世界的美妙，互相露出会心的微笑；而右侧菩萨与比丘组合，又仿佛是人间的一对少男少女在脉脉含情、窃窃私语、互吐心曲。这种只有在世俗人生中才可以见到的情景，却出现在麦积山石窟的佛教造像群中，完全冲破了佛教禁欲的表现模式，突出了世俗人情的趣味，具有浓烈的中国化、民族化、人格化、世俗化特征。匠心独具、巧妙的组合，充满生活气息又极富人情味的造型艺术正是麦积山石窟跨越历史的艺术魅力之所在。（张萍）

第 121 窟实景图
Real image of Cave 121

Restored Cave 121

Cave 121 is located at the western end of the upper level of the western cliff, initially carved during the late Northern Wei period and later restored in the Song Dynasty. It is a representative cave of the Northern Wei period in the Maijishan Grottoes.

The cave is designed with a square plan and an inverted-bowl shaped ceiling. It measures 2.55 meters in height, 2.36 meters in width, and 2.15 meters in depth. Each of the front, left, and right walls features a niche, each housing a Buddha statue, collectively forming a triad of the Buddhas of Three Times. Currently, the niches on the left and right walls have been altered to house Bodhisattva statues, although the original robes remain preserved. The Buddha statue on the front wall was also restored during the Song Dynasty. On the upper sides of the front wall's niche, there are clay-molded sculptures representing the Buddha's disciples, arranged in a row of five on each side, making up the Ten Great Disciples. Each figure stands approximately 0.30 meters high. On either side of the door in the front wall are sculptures of warrior guardians, with their heads being Song Dynasty recreations. The left guardian is depicted with a bare upper body, wearing a skirt and a sash around his waist, draped in a circular cross pattern. He stands holding a vajra staff in his left hand, with his right hand grasping a wind-swept ribbon. The right guardian wears a wide-sleeved upper garment and a long skirt, standing with arms lowered, clad in protective armor. His form embodies a robust and commanding presence.

The upper body of the Buddha statue was reconstructed during the Song Dynasty, while the lower body features a skirt draped in a three-petal style over the front of the seat, seated in a lotus position on a square platform. The disciples are depicted wearing robes with skirts. Particularly noteworthy are the two groups of figures flanking the main Buddha niche, which are considered masterpieces of Northern Wei sculpture at the Maijishan Grottoes. On the left, a group leans slightly forward, with elbows, shoulders, and heads closely nestled together, as if whispering secrets. They appear to have grasped the wonders of the Buddhist realm, sharing knowing smiles. On the right, the combination of a Bodhisattva and a bhikkhu resembles a pair of young lovers from the human world, exchanging tender glances and whispers of affection. These scenes, typically found in secular life, appear within the Buddhist sculptures of the Maijishan Grottoes, breaking away from the traditional ascetic representations of Buddhism and highlighting the charm of human emotions. The sculptures are characterized by strong elements of Sinicization, national identity, personalization, and secularization. The ingenious design, skillful composition, and lifelike, emotionally rich artistic expressions are what endow the Maijishan Grottoes with their timeless artistic allure.(By Zhang Ping)

第 121 窟弟子与菩萨像线描图
Line drawing of Disciple and Bodhisattva in Cave 121

弟子与菩萨像 第 121 窟正壁右侧与右壁左侧
Disciple and Bodhisattva Statues, on the right side of the main wall and
the left side of the right wall of Cave 121

22 螺髻梵王与菩萨像

毛建鸿临摹
北魏
左菩萨：高 137 厘米　宽 83 厘米　厚 31 厘米
右菩萨：高 137 厘米　宽 83 厘米　厚 31 厘米
第 121 窟
麦积山石窟艺术研究所藏

　　第 121 正壁龛外左侧，螺髻梵王与菩萨头部紧贴，比肩而立，好似耳语，俗称此像为"窃窃私语"。螺髻梵王头束螺旋高发髻，低首下视，眉目细长，双手合十，身穿翻边双领下垂的袈裟，内着僧祇支，下着长裙，似开似闭的双眼和抿起的嘴唇，露出了专心聆听的表情。左菩萨顶束扇形高髻，头微侧，发髻前倾，五官清秀俊美，右手握莲，身材修长，细颈削肩，身穿褒衣博带式上衣，下着长裙，肩披宽边大披巾，足穿云头履。

"窃窃私语"匠心独运、构思巧妙，充满生活气息又极富人情味，是当之无愧的艺术佳作。

　　最为精彩的是迎门而立的螺髻梵王衣袖下摆微微地向两侧敞开，好像是一股轻风从窟门吹入，袈裟衣袖被风轻轻荡起。久而视之，似乎可以感受到一缕清风拂面而过，荡人肺腑。古代艺术家对这一细节恰到好处地把握，为这一组雕塑增添了无限的生命力。（张萍、谈叶闻）

Statues of Brahma with Spiral Hair and Bodhisattva

Copy by Mao Jianhong
Northern Wei Dynasty
Left Bodhisattva: Height: 137 cm, Width: 83 cm, Thickness: 31 cm
Right Bodhisattva: Height: 137 cm, Width: 83 cm, Thickness: 31 cm
Cave 121
Art Institute of Maijishan Cave-Temple Complex

On the left side outside the main wall niche of Cave 121, the Brahma with spiral hair and the Bodhisattva stand shoulder to shoulder, their heads close together as if engaged in a whisper, commonly referred to as "Whispering". The Brahma features a high spiral bun, looking down with slender eyebrows and elongated eyes. His hands are joined in a gesture of reverence. He is adorned in a kasaya with turned-up double collars, layered with a sanghati underneath, and a long skirt. His half-closed eyes and pursed lips convey an expression of attentive listening. The Bodhisattva on the left sports a high fan-shaped bun, slightly tilted forward. With delicate and handsome features, he holds a lotus in his right hand. His slender figure is complemented by a graceful neck and sloping shoulders. He wears a wide-sleeved upper garment styled with a flowing robe and broad belts, a long skirt, and a wide shawl draped over his shoulders, along with cloud-patterned shoes.

The piece titled "Whispering" showcases exceptional craftsmanship and ingenious conception. It is imbued with a vibrant atmosphere of life and rich in human emotion, making it a well-deserved artistic masterpiece.

The most remarkable aspect of this sculpture is the way the lower hem of the sleeve of Brahma with spiral hair, standing facing the door, is slightly opened to both sides. This detail evokes the sensation of a gentle breeze flowing in from the cave entrance,

causing the kasaya sleeves to flutter softly. Upon closer observation, one can almost feel a refreshing wisp of breeze brushing against the face, invigorating the spirit. The ancient artists' masterful attention to this detail has infused this group of sculptures with an extraordinary sense of vitality. (By Zhang Ping and Tan Yewen)

第 121 窟左侧菩萨线描图
Line drawing of Bodhisattva on the left side of Cave 121

螺髻梵王与菩萨像 第 121 窟正壁左侧与左壁右侧
Brahma with spiral hair and Bodhisattva statue, on the left side on the main
wall and the right side of the left wall of Cave 121

二

造像

Statues

　　佛陀自西方而来，到达麦积山时却神奇地改变了他的样貌。人们把自己对美的独特见解融入其间，营造浓郁的人情趣味，在一千多年的时间里创造了一批划时代的佳作，达到了人神交融的高度。

The Buddha came from the west. When he arrived at Maijishan, his appearance miraculously transformed. People integrated their unique insights of beauty into this transformed image, leading to the creation of a series of epoch-making masterpieces enduring over a period of more than 1,000 years, leaving the Buddha's form as an eternal mark at Maijishan.

23 影塑佛坐像

Clay-Molded Sculpture of Seated Buddha

北魏晚期
高 18.9 厘米　宽 10.5 厘米　厚 4.6 厘米　重 392 克
第 162 窟
麦积山石窟艺术研究所藏

Late Northern Wei Dynasty
Height: 18.9 cm, Width: 10.5 cm, Thickness: 4.6 cm, Weight: 392 g
Cave 162
Art Institute of Maijishan Cave-Temple Complex

　　佛头部为柱状高肉髻，面部长方，弯眉新月目，眉宇高朗，双目平视半睁，鼻隆且直，与眉骨相连；两颊略瘦，嘴小内敛微微上翘，双耳紧贴于两侧后颊。面容清秀，微微俯视，细颈削肩，躯体扁平。左手屈肘抚于腹部，右手掌心朝外贴于胸前。内着僧祇支，腰间束带，外披偏右袒袈裟，衣摆外搭于左臂分两瓣垂于佛座之下。衣褶处有阴刻线装饰，宽边衣饰线条流畅，衣褶反转自如，体现娴熟的技艺。整体敷彩，色泽鲜艳。面部有清代重新彩绘。局部虽有磨蚀，仍不失北魏"秀骨清像""褒衣博带"造像之风格。

　　20 世纪 80 年代麦积山石窟山体加固维修工程期间由第 162 窟移入文物库房保存。（张萍）

　　The Buddha's head features a columnar high usnisa, with a rectangular face adorned with crescent-shaped eyebrows and eyes. His forehead is high and clear, and his eyes are half-open, looking straight ahead. The nose is prominent and straight, connecting seamlessly to the brow bone, while the cheeks are slightly thin. His mouth is small, restrained, and slightly upturned, with ears closely attached to the back of the cheeks on both sides. The Buddha's face is handsome, with a slight downward gaze, a slender neck, and sloping shoulders, culminating in a flat body. The left hand is bent at the elbow and rests on the abdomen, while the right hand is placed against the chest with the palm facing outward. He wears a sanghati underneath, secured with a belt at the waist, and a kasaya that exposes the right shoulder. The hem of the kasaya drapes over the left arm, falling in two flaps beneath the Buddha seat. The folds of the clothing are decorated with intaglio lines. The folds are fluid, showcasing skilled craftsmanship. The entire statue is painted in vibrant colors, with the face having been repainted in the Qing Dynasty. Despite some abrasions in certain areas, the statue retains the Northern Wei Dynasty style characterized by "elegant bones and clear features" and "flowing robes and broad belts".

　　During the mountain reinforcement and maintenance project of the Maijishan Grottoes in the 1980s, the statue was relocated from Cave 162 and stored in the cultural relics warehouse. (By Zhang Ping)

24 影塑佛立像

Clay-Molded Sculpture of Standing Buddha

北魏晚期
高 26.2 厘米　宽 10.4 厘米　厚 4.9 厘米　重 700 克
第 162 窟
麦积山石窟艺术研究所藏

Late Northern Wei Dynasty
Height: 26.2 cm, Width: 10.4 cm, Thickness: 4.9 cm, Weight: 700 g
Cave 162
Art Institute of Maijishan Cave-Temple Complex

　　佛像柱状磨光高肉髻，广额，额际略向下呈弧形，面型长圆，长弯眉细目，鼻梁高直，连接于眉骨，小口内敛；嘴角微微上翘，面带微笑，细颈端肩，平胸鼓腹。跣足立于半圆形连台之上。内着僧祇支，外披宽博双领下垂式通肩袈裟，胸前衣领外翻，左手屈肘持巾抚腹部，右手贴于胸前。衣纹阴刻线稀疏且刚劲有力。袈裟衣角搭于手臂自然下垂，中间衣褶呈 U 字状。面目清新秀美，体态端庄挺拔，给人恬静优雅之美。通体施彩，脱落所剩无几。虽有磨蚀痕迹，且颈部已经出现断裂纹，却更增添了历史的沉淀之美。为麦积山北魏立佛之代表作品。

　　20 世纪 80 年代麦积山石窟山体加固工程期间从 162 窟移入文物库房保存。（张萍）

　　The Buddha statue features a columnar, highly polished usnisa, with a broad forehead that curves slightly downward. The face is elongated and oval, adorned with long, curved eyebrows and narrow eyes. The bridge of his nose is high and straight, seamlessly connecting to the brow bone, while the mouth is small and restrained, with corners slightly upturned in a gentle smile. The statue has a slender neck, straight shoulders, a flat chest, and a bulging abdomen, standing barefoot on a semicircular pedestal. He wears a sanghati underneath and a broad, full-length kasaya with double collars draping down over it. The collar in front is turned outward. The left hand is bent at the elbow, holding a scarf against the abdomen, while the right hand rests against the chest. The intaglio lines on the clothing are sparse yet vigorous, and the hem of his kasaya naturally drapes over the arm. The middle fold of the clothing forms a U shape. The statue's face is fresh and beautiful, with dignified and upright posture that conveys a serene and elegant beauty. The entire body is painted, though very little paint remains. Despite signs of abrasion and a crack appearing on the neck, these features enhance the beauty of its historical depth. This statue is a representative work of the standing Buddha from the Northern Wei Dynasty at Maijishan.

　　During the mountain reinforcement and maintenance project of the Maijishan Grottoes in the 1980s, the sculpture was relocated from Cave 162 and stored in the cultural relics warehouse. (By Zhang Ping)

影塑菩萨立像

25

Clay-Molded Sculpture of Standing Bodhisattva

北魏晚期
高 25.3 厘米　宽 8.8 厘米　厚 5.5 厘米　重 594 克
第 162 窟
麦积山石窟艺术研究所藏

Late Northern Wei Dynasty
Height: 25.3 cm, Width: 8.8 cm, Thickness: 5.5 cm, Weight: 594 g
Cave 162
Art Institute of Maijishan Cave-Temple Complex

　　菩萨面型长方，宽额，弯眉细目，直鼻，嘴角内敛，下颌上翘，双耳下垂，细颈端肩，平胸鼓腹。左臂屈肘，左手轻贴于胸前，右臂屈肘，右手抚于腹部。上着交领襦衫，下着长裙。披巾自双肩下垂交叉于腹部。躯体微微向左侧扭动，体态柔美轻盈，委婉多姿；服饰层次清晰、厚重且富于质感，含笑的神态，深刻地塑造出菩萨女性般的温柔与恬静，给人以高雅、豁达之感。

　　20 世纪 80 年代麦积山石窟山体加固工程期间从 162 窟移入文物库房保存。（张萍）

　　The Bodhisattva features an oblong face with a broad forehead, curved eyebrows, and slender eyes. She has a straight nose, inwardly curved corners of her mouth, an upturned jaw, and drooping ears. Her neck is slender, with straight shoulders, a flat chest, and a bulging abdomen. The left arm is bent at the elbow, with the left hand lightly resting on the chest, while the right arm is also bent at the elbow, with the right hand placed on the abdomen. She wears a cross-collared jacket on the upper body and a long skirt on the lower body, with a shawl draping down from both shoulders and crossing at the abdomen. Her body is slightly twisted to the left, showcasing a soft, light posture and graceful charm. The clothing displays clear layers and is thick, rich in texture. Her smiling expression profoundly conveys the tenderness and tranquility of a feminine Bodhisattva, imparting a sense of elegance and open-mindedness.

　　During the mountain reinforcement and maintenance project of the Maijishan Grottoes in the 1980s, the sculpture was relocated from Cave 162 and stored in the cultural relics warehouse. (By Zhang Ping)

影塑弟子立像

26

北魏
高 24.5 厘米　宽 9.3 厘米　厚 4.1 厘米　重 470 克
第 20 窟
麦积山石窟艺术研究所藏

第 20 窟影塑弟子立像线描图
Line Drawing of Standing Disciple in Cave 20

　　弟子面型长方圆润，弯眉细目，鼻梁直通额际，双唇薄，嘴角内敛，低眉微笑。细颈削肩，平胸鼓腹。内着僧祇支，下穿长裙，外披圆领通肩袈裟；衣角外搭于左臂自然下垂；右手托一方形物品，置于胸前，左手持一莲蕾贴于腹部。服饰上阴刻线疏密有致、简洁流畅，彰显厚重沉稳之感。修长的身躯略前倾，上身微微扭动，作举步前行状。面容丰润隽秀，神态稚嫩，体姿端庄挺拔，雕塑技法娴熟，准确地刻画了人物内心世界，表现出一位眉清目秀、温婉敦厚、虔诚舒朗的英俊少年模样。

　　20 世纪 80 年代麦积山石窟山体加固工程期间由第 20 窟移入麦积山石窟文物库房存放。（张萍）

Clay-Molded Sculpture of Standing Disciple

Northern Wei Dynasty
Height: 24.5 cm, Weight: 9.3 cm, Thickness: 4.1 cm, Weight: 470 g
Cave 20
Art Institute of Maijishan Cave-Temple Complex

The disciple has a long, smooth and rounded face, with curved eyebrows and slender eyes. The bridge of his nose extends straight to the forehead, and he has thin lips with the corners of his mouth inwardly curved. He smiles with lowered eyebrows. His slender neck and sloping shoulders complement a flat chest and a bulging abdomen. He wears a sanghati undergarment, a long skirt, and a round-necked, full-shouldered kasaya. The corner of the robe drapes over his left arm and hangs naturally. His right hand holds a square object placed on the chest, while his left hand holds a lotus bud against the abdomen. The incised lines on the clothing are well-proportioned in density, simple and smooth, conveying a sense of thickness and stability. The slender body leans slightly forward, and the upper body twists slightly, as if taking a step forward. His face is plump and handsome, with a youthful expression, and he maintains a dignified and upright posture. The sculpting technique is skillful and accurately portrays the figure's inner world, presenting a handsome young man with clear features, gentle and honest demeanor, and a devout, open-minded spirit.

During the mountain reinforcement and maintenance project of the Maijishan Grottoes in the 1980s, the sculpture was relocated from Cave 20 and stored in the cultural relics warehouse of the Maijishan Grottoes. (By Zhang Ping)

第 20 窟全景图
Panoramic View of Cave 20

27 泥塑菩萨立像

北魏
高 90 厘米　宽 25 厘米　厚 17 厘米　重 9.25 千克
第 165 窟
麦积山石窟艺术研究所藏

第 165 窟泥塑菩萨立像线描图
Line Drawing of Standing Bodhisattva in Cave 165

　　菩萨束发高冠，面型长方，弯眉细目，高鼻薄唇，嘴角上翘内敛，下颌微微上翘，长颈溜肩，平胸鼓腹。着内衣及僧祇衼，外披通肩宽袖长衫，披巾自双肩自然下垂，腹部腰带打结下垂，左手持环，环内饰带打结分三条自然下垂，右手臂横置于胸前，体态端庄秀美，为麦积山北朝典型的"秀骨清像"。

　　165 窟建于第 78 窟正上方，开凿于后秦，也是麦积山最早的洞窟之一，窟内现存 6 身造像俱为北宋重塑。此像与麦积山第 165 窟宋代造像不同，或不属于该窟，可能是其他洞窟残损后移入第 165 窟保存的。

　　现存于文物库房。（张萍、谈叶闻）

Clay Sculpture of Standing Bodhisattva

Northern Wei Dynasty
Height: 90 cm, Width: 25 cm, Thickness: 17 cm, Weight: 9.25 kg
Cave 165
Art Institute of Maijishan Cave-Temple Complex

The Bodhisattva wears a high headdress for tied-up hair and has an oblong face, with curved eyebrows and slender eyes, a high nose and thin lips. The corners of the mouth are upturned and inwardly curved, and the jaw is slightly raised. The figure has a long neck and sloping shoulders, with a flat chest and a bulging abdomen. The Bodhisattva wears undergarments and a sanghati underneath, and a wide-sleeved long robe that drapes over the shoulders, with a shawl naturally hanging down from both shoulders. A belt at the abdomen is knotted and hangs down. The left hand holds a ring, within which a belt is knotted and divided into three parts that hang down naturally. The right arm is positioned horizontally across the chest. The posture is dignified and graceful, representing the typical style of "elegant bone and clear features" from the Northern Dynasties at Maijishan.

Cave 165, built directly above Cave 78 and carved in the Later Qin Dynasty, is also one of the earliest caves at Maijishan. The cave currently houses six statues, all remolded in the Northern Song Dynasty. Based on the characteristics of this statue, it's different from the Song Dynasty statues typically found in Cave 165. Therefore, it may not originally belong to this cave, and could have been relocated here for preservation after being damaged in other caves.

The Bodhisattva statue is currently stored in the cultural relics warehouse. (By Zhang Ping and Tan Yewen)

第 165 窟正壁右侧供养人线描图
Line Drawing of a Patron on the Right Side
of the Main Wall of Cave 165

第 165 窟左壁菩萨像线描图
Line Drawing of a Bodhisattva on
the Left Wall of Cave 165

第 165 窟右侧供养菩萨
Bodhisattva and Patron on the Right Side of Cave 165

第 165 窟正壁及左壁菩萨像
Bodhisattva statues on the main wall and left wall of Cave 165.

28 泥塑弟子立像

Clay sculpture of Standing Disciple

北魏晚期
高 70 厘米　宽 21.3 厘米　厚 13.5 厘米　重 11.39 千克
第 139 窟
麦积山石窟艺术研究所藏

Late Northern Wei Dynasty
Height: 70 cm, Width: 21.3 cm, Thickness: 13.5 cm, Weight: 11.39 kg
Cave 139
Art Institute of Maijishan Cave-Temple Complex

139 窟位于西崖东侧，平面方形，平顶。全窟被香火熏黑，壁画皆已剥落。

弟子面目清瘦，前额有明显的皱纹，眼眶及颧骨突出，双眼及脸颊内陷，薄唇，嘴角内敛，长颈圆肩。内着僧祇衩，外着偏袒右肩袈裟，双手合抱腹前隐于袈裟外翻的下摆内。造像形体消瘦，筋骨清晰可见，表现了苦行僧的形象。（王通玲、谈叶闻）

Cave 139 is located on the east side of the western cliff and features a square plan with a flat ceiling. The interior of the cave is blackened by incense smoke, and all the murals have suffered from peeling.

The disciple is depicted with a thin face, characterized by prominent wrinkles on the forehead, protruding eye sockets, and cheekbones. His eyes and cheeks appear sunken, and he has thin lips with inwardly curved corners. The figure features a long neck and rounded shoulders. He is dressed in a sanghati underneath and a kasaya draped over the right shoulder. His hands are clasped in front of the abdomen, concealed within the turned-out hem of the kasaya. The statue's emaciated form reveals clear outlines of bones and tendons, effectively conveying the image of an ascetic monk. (By Wang Tongling and Tan Yewen)

29 石雕佛立像

段一鸣临摹
北魏
高250厘米　宽95厘米　厚86厘米
第135窟
麦积山石窟艺术研究所藏

石雕佛立像线描图
Line Drawing of Stone-Carved Standing Buddha

　　麦积山石窟洞窟内保存了大量泥塑造像，也保存了一些石刻造像。这些石雕石质细腻，色泽明显与麦积山本体的红色砂砾岩石不同，麦积山石窟周边没有这些石质，应是在其他地方雕凿好以后运输过来的。更为疑惑的是，古人是如何在接近80米的高度将这座重达两吨半的石雕造像置入窟内的，这实在令人惊叹。

　　这是麦积山最大的石雕造像，漩涡纹高肉髻，面相长圆，细眉入鬓，眼睛微睁，直鼻与弯眉相连，唇厚且饱满，肩宽而浑圆，平胸鼓腹，内着僧祇支，中衣在胸前打结相连，外穿双领下垂宽博的袈裟，右领搭于左臂，衣褶厚重，体积感强。左手施与愿印，右手屈肘向前，手部缺失。袈裟的衣纹雕刻流畅自如，脚踩覆钵莲花，莲瓣饱满尖部翘起。尤其是大拇指与中指之间雕一莲苞，四指背部被衣袖内伸出一盛开的莲花所托举，肌理丰腴秀润，似有弹性，手指纤细，从外观上感觉非常唯美，装饰性极强，同时也解决了受力的问题，一举两得，妙手佳境。全像雕刻精美，动态自然，显示出较高的雕琢水平，为麦积山少数北魏单体圆雕造像之佳作。（张萍、谈叶闻）

第 135 窟石雕立佛（局部）
Standing Buddha (Detail) of Cave 135

Stone Sculpture of Standing Buddha

Copy by Duan Yiming
Northern Wei Dynasty
Height: 250 cm, Width: 95 cm, Thickness: 86 cm
Cave 135
Art Institute of Maijishan Cave-Temple Complex

The Maijishan Grottoes contain a significant number of clay sculptures, as well as some stone carvings characterized by a fine texture. The colors of these stone carvings are noticeably inconsistent with the red sandy conglomerate rock native to Maijishan. Since such stone quality is not found in the vicinity of the Maijishan Grottoes, it is likely that these carvings were transported here after being carved elsewhere. What is even more astonishing is how the ancients managed to place these stone carvings, weighing two and a half tons, into the cave at a height of nearly 80 m.

This is the largest stone carving statue at Maijishan. It features a high spiral-patterned ushnisha and an oblong face with slender eyebrows extending into the temples. The eyes are slightly open, complemented by a straight nose that connects to the curved eyebrows, and the lips are thick and full. The shoulders are wide and rounded, with a flat chest and a bulging abdomen. The figure wears a sanghati underneath, with the middle garment knotted at the chest. Over this,

he dons a broad kasaya with double collars that hangs down, the right collar draped over the left arm. The folds of the garment are thick, giving a strong sense of volume. The left hand is in the vara mudra, while the right arm is bent forward at the elbow, with the hand missing. The carving of the kasaya's folds is smooth and natural. He stands on a lotus with an inverted bowl, featuring full lotus petals with upward-turned tips. Notably, a lotus bud is carved between the thumb and middle finger, while a blooming lotus flower, extending from the sleeve, supports the back of the four fingers. The texture is plump, smooth, and moist, appearing elastic, with slender fingers that enhance its beauty and decorative quality. This design also addresses the issue of force, showcasing remarkable craftsmanship. The entire statue is exquisitely carved, with a natural posture that reflects a high level of artistry. It is one of the masterpieces among the few individual round sculptures from the Northern Wei Dynasty at Maijishan. (By Zhang Ping and Tan Yewen)

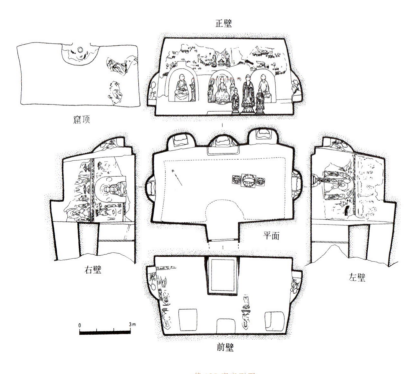

第 135 窟实测图
Surveyed drawing of Cave 135

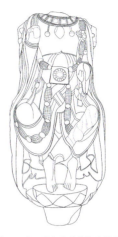

第 135 窟石雕交脚菩萨像线描图
Line Drawing of Cross-Legged Bodhisattva in Cave 135

石雕交脚菩萨像

30

Stone Sculpture of Cross-Legged Bodhisattva

北周
高 81.5 厘米　宽 35 厘米　厚 22 厘米　重 62.1 千克
第 135 窟
麦积山石窟艺术研究所藏

Northern Zhou Dynasty
Height: 81.5 cm, Width: 35 cm, Thickness: 22 cm, Weight: 62.1 kg
Cave 135
Art Institute of Maijishan Cave-Temple Complex

　　菩萨头部缺失。平肩、平胸鼓腹，身躯饱满，双脚相互交叉，双足外翻直立于莲座之上。宝缯分搭于双臂两侧。外搭披巾，内着僧祇枝，腰系长裙，戴项圈，披璎珞。披巾自肩分搭两侧下垂，在腹部相交穿环后于双小腿处外绕回环。璎珞叠压在披巾上，自双肩下垂在腹前相交绕膝后搭。衣纹线条流畅，雕刻细致。

　　2009 年从 135 窟移入文物库房保存。从此造像特点上看，与麦积山第 135 窟造像不同，故不属于该窟，应是其他洞窟残损后移入第 135 窟保存的。（张萍）

　　The head of the Bodhisattva is missing. The statue has square shoulders, a flat chest, and a bulging abdomen, with a full body. The feet are crossed and turned outward, standing upright on a lotus pedestal. Precious ribbons are draped along both sides of the arms. The figure wears a scarf over an inner sanghati robe, a long skirt around the waist, a necklace, and pendants. The scarf drapes down from the shoulders, intersecting at the abdomen and passing through a ring, before looping back around the lower legs. The pendants are layered over the scarf, hanging down from the shoulders, intersecting in front of the abdomen, and then draping over the knees. The clothing lines flow smoothly, and the carving is executed with meticulous details.

　　In 2009, the statue was relocated from Cave 135 and stored in the cultural relics warehouse. Based on the features of this statue, it is different from the statues in Cave 135 of Maijishan, so it does not belong to this cave. It should have been moved to Cave 135 for preservation after being damaged in other caves. (By Zhang Ping)

第 135 窟 北壁正中 交脚菩萨
Cave 135, Center of the North Wall, Cross-Legged Bodhisattva

31 小沙弥像

董晴野临摹
北魏
高 95 厘米　宽 40 厘米　厚 23 厘米
第 133 窟
麦积山石窟艺术研究所藏

　　在 133 窟第 9 龛右壁外侧有一身弟子，俗称小沙弥，他高度不足一米，头微偏向右侧，脸形椭圆，面带微笑，细颈削肩，挺胸鼓腹而立，左臂略屈肘下垂，左手于腹侧持一莲包（现莲包无存），右手上扬、手心向外置于肩前，手部残失，内着僧祇枝，外着袈裟，身体略前倾而立。

　　微笑是人与人之间最短的距离。此微笑小沙弥，双唇轻闭而嘴角上扬，一双细长凤眼满含天真笑意，难掩心中的欢欣与喜悦。于心底流露出的那份真情实感，如此生动鲜活，仿佛生活在我们身边的一个可爱孩童，尤为传神。俯身去看他的脸，眉宇间尚未脱去天真无邪的稚气，让观者也不禁会心一笑，有一种烦恼都被治愈的感觉，唤起了人们内心对美好生活的向往和憧憬。整体造像简洁明快，没有过多的刻画，是麦积山石窟北魏精品造像。（张萍、谈叶闻）

Statue of Novice Monk

Copy by Dong Qingye
Northern Wei Dynasty
Height: 95 cm, Width: 40 cm, Thickness: 23 cm
Cave 133
Art Institute of Maijishan Cave-Temple Complex

Located outside the right wall of Niche 9 in Cave 133, this statue represents a disciple, commonly referred to as a novice monk. Standing at less than 1 meter tall, the figure has a slightly tilted head facing right and an oval-shaped face adorned with a gentle smile. The statue features a slender neck and sloping shoulders. It stands with a proud chest and a bulging belly. The left arm is slightly bent at the elbow and hangs down, with the left hand originally holding a lotus bud at the abdomen (the lotus bud is now missing). The right hand is raised upward with the palm facing outward, positioned in front of the shoulder, though the hand is partially damaged. The monk is depicted in traditional attire, wearing a sanghati underneath and a kasaya over it, with his body slightly leaning forward.

A smile is the shortest distance between people. This smiling novice monk features gently closed lips and raised corners of his mouth, with long, slender phoenix eyes that radiate innocent joy. His expression reveals a heartfelt happiness that is both vivid and refreshing, reminiscent of a charming child living among us. Upon closer inspection, one can see the lingering innocence in his eyebrows, evoking a knowing smile from viewers. This expression creates a sense of healing, as if all troubles are alleviated, stirring a deep yearning for a better life within the hearts of those who gaze upon him. The overall design of the statue is simple yet lively, avoiding excessive detail. It stands as a remarkable example of the Northern Wei artistry within the Maijishan Grottoes. (By Zhang Ping and Tan Yewen)

第 133 窟东壁佛龛比丘
Bhiksu in Niche 9 on the East Wall of Cave 133

32 弟子像

Disciple Statue

中央勘察团翻模、唐冲做旧
北周
高 78 厘米　宽 27 厘米　厚 22 厘米
第 94 窟
麦积山石窟艺术研究所藏

Mold Created by the Central Survey Team and Aging Process Carried out
by Tang Chong
Northern Zhou Dynasty
Height: 78 cm, Width: 27 cm, Thickness: 22 cm
Cave 94
Art Institute of Maijishan Cave-Temple Complex

第 94 窟弟子像位于主佛左壁右侧，为一青年弟子造像。面形饱满圆润，弯眉细目，高鼻薄唇，下颌微微上翘，面部丰润敦实，面带微笑，短颈端肩，臂膊浑圆。左手下垂置于腹侧，右手上举，轻抚衣领。内着僧祇衼，腰间结带，着双领下垂僧衣，跣足立于半圆形台基上，神态祥和自然，具有北周"珠圆玉润"的特点。

石膏翻模是 20 世纪 50 年代考察团研究和保护石窟的方式之一。1953 年，中央勘察团在第 133 窟首次开启翻模工作，共计翻模石膏 19 件。

（张萍）

The disciple statue in Cave 94 is located on the right side of the left wall of the main Buddha. This statue depicts a young disciple characterized by a full and rounded face, featuring curved eyebrows, slender eyes, a high nose, and thin lips, with the lower jaw slightly upturned. His face exudes a plump and solid appearance, complemented by a gentle smile. He has a short neck, square shoulders, and rounded arms. The left hand hangs down at his abdomen, while the right hand is raised, gently touching the collar of his robe. He is dressed in a sanghati underneath, secured with a belt at the waist, and adorned with a monk's robe featuring double collars that drape down. Standing barefoot on a semicircular pedestal, the disciple's expression is peaceful and natural, reflecting the perfectly round and lustrous characteristics typical of the Northern Zhou Dynasty.

Plaster molding was one of the techniques used by the Survey Team in the 1950s to study and protect grottoes. In 1953, the Central Survey Team initiated the plaster molding process in Cave 133, resulting in a total of 19 plaster casts. (By Zhang Ping)

33 影塑飞天

北魏晚期
高 22 厘米　宽 9 厘米　厚 2.5 厘米　重 1.929 千克（含边框）
第 133 窟
麦积山石窟艺术研究所藏

20 世纪 50 年代在清理第 133 窟时发现，原为第 133 窟第 11 龛龛楣影塑。20 世纪 80 年代麦积山石窟山体加固工程期间，由 133 窟移入文物库房保存。

头部采用圆雕，身体采用高浮雕，衣带采用浅浮雕的技法制作。飞天束扇形高发髻，面型长方，弯眉细目，眉宇舒展，目视前方。长颈，平胸鼓腹。右手手掌向上举于肩部，左手于腹部握莲蕾。双腿作弯曲状。内着僧祇衣，外穿汉式交领宽袍大袖束腰长衫，披帛自双肩穿肘向后，裙裾飞扬，尽显飘逸灵动之感。（张萍）

影塑就是模制泥塑，是采用预先制作好的模子进行大量的塑像制作，一般的小型塑像都是采用这种方法。麦积山石窟在北朝时期信仰千佛，在洞窟壁面上大量地贴敷，这些千佛都是通过模塑的方法来制作的，其高度一般在 10—20 厘米左右，厚度在 2 厘米左右。由于同一个模子可以大量制作，所以我们在同时期的各个洞窟中都可以看到同样的影塑。除了这些千佛外，供养人也常用模塑的方法。

Clay-Molded Sculpture of Flying Apsara

Late Northern Wei Dynasty
Height: 22 cm, Width: 9 cm, Thickness: 2.5 cm, Weight: 1.929 kg
(including the frame)
Cave 133
Art Institute of Maijishan Cave-Temple Complex

In the 1950s, during the clearance of Cave 133, it was discovered that the clay-molded sculpture originally formed part of the lintel of Niche 11 in Cave 133. Subsequently, in the 1980s, during the mountain reinforcement project of the Maijishan Grottoes, the sculpture was relocated from Cave 133 and stored in the cultural relics warehouse for preservation.

The sculpture features a head crafted in round carving, a body rendered in high relief, and a clothing belt created using low relief techniques. The flying apsara sports a fan-shaped high bun, characterized by a rectangular face, curved eyebrows, and slender eyes, with a relaxed expression gazing forward. She has a long neck, a flat chest, and a bulging abdomen. The right hand is raised with the palm positioned at shoulder height, while the left hand holds a lotus bud at the abdomen, and her legs are bent. Her attire includes a sanghati underneath and a Han-style cross-collared long robe with wide sleeves and a waist-tied long gown outside. A silk scarf flows from her shoulders through her elbows to the back, and her skirt billows, conveying a sense of elegance and agility. (By Zhang Ping)

Clay molding refers to the process of using molds to shape clay into various sculptures, allowing for the production of a large number of identical pieces using pre-made molds. Generally, small statues are made by this method.During the Northern Dynasties, the Maijishan Grottoes featured a significant number of sculptures representing Thousand Buddhas, which were affixed to the cave walls. These Thousand Buddhas were crafted using molding technique, typically measuring about 10-20 cm in height and approximately 2 cm in depth. The use of the same mold for mass production allowed for the replication of identical clay-molded sculptures across various caves from the same period. In addition to these Thousand Buddhas, patrons were often created utilizing the molding method.

第 133 窟飞天线描图
Line Drawing of Flying Apsara in Cave 133

第 133 窟第 11 龛飞天
Flying Apsara in Niche 11 of Cave 133

34

泥塑菩萨立像

Clay Sculpture of Standing Bodhisattva

张北平临摹
北魏
高 155 厘米　宽 67 厘米　厚 40 厘米
第 135 窟
麦积山石窟艺术研究所藏

Copy by Zhang Beiping
Northern Wei Dynasty
Height: 155 cm, Width: 67 cm, Thickness: 40 cm
Cave 135
Art Institute of Maijishan Cave-Temple Complex

　　第 135 窟正壁龛内左侧菩萨像，菩萨扇形高髻宝冠，发际线中分，面型扁平，弯眉细目，嘴角内敛，下颌微微上翘，面带微笑。宝缯发辫自双肩下垂，长颈溜肩，双肩饰宝珠，身着"三重"交领衣饰，束腰，外披披帛，飘带及地，足穿云头履，左手下提如意，右手抚于胸前。身材修长，神情恬静淡然。服饰多重华丽，风姿绰约，笑靥可亲，表现出一个温婉秀丽、宁静谦和的形象，其形成是受南朝文化之影响。在整体造型上比例准确，姿态生动，力求突出菩萨清秀的仪容。在服饰的处理上采用概括简练的手法，衣着粗中有细，厚中见薄，拙中见巧，主次分明，充分体现了"秀骨清像"的艺术风格。（张萍）

　　The Bodhisattva statue on the left inside the main wall niche of Cave 135 features a high fan-shaped bun adorned with a jeweled crown, with hair neatly parted down the middle. The statue has a flat face characterized by curved eyebrows and slender eyes, while the corners of his mouth are restrained, complemented by a slightly upturned lower jaw that creates a serene smile. The Bodhisattva's braided hair, embellished with jewels, cascades down from both shoulders, framing a long neck and sloping shoulders, both adorned with additional jewelry. Dressed in "triple" cross-collared garments, the figure is cinched at the waist and draped in a flowing shawl, with ribbons extending to the ground. It wears cloud-patterned shoes, with the left hand holding a Ruyi beneath the body, and the right hand gracefully positioned on the chest. This slender figure conveys a calm and peaceful demeanor, with its clothing intricately layered and resplendent, exuding grace and an approachable smile. The representation encapsulates a gentle, beautiful, tranquil, and modest image, influenced by the culture of the Southern Dynasties. In terms of overall form, the proportions are accurate, and the postures are vivid, emphasizing the delicate appearance of the Bodhisattva. The treatment of clothing employs a concise and generalized technique, balancing rough and detailed elements while clearly distinguishing focal points, fully reflecting the artistic style of "elegant bones and clear features". (By Zhang Ping)

第 135 窟正壁中龛照
Photo of the Central Niche on the Main Wall of Cave 135

第 135 窟正壁右侧菩萨特写
Close-up Photo of Bodhisattva on the Right Side of the Main Wall of Cave 135

《法华经变》壁画

35

唐冲临摹
北魏
长 209 厘米　宽 84 厘米
第 110 窟
麦积山石窟艺术研究所藏

经是佛经，变是"变相"或"变现"，也就是形象化的意思。换句话说，经变就是以图像的形式来说明某部佛经的思想内容。

《法华经》是大乘佛教初期的典籍，约成稿于公元1世纪前后的印度。公元3世纪，《法华经》经中亚沿着丝绸之路传入中国，逐渐受到推崇，之后更影响至韩国、日本。《法华经》推崇写刻佛经

与造像，因此造就了相当数量的美术遗存。麦积山石窟第110窟的法华变是北朝壁画的代表作品。

此壁画位于窟龛前壁门上，居中画一佛二菩萨。左、右菩萨题名分别为"此事观世音菩萨""此是无尽意菩萨"。两侧各画比丘、比丘尼、优婆塞、优婆夷共四身。两侧上部绘飞天各一身、莲花化生一身。（张萍、谈叶闻）

Mural Painting of *the Lotus Sutra Illustrations*

Copy by Tang Chong
Northern Wei Dynasty
Length: 209 cm, Width: 84 cm
Cave 110
Art Institute of Maijishan Cave-Temple Complex

In this context, "Jing (sutra)" refers to Buddhist scriptures, while "Bian" means "transformation" or "manifestation", which relates to the concept of visualization. In other words, "Jing Bian" refers to the practice of illustrating the ideological content of a specific Buddhist sutra through visual imagery.

Fahuajing (The Lotus Sutra) is a foundational text of early Mahayana Buddhism, believed to have been completed in India around the 1st century AD. In the 3rd century AD, it was introduced to China via the Silk Road through Central Asia, where it gradually gained prominence and later became highly revered in Korea and Japan. The Lotus Sutra emphasizes the importance of writing, engraving Buddhist scriptures, and creating statues, which led to the production of a significant number of artistic relics. Notably, the Illustration of the Lotus Sutra in Cave 110 of the Maijishan Grottoes stands as a representative example of mural art from the Northern Dynasties.

This mural is situated on the door of the front wall of the niche. At its center, it features one Buddha flanked by two Bodhisattvas. The inscriptions identifying the Bodhisattvas read: "This is Avalokitesvara Bodhisattva" on the left and "This is Akshayamati Bodhisattva" on the right. On each side of the mural, there are four figures representing bhikshus, bhikshunis, upasakas, and upasikas. Additionally, in the upper sections on both sides, there is one apsara and one figure representing lotus transformation. (By Zhang Ping and Tan Yewen)

《法华经变》壁画局部
Mural of Fahuajing Bian (Illustrations of the Lotus Sutra) – Detail

36 泥塑维摩诘坐像

张北平临摹
西魏
高 145 厘米　宽 102 厘米　厚 70 厘米
第 102 窟
麦积山石窟艺术研究所藏

泥塑维摩诘坐像线描图
Line Drawing of Clay-Covered Sculpture of Seated Vimalakirti

西魏文帝元宝炬笃信佛教，注意经营秦州。他出于政治原因不得不将其钟爱的皇后乙弗氏废黜为尼，并迁居秦州；同时将自己年幼的爱子武都王元戊封为秦州刺史，以慰藉其母乙弗氏忧戚的心情。这样的处置势必给西魏初年的麦积山石窟带来巨大的影响。麦积山自西魏大统（535—551）初年即已出现技艺高超的龛像，比北魏晚期有了明显的发展，来自西魏王朝的直接眷顾显然是决定性因素之一。

在西崖的上层，出现了一批精美的西魏窟。其中稍靠下的第 102 窟，以精湛的技艺，表现了新颖的造像题材维摩变。

第 102 窟维摩诘像，位于龛内左壁。头戴卷荷帽，宽额长眉。五官较为集中，棱角分明，双目有神。内穿圆领内衣，中衣胸前打结，外穿双领下垂长袍，结跏趺坐。左手抚膝，右臂屈于胸前，右手已残缺。（王通玲、谈叶闻）

Clay-Covered Sculpture of Seated Vimalakirti

Copy by Zhang Beiping
Western Wei Dynasty
Height: 145 cm, Width: 102 cm, Thickness: 70 cm
Cave 102
Art Institute of Maijishan Cave-Temple Complex

Yuan Baoju, Emperor Wen of the Western Wei Dynasty, was a devout Buddhist who focused on managing Qinzhou. Due to political circumstances, he had to depose his beloved empress, Yifu, forcing her to become a nun and relocating her to Qinzhou. To alleviate her sorrow, he granted their young son, Yuan Wu, Prince of Wudu, the title of governor of Qinzhou. This situation undoubtedly influenced the early years of the Maijishan Grottoes. From the inception of the Datong era (535—551) of the Western Wei Dynasty, the grottoes began to feature niche statues crafted with exceptional skill, marking a significant advancement compared to those of the late Northern Wei Dynasty. The direct patronage by the Western Wei Dynasty played a crucial role in this development. On the upper layer of the western cliff, a series of exquisite Western Wei caves emerged. Notably, Cave 102, positioned slightly lower, showcases the innovative statue theme of Vimalakirti Transformation, exemplifying remarkable craftsmanship.

The Vimalakirti statue in Cave 102 is situated on the left wall within the niche. The figure is adorned with a lotus-leaf-shaped hat, characterized by a broad forehead and long eyebrows. His facial features are concentrated, with distinct contours and bright, expressive eyes. He is dressed in a round-necked undergarment, with a knot tied at the chest of the middle garment. Over this, he wears a long robe featuring double collars that drape down, and he is seated in full lotus position. His left hand rests on the knee, while his right arm is bent in front of the chest; however, the right hand is incomplete. (By Wang Tongling and Tan Yewen)

第 102 窟全景图
Full view of Cave 102

37

第44窟整体复原窟

第44窟正壁龛内塑一身坐佛，龛外两侧各塑一身胁侍菩萨，左壁塑一身立弟子。共计4身。

坐佛水涡纹高肉髻，面形方圆适中，薄唇小口，低眉浅笑，微微俯视观者，内穿僧祇支，胸前系结，外披通肩袈裟，结跏趺坐。覆于佛座前的悬裳衣褶俱呈圆转的线条，质感厚重，层次分明，富有装饰趣味。造像端庄典雅、微微俯视、和蔼可亲，集中体现了西魏造像的美感。传说她是西魏武都王仿母亲的形象所塑，即西魏文帝皇后乙弗氏。因此气质格外慈祥，极具女性化特征。发髻、胸前、衣裙的彩绘，如今褪成淡淡的青绿色，衣褶从佛座垂下，层层叠叠如涟漪般晕开，高贵、飘逸、圣洁。

龛外左、右胁侍菩萨各一身。头戴花冠，低平发髻，面型丰满圆润，眉长眼小。双眼微开下视，鼻高修直，戴项圈。上身袒露，下着长裙，帛带于身体两侧飘然而下；面容秀美，体型适中，和主佛相互映衬，给人一种极强的美感。飘带的残破处露出内部的铁条，这是为了适应飘带独立且自然弯曲的形态而采取的工艺，这些成熟的工艺方法在中国古代泥塑作品中很有自身的特点。

窟内东壁靠后侧位置，保存着一身弟子造像，面型方圆，身披双领下垂袈裟，双手合十，手指残损处露出铁条，足蹬方头履。造像简洁质朴，清新自然。弟子面部朝向特别引人注意，其并不是朝向主佛，而是朝向洞窟门口，似乎是透过窟门口向外眺望。这显然是当时的工匠有意而作，将身处庄严佛国的一名年轻弟子的小心思在不经意间表达出来。（张萍）

Restored Cave 44

In the niche on the main wall of Cave 44, there is a seated Buddha statue. On both sides of the niche, there are Bodhisattva attendant statues, and on the left wall, there is a standing disciple statue. In total, there are four statues.

The seated Buddha features a high spiral bun adorned with water-vortex patterns, a face that is both moderately square and round, thin lips, a small mouth, low eyebrows, and a faint smile, slightly looking down at the viewers. She wears a sanghati underneath, tied at the chest, and a kasaya draped over the shoulders, sitting in full lotus position. The folds of the hanging skirt in front of the Buddha seat are characterized by rounded lines, with a thick texture, distinct layers, and rich decorative details. The statue exudes dignity and elegance, with a gentle demeanor that embodies the beauty of statues in the Western Wei Dynasty. Legend has it that this statue was molded by the Prince of Wudu of the Western Wei Dynasty after his mother, Empress Yifu, the consort of Emperor Wen. This connection lends the figure an exceptionally kind temperament and distinctly feminine features. The painted patterns on the bun, chest, and dress have now faded to a soft bluish-green. The folds of the dress cascade down from the Buddha seat, layered like ripples, conveying a sense of nobility, grace, and sanctity.

On each side outside of the niche, there is an attendant Bodhisattva. They wear a flower crown and a low flat bun, with a plump and rounded face, long eyebrows, and small eyes. Their eyes are slightly open and looking down, complemented by a tall, straight nose and a necklace. Their upper bodies are exposed, and they wear a long skirt, with silk ribbons gracefully cascading down on both sides. With their beautiful faces and moderate figures, they enhance the presence of the main Buddha, creating a strong sense of beauty. In the broken part of the ribbon, iron bars are exposed, a technique used to maintain the independent and naturally curved shape of the ribbons. These sophisticated methods are characteristic of ancient Chinese clay sculpture.

On the back side of the east wall inside the cave, there is a preserved statue of a disciple. The face is both square and round, and the figure is draped in a kasaya with double collars hanging down, with hands joining together in prayer. In the damaged areas of the fingers, iron bars are exposed. The statue features square-toed shoes and has a simple, unadorned appearance that feels fresh and natural. What is particularly striking is the direction of the disciple's gaze; rather than facing the main Buddha, he looks toward the cave entrance, as if peering out into the world beyond. This was clearly an intentional choice by the craftsmen, subtly expressing the thoughts of a young disciple within the solemnity of the Buddhist realm. (By Zhang Ping)

第 44 窟主佛线描图
Line Drawing of the Main Buddha in Cave 44

第 43 窟西魏皇后乙弗氏墓葬
Cave 43, the Tomb of Empress Yifu of the Western Wei Dynasty

①
②

①②③泥塑一佛二菩萨（Clay Sculptures of one Buddha and two Bodhisattvas）
孙靖临摹（Copy by Sun Jing）
西魏（Western Wei Dynasty）
1 组 3 身（Three Statues of one Group）
主佛：高 171 厘米　宽 106 厘米　厚 16 厘米（Main Buddha: Height: 171 cm　Width: 106 cm　Thickness: 16 cm）
菩萨：高 140 厘米　宽 68 厘米　厚 16 厘米（Bodhisattvas: Height: 140 cm　Width: 68 cm　Thickness: 16 cm）
第 44 窟（Cave 44）
麦积山石窟艺术研究所藏（Art Institute of Maijishan Cave-Temple Complex）

③

④

④泥塑弟子立像（Clay Sculpture of Standing Disciple）

孙靖临摹（Copy by Sun Jing）

西魏（Western Wei Dynasty）

高 113 厘米　宽 40 厘米　厚 33 厘米

（Height: 113 cm　Width: 40 cm　Thickness: 33 cm）

第 44 窟（Cave 44）

麦积山石窟艺术研究所藏（Art Institute of Maijishan Cave-Temple Complex）

38 泥塑佛头像

Clay Sculpture of Buddha Head

西魏
高 32.7 厘米　宽 9.9 厘米　厚 9.3 厘米　重 1.37 千克
第 110 窟
麦积山石窟艺术研究所藏

Western Wei Dynasty
Height: 32.7 cm, Width: 9.9 cm, Thickness: 9.3 cm, Weight: 1.37 kg
Cave 110
Art Institute of Maijishan Cave-Temple Complex

　　佛头像高肉髻，发际线平整，面形长方，平额，弯眉如满月，高鼻薄唇，嘴角内敛，双耳紧贴后颊，下颌微翘。面容清俊秀美，温婉可亲，有一种超凡脱俗之感。此造像的工匠们摆脱了早期印度造像的风格，塑造出一个具有典型的汉民族造像特点的艺术佳作。

　　20 世纪 60 年代麦积山石窟山体加固工程前从 110 窟移入文物库房保存。（张萍）

　　The Buddha head features a high spiral bun and a straight hairline. Its face is rectangular, with a flat forehead and curved eyebrows resembling a full moon. The nose is high, and the lips are thin, with the corners of the mouth slightly restrained. The ears are closely positioned against the back of the cheeks, and the lower jaw is slightly upturned. His face is handsome, gentle and amiable, exuding a sense of transcendence. The craftsmen of this statue have moved away from the style of early Indian sculptures, creating an artistic masterpiece that embodies the typical characteristics of Han statue art.

　　Before the mountain reinforcement project of the Maijishan Grottoes in the 1960s, the statue was relocated from Cave 110 and stored in the cultural relics warehouse. (By Zhang Ping)

39 泥塑弟子头像

Clay Sculpture of Disciple Head

西魏
通高 24.8 厘米　宽 12.3 厘米　厚 12.3 厘米
佛头：高 21.5 厘米　宽 12.3 厘米　重 2.622 千克
第 146 窟
麦积山石窟艺术研究所藏

Western Wei Dynasty
Total height: 24.8 cm, Width: 12.3 cm, Thickness: 12.3 cm
Disciple head: Height: 21.5 cm, Width: 12.3 cm, Weight: 2.622 kg
Cave 146
Art Institute of Maijishan Cave-Temple Complex

弟子面型方圆丰润，宽额，眉宇舒朗、高耸弯曲，高鼻，薄唇小口，嘴角内敛。下颌丰润，双耳紧贴于两侧。面容饱满，双目微睁下视，嘴角挂着微微的笑意，眉宇间尚未脱去孩童天真无邪的稚气，脸上喜悦和羞涩的神情被刻画得惟妙惟肖，神态安详恬静。

20 世纪 60 年代麦积山石窟山体加固工程前从 146 窟移入文物库房保存。（张萍）

The disciple has a square and plump face, characterized by a broad forehead and lofty, curved eyebrows. He has a high nose, thin lips, and a small mouth, with the corners of his mouth restrained. His lower jaw is plump, and his ears are closely positioned to the sides of his head. His face is full, and his eyes are slightly open, gazing downward, accompanied by a faint smile at the corners of the mouth. There remains a trace of the innocent childishness in his expression. The joy and shyness on his face are vividly depicted, bearing a serene and tranquil expression.

Before the mountain reinforcement project of the Maijishan Grottoes in the 1960s, the statue was relocated from Cave 146 and stored in the cultural relics warehouse. (By Zhang Ping)

第 146 窟正壁龛佛像
Buddha Statue in the Niche on the Main Wall of Cave 146

石雕佛头像线描图
Line Drawing of Stone Carving of Buddha Head

Stone Carving of Buddha Head

40 石雕佛头像

西魏
高 21 厘米　宽 18 厘米　厚 13 厘米　重 4.57 千克
西崖
麦积山石窟艺术研究所藏

Western Wei Dynasty
Height: 21 cm, Width: 18 cm, Thickness: 13 cm, Weight: 4.57 kg
Western cliff
Art Institute of Maijishan Cave-Temple Complex

　　此石雕佛头像是 20 世纪 50 年代麦积山石窟加固工程前期由中央考察团在西崖发掘出土。

　　发髻为旋涡纹高平肉髻，左侧有头光残迹。面型圆润，弯眉细目，直鼻小口，嘴角内敛，双唇微启，面颊丰满，方圆适中，下颌有一道阴刻线，双耳紧贴于后颊。眉清目秀，微露笑意，神态沉静，肃穆中流露出慈祥与恬静，体现出温婉可亲之模样。石质细腻，发髻采用阴刻线雕琢，造像比例准确，手法娴熟精细，它突破了北魏"秀骨清像"的艺术风格，人物造型已经开始有圆润之感，注重"以形写神、重在写神、形神兼备"。雕凿技艺精湛，是不可多得的石雕佳作。

（张萍）

This stone-carved Buddha head was unearthed on the western cliff by the Central Survey Group in the initial phase of the reinforcement project of the Maijishan Grottoes in the 1950s.

The statue features a high, flat spiral bun, with remnants of a halo preserved on the left side. His face is round, adorned with curved eyebrows and slender eyes, a straight nose and a small mouth. The corners of his mouth are restrained, and the lips are slightly parted, set against full cheeks that are moderately square and round. An engraved line runs along the lower jaw, with two ears closely positioned to the back of the cheeks. The features are delicate, and a faint smile graces the face, which bears a calm expression. Amidst the solemnity, kindness and tranquility are revealed, reflecting a gentle and amiable appearance. The stone is finely textured, and the bun is intricately carved with engraved lines. The proportions of the statue are accurate, showcasing proficient and meticulous craftsmanship. This work broke through the Northern Wei Dynasty's artistic style of "elegant bones and clear features", as the figure modeled has begun to exhibit a sense of roundness, emphasizing the principle of "depicting the spirit through form, focusing on depicting the spirit, and achieving both spirit and form". The superb carving technique makes it a rare masterpiece of stone sculpture. (By Zhang Ping)

41

石雕佛坐像

第 117 窟石雕佛坐像线描图
Line Drawing of Seated Buddha in Cave 117

Stone Carving of Seated Buddha

西魏
高 89 厘米　宽 61 厘米　厚 25 厘米　重 67 千克
第 117 窟
麦积山石窟艺术研究所藏

Western Wei Dynasty
Height: 89 cm, Width: 61 cm, Thickness: 25 cm, Weight: 67 kg
Cave 117
Art Institute of Maijishan Cave-Temple Complex

　　原为麦积山石窟第 117 窟主尊坐佛，高肉髻、面型方圆，脸颊饱满、短颈、圆肩，左手施与愿印，右手残缺。内着僧祇衣，胸前束带，外着厚重的袈裟，结跏趺坐于"工"字形须弥座之上。身后圆形头光和椭圆形身光，以莲瓣作装饰。两侧原有两身弟子造像，但左侧弟子残缺，仅存右面的一身弟子像，侧身面朝主尊，一手持净瓶，姿态恭谨。

　　主尊造像端庄典雅、微微俯视、和蔼可亲，集中体现了西魏造像的美感。西魏造像继承了北魏造像传统，人物仍具有秀骨清像特征，但身躯更为饱满，富有张力。覆于佛座前的悬裳衣褶，多采用弧形曲线，叠压的纹饰，层次分明，有厚重的质感，富有装饰趣味。（张萍）

Originally, this statue was the main seated Buddha in Cave 117 of the Maijishan Grottoes. It features a high bun, a square and round face, full cheeks, a short neck, and rounded shoulders. The left hand is positioned in the vara mudra, while the right hand is incomplete. He wears a sanghati underneath, secured with a belt at the chest, and drapes a thick kasaya over his body, sitting in full lotus position on an I-shaped pedestal. Behind him, there are a circular halo around the head and an oval halo around the body, both decorated with lotus petals. Originally, there were two disciple statues on either side, but the disciple on the left is incomplete. Only the disciple statue on the right remains, standing sideways facing the main statue, holding a pure vase in one hand, in a respectful posture.

The main statue is dignified and elegant, with a slight downward gaze that conveys an amiable demeanor, embodying the beauty of statues from the Western Wei Dynasty. The statues of the Western Wei Dynasty inherit the tradition of the Northern Wei Dynasty statues, retaining the characteristics of "elegant bones and clear features", but with fuller bodies that exhibit more tension. The folds of the hanging skirt in front of the Buddha seat predominantly utilize arc-shaped curves. The superimposed patterns are distinct in layers, with a thick texture and rich decorative interest. (By Zhang Ping)

42

泥塑坐佛

Clay-Covered Sculpture of Seated Buddha

北周
高 38 厘米　宽 26.6 厘米　厚 14.8 厘米
第 127 窟
麦积山石窟艺术研究所藏

Northern Zhou Dynasty
Height: 38 cm, Width: 26.6 cm, Thickness: 14.8 cm
Cave 127
Art Institute of Maijishan Cave-Temple Complex

20 世纪 80 年代麦积山石窟山体加固维修工程期间由原存放第 127 窟移入文物库房保存，从造像特征来看，与 127 窟明显不是同时代作品。2000 年被定为国家三级文物。

圆塑。佛像低平肉髻，面形方圆饱满，鼻梁高直、双眉弯曲，眼细长如月，半闭半睁。嘴唇圆润，嘴角微微上翘。双耳紧贴两侧面颊，短颈圆肩。双手结禅定印隐于袈裟内，呈跏趺坐。内着僧祇衼，外披垂领式袈裟，纹饰采用刻、塑相结合的手法，线条简洁，纹饰清晰可见。整体造型呈"三角"状，彰显沉稳敦实之感；造像虽有磨损，仍体现出神情安详、温和质朴之感。体态敦厚端庄的造像风格，是麦积山北周塑像中的代表作品之一。（张萍）

During the reinforcement and maintenance project of the Maijishan Grottoes in the 1980s, this clay sculpture was relocated from Cave 127 to a cultural relics warehouse. Its stylistic features indicate that it is not contemporaneous with other works in Cave 127. In 2000, it was classified as a National Grade III Cultural Relic.

This sculpture is carved in the round. The Buddha sculpture features a low, flat ushnisha, and a full, square-round face with a high, straight nose. The eyebrows are curved, and the eyes are long and slender, resembling a crescent moon, half-closed in a serene expression. The lips are rounded, with the corners slightly upturned. The ears are closely aligned with the cheeks, and the figure has a short neck and rounded shoulders. The hands are positioned in the Dhyana Mudra, concealed within the robes, and the figure is seated in a lotus position. The figure is dressed in an inner garment known as a "sanghati," with an outer robe draped in a hanging-collar style. The decorative patterns are crafted using a combination of carving and sculpting techniques, resulting in simple lines and clearly visible ornamentation. The overall form of the sculpture is triangular, conveying a sense of solidity and stability. Despite some wear, the sculpture still exudes a serene, gentle, and unpretentious expression. Its robust and dignified posture exemplifies the style of Northern Zhou sculptures from the Maijishan Grottoes, making it one of the representative works of this period. (By Zhang Ping)

43 泥塑坐佛

Clay-Covered Sculpture of Seated Buddha

隋
高 46 厘米　宽 43 厘米　厚 19 厘米
第 141 窟
麦积山石窟艺术研究所藏

Sui Dynasty
Height: 46 cm, Width: 43 cm, Thickness: 19 cm
Cave 141
Art Institute of Maijishan Cave-Temple Complex

20 世纪 80 年代麦积山石窟山体加固维修工程期间，由第 141 洞窟移入文物库房保存。2000 年被定为国家一级文物。

圆塑。佛像低平肉髻、宽额，高眉深目，双眉弯曲，两眼半睁，直鼻，鼻翼较大，鼻梁连接眉宇；双唇紧闭，嘴角平直，唇两侧下方有明显的两条深纹，突出圆润的下颌；大耳下垂并紧贴于后颊；短颈端肩，平胸略鼓腹。内着束腰结带僧祇支，外穿垂领式宽边袈裟。左手屈肘贴于胸前，右手抚膝，呈结跏趺坐状，可见脚心朝上的右足。衣纹简洁，线条清晰且刚柔并济，塑像形体饱满，神情庄重威严，体现出气势雄健、法相庄严的佛教造像特点。整体造型均有磨蚀、微残、烟熏痕迹，但泥质坚硬、厚重，有烧陶之感。为麦积山隋代代表作品。（张萍）

During the reinforcement and restoration project of the Maijishan Grottoes in the 1980s, this sculpture was relocated from Cave 141 to a cultural relics warehouse for preservation. In 2000, it was designated as a National Grade I Cultural Relic.

This sculpture is carved in the round. The Buddha sculpture features a low, flat ushnisha and a broad forehead. It has high, deep-set eyes beneath curved eyebrows, with the eyes half-open. The nose is straight with prominent nostrils, and the bridge seamlessly connects to the brow. The lips are tightly closed with straight corners, and two distinct deep lines extend downward from the sides of the lips, accentuating the rounded chin. The large ears hang down closely against the back of the cheeks. The figure has a short neck, well-defined shoulders, a flat chest, and a slightly protruding abdomen. The figure is depicted wearing an inner garment with a cinched waist and tied belt, beneath an outer robe with hanging collars and broad edges. The left arm is bent at the elbow, resting against the chest, while the right hand is placed on the knee, in a lotus position with the sole of the right foot facing upwards. The robe features simple drapery with clear lines that are both strong and gentle, complementing the sculpture's full form. The expression is dignified and solemn, embodying the commanding presence and majestic characteristics typical of Buddhist statues. The sculpture shows signs of erosion and minor damage, along with smoke stains. However, the clay remains hard and solid, reminiscent of fired terracotta. This piece is a representative work from the Sui Dynasty at Maijishan. (By Zhang Ping)

中区 25 窟附近崖面情况，1952 年拍摄
The Cliff Surface near Cave 25 in the Central Area, Photographed in 1952

泥塑佛头像

44

Clay Sculpture of Buddha Head

北周
高 25.5 厘米　宽 11.8 厘米　厚 12.2 厘米　重 2.479 千克
第 25 窟
麦积山石窟艺术研究所藏

Northern Zhou Dynasty
Height: 25.5 cm, Width: 11.8 cm, Thickness: 12.2 cm, Weight: 2.479 kg
Cave 25
Art Institute of Maijishan Cave-Temple Complex

　　佛头像磨光低平肉髻，面型长圆，弯眉细长目，眼角细长，眼睑突鼓，双眼微下视，直鼻，小口，嘴角平直，双耳平贴后颊。神态庄严肃穆，北周造像风格。

　　20 世纪 60 年代麦积山石窟山体加固工程前从 25 窟移入文物库房保存。25 窟为隋开窟、明重修，从造像看，此泥塑佛头像应不是 25 窟内塑像，根据造像风格分析，其有 140 窟内佛的特征。(张萍)

The Buddha head features a polished, low, flat ushnisha, with a long and round face. It has curved eyebrows and elongated eyes, with the corners being thin and the eyelids slightly bulging. The eyes gaze down, complemented by a straight nose and a small mouth with straight corners. The ears are flat against the cheeks. The overall expression is solemn and dignified, reflecting the style of statues from the Northern Zhou Dynasty.

Before the mountain reinforcement project of the Maijishan Grottoes in the 1960s, the statue was relocated from Cave 25 and stored in the cultural relics warehouse. Cave 25 was excavated during the Sui Dynasty and renovated in the Ming Dynasty. Based on the characteristics of the statues, this clay-covered sculpture of the Buddha head should not belong to the statues inside Cave 25. Some analysis suggests that it features characteristic of the Buddha in Cave 140. (By Zhang Ping)

45 | 泥塑佛头像

Clay Sculpture of Buddha Head

北周
高 25.5 厘米　宽 13.6 厘米　厚 12.8 厘米　重 3.07 千克
第 140 窟
麦积山石窟艺术研究所藏

Northern Zhou Dynasty
Height: 25.5 cm, Width: 13.6 cm, Thickness: 12.8 cm, Weight: 3.07 kg
Cave 140
Art Institute of Maijishan Cave-Temple Complex

　　此佛头像磨光低平肉髻，发际线平整规则，面型长圆，弯眉细长目，眼睑突鼓，双目下视，悬胆鼻，小口，嘴角平直，双耳平贴后颊。饱满的面容和恬静庄重的神情，体现出北周匠师独有的造像艺术风格。

　　20 世纪 60 年代麦积山石窟山体加固工程前从 140 窟移入文物库房保存。（张萍）

　　The statue features a polished, low, flat ushnisha with a neat and regular hairline, complemented by a long and round face. His eyebrows are curved and the eyes are long and thin, set behind bulging eyelids that gaze down. The nose resembles a hanging gallbladder, and the mouth is small with straight corners. His ears are flat against the cheeks. The statue's full face and serene, solemn expression reflect the unique statue-making art style of craftsmen from the Northern Zhou Dynasty.

　　Before the mountain reinforcement project of the Maijishan Grottoes in the 1960s, the statue was relocated from Cave 140 and stored in the cultural relics warehouse. (By Zhang Ping)

壁画

Murals

　　飞天与火焰，"薄肉塑"与大型经变，霞色云海，天女散花，位于丝绸之路要冲的麦积山，既受到来自于西域的影响，也受到中原地区以及南方地区文化的影响，进而形成了独具特色的壁画艺术风格。

Due to their strategic location on the Silk Road, the Maijishan were influenced by the cultures of the Western Regions, the Central Plains, and southern China, resulting in a distinctive artistic style of sculptures and murals.

46

《明代冯惟讷重刻庾信
麦积山七佛龛铭并序》
拓片

Rubbing of "Yu Xin's Inscription and Preface
for the Seven-Buddha Niche in Maijishan Re-engraved
by Feng Weine during the Ming Dynasty"

民国
长 268 厘米　宽 115 厘米
麦积山石窟艺术研究所藏

the period of the Republic of China
Length: 268 cm, Width: 115 cm
Art Institute of Maijishan Cave-Temple Complex

　　拓片为冯国瑞先生捐赠。原碑现存于瑞应寺天王殿左侧，碑文刻于明嘉靖四十三年（1564）。碑阴为甄敬题诗刻石。冯惟讷跋识，甘茹书丹。螭首方座，青岩石质，碑身断裂数块后又重新粘接。在碑文中，南北朝文学家庾信记述了当时开凿麦积山石窟的盛况，认为"兹山名胜，独冠陇右"，故此碑又名《庾信碑》。

　　《庾信碑》是麦积山极为珍贵的碑刻之一，许多撰文中均有提及，原碑已经佚失，故此碑为重刻。首行刻碑题，碑文楷书，18行，满行45字，书写规矩，遒劲有力。（谈叶闻）

　　The rubbing was donated by Mr. Feng Guorui. The original stele is currently located on the left side of the Heavenly Kings Hall in the Ruiying Temple, and its inscription on the stele was carved in 1564, the 43rd year of Jiajing period of the Ming Dynasty. On the back of the stele are stone carvings of poems inscribed by Zhen Jing, along with postscripts by Feng Weine and calligraphy by Gan Ru. The stele has a dragon-head top and a square base made of bluestone. It is broken into several pieces and has been reattached. In the inscription, Yu Xin, a literary figure of the Southern and Northern Dynasties, described the grand occasion of excavating the Maijishan Grottoes at that time, stating that "this famous mountain is unrivaled in Longyou (now part of Gansu)."

　　The "Yu Xin Stele" at Maijishan is one of the most precious steles, frequently referenced in many writings. The original stele is now missing, which is why this version is a re-engraving. The title of the stele is engraved on the first line, and the inscription is in regular script, with eighteen lines and forty-five characters per line. The writing is neat and powerful. (By Tan Yewen)

秦州天水郡麥積崖佛龕銘并序　周庾信子山

麥積崖者乃隴坻之名山河西之靈嶽高峯尋雲深谷無量方之鷲島迹遁三禪譬彼鶴鳴虛飛六甲鳥
道乍窮羊腸或斷雲如鵬翼忽已垂天樹若桂華翻能拂日是以飛錫遙來乘杯遠至疏山鑿洞鬱爲淨
土拜燈王於石室乃假馭風禮花首於山龕方資控鶴大都督李允信者籍以宿植深悟法門乃於壁之
南崖梯雲鑿道奉爲亡父造七佛龕似刻浮檀如攻水玉從容滿月照耀青蓮影現須彌香聞忉利如斯
塵野還開說法之堂猶彼香山更對安居之佛昔者如來追福有報恩之經菩薩去家有思親之供敢緣
斯義乃作銘曰
鎮地鬱盤基乾峻極石關千上銅梁九息百仞崖橫千尋松直陰兔假道陽烏飛翼載輦疏山穿龕架嶺
糺紛星漢迴旋光景壁累經文龕重佛影雕輪月殿刻鏡花堂鏤石壁寫山梁雷乘法鼓樹積天香
嗽泉珉谷吹塵石林集靈真館藏仙冊府芝洞秋房檀林春乳水谷銀山樓石柱異嶺共雲同峯別雨
冀城餘俗河西舊風水聲幽咽山勢崆峒法雲常住慧日無窮方城芥盡不變天宮

茲山名勝獨冠隴右其開刱之始不可攷而志籍所存惟子山是銘最古觀其圖寫山形標揚法界事
綜理該辭義典則而碑版不傳遺文湮滅乃命工伐石刊置山陽將以貽之同好俾後來者有所考焉
子山新野人仕梁累官右衛將軍聘于西魏屬魏師南討遂留長安江陵平累遷開府儀同三司司宗
中大夫博學工文辭尤長于詩有集若干卷傳于世

賜進士出身朝列大夫河南布政司右參議前陝西按察司分巡隴右道僉事北海馮惟訥識
嘉靖歲次甲子孟秋吉日
賜進士出身奉議大夫陝西等處提刑按察司分巡隴右道僉事甘茹書

碑文:

《秦州天水郡麦积崖佛龛铭》(并序):麦积崖者,乃陇坻之名山,河西之灵岳。高峰寻云,深谷无量,方之鹫岛,迹循三禅。譬彼鹤鸣,虚飞六甲。鸟道乍穷,羊肠或断。云如鹏翼,忽已垂天。树若桂华,翻能拂日。是以飞锡遥来,乘杯远至,疏山凿洞,郁为净土。拜灯王于石室,乃假驭风。礼花首于山龛,方资控鹤。大都督□□□者,籍以宿植,深悟法门,乃于壁之南崖,梯云凿道,奉为王父造七佛龛,似刻浮檀,如攻水玉。从容满月,照耀青莲。影现须弥,香闻忉利。如斯尘野,还开说法之堂,犹彼香山,更对安居之佛。昔者如来追福,有报恩之经。菩萨去家,有思亲之供。敢缘斯义,乃作铭曰:

"镇地郁盘,基乾峻极。石关十上,铜梁九息。百仞崖横,千寻松直。阴兔假道,阳乌飞翼。载华疏山,穿龛架岭。纠纷星汉,回旋光景。壁累经文,龛重佛影。雕轮月殿,刻镜花堂。(横)镌石壁,暗凿山梁。雷乘法鼓,树积天香。嗽泉珉谷,吹尘石床。集灵真馆,藏仙册府。芝洞秋房,檀林春乳。水谷银沙,山楼石柱。异岭共云,同峰别雨。冀城余俗,河西旧风。水声幽咽,山势崆峒。法云常住,慧日无穷。方城芥尽,不变天宫。"兹山名胜,独冠陇右,其开创之始不可考,而志籍所存,惟子山是铭最古。

观其图写山形,标扬法界。

事综理该,辞义典则,而碑版不传,遗文湮灭,乃命工伐石,刊置山隅,将以贻之同好。俾后来者,有所考焉。

子山,新野人,仕梁,累官右卫将军,聘于西魏,属魏师南讨,遂留长安。江陵平,累迁开府仪同三司。司宗中大夫,博学、工文辞,尤长

于诗。有集若干卷传于世。

赐进士出身,朝列大夫,河南布政司右参议,前陕西按察司分巡陇右道佥事,北海冯惟讷识。

嘉靖岁次甲子孟秋吉日。

赐进士出身,奉议大夫,陕西等处提刑按察司分巡陇右道佥事,甘茹书。(沈玉璋)

Stele Inscription: *Inscription on the Buddha Niches on the Maiji Cliff, Tianshui Prefecture, Qinzhou* (with a preface): Maiji Cliff is a renowned mountain in Longcheng and a sacred hill in Hexi (west of the Yellow River). It features a lofty peak reaching for the clouds and boundless deep valleys. Compared to Vulture Peak, it vanished into the Third Dhyana Heaven. Hearing the call of cranes, it's as if one is flying through the air. The narrow trail suddenly ends. The clouds are like the wings of a roc, suddenly hanging down from the sky. The trees are like laurel blossoms, brushing against the sun. Therefore, there were flying monk coming from afar, and travelers arriving by boat. They carved caves on the sparse mountain, creating a pure land. Worshiping the lamp king in the stone chamber, they borrowed the wind for their journey. Offering flowers to the Buddha in the mountain niche, they relied on the cranes for support. Li Yunxin, the governor-general, was endowed with past good deeds and deeply comprehended the Dharma. On the southern cliff of the wall, he cut a path through the clouds and built a Seven-Buddha niche for his grandfather, akin to carving sandalwood and shaping jade. The serene full moon shines on the blue lotus, while shadows appear on Mount Sumeru, and the fragrance reaches in Trayastrimsa. In such a dusty world, a hall for preaching the Dharma was still opened, just like that soaring mountain, where Buddhas face those who dwell in peace. In the past, when the Tathagata sought blessings, there was the Sutra of Repaying Kindness. When Bodhisattvas left home, offerings were made to remember their parents. Daring to follow this meaning, an inscription was made as follows:

"The town is majestic and coiled, with the foundation that is lofty and steep. The stone pass is tenfold, and the copper pillar is ninefold. The hundred-foot cliff is horizontal, while the thousand-foot pine stands straight. The shade allows passage, and the sunbird spreads its wings. People lifted and built on the sparse mountain, carving niches and spanning ridges. Confused by the stars and the Milky Way, people enjoy the scenery. The walls are adorned with scriptures, and the niches are filled with Buddha images. The carved wheels embellish the moon palace, and the engraved mirrors decorate the flower hall. (Horizontal) There are engravings on the stone wall, secretly cutting through the

麦积山石窟及瑞应寺
Maijishan Grottoes and Ruiying Temple

mountain ridge. Thunder accompanies the Dharma drum, and the trees accumulate like heavenly clouds. Drinking from the spring and sleeping in the valley, the wind blows away dust on the stone bed. People gather at the true pavilion of spirits, storing volumes in the library of immortals. We can see the autumn room in the mushroom cave and the spring milk in the sandalwood forest, the silver sand in the water valley, and the stone pillars in the mountain pagoda. Different ridges share clouds, while the same peak experiences different rains. We witness the remaining customs of Jicheng and the old customs of Hexi. The sound of water is mournful, and the mountain is vast and empty. The Dharma cloud is ever-present, and the sun of wisdom is infinite. Even when the mustard seed of the fortified city is exhausted, the heavenly palace remains unchanged." This mountain is renowned and scenic, surpassing all others in Longyou. The beginning of its creation cannot be traced, but among the records and annals, only this inscription by Zishan is the oldest.

Looking at the pictures that depict the mountain's shape, we extol the Dharma realm.

The matters are comprehensive and well-organized, and the words and meanings are canonical and proper. However, the stele version has not been passed down, and the remaining writings are obliterated. Therefore, I ordered workers to cut stones and erect it at the foot of the mountain, intending to present it to like-minded people. So that later

generations can have something to refer to.

Zishan, from Xinye, served in the Liang Dynasty and held successive official positions, ultimately rising to General of the Right Guard. He was sent on a diplomatic mission to the Western Wei Dynasty. When the Wei army launched a southern expedition, he chose to remain in Chang'an. After the pacification of Jiangling, he was successively promoted to the rank of Kaifu, with ceremonial rank equivalent to the Three Departments, and Ancestral Worship Minister. He was erudite and skilled in literary composition, particularly in poetry. Several volumes of his collected works have been passed down through the ages.

He was granted the title of Jinshi and held an official position of Chaolie Dafu, and served as the Right Counselor of the Henan Provincial Administration Commission. Previously, he had been appointed as the Deputy Commissioner overseeing the Longyou Circuit in Shaanxi Province. This postscript is written by Feng Weine of Beihai.

This is an auspicious day in the early autumn of the Jiazi year during the Jiajing era.

He was awarded the title of Jinshi, held an official position of Fengyi Dafu, and served as the Surveillance Commissioner of the Longyou Circuit, Shaanxi Provincial Surveillance Commission for Punishment and Supervision. This was written by Gan Ru. (By Shen Yuzhang)

47 《车马出行图》壁画

冯仲年临摹
北周
长 117 厘米　宽 93 厘米
第 4 窟
麦积山石窟艺术研究所藏

　　原壁画位于第 4 窟第 7 龛顶部平棋右起第二排自内至外第一格，边缘棱框大多残损，壁画边缘残破多（已修补），内容为贵妇出行场景。

　　《车马出行图》画一辆由四匹马拉的车，车中坐一位头戴花冠、身穿高领襦服的贵妇，前面有侍从开道，周围侍从护卫头戴巾、身穿圆领窄袖束腰短袍胡服，有骑马的，也有步行的。不论是人物还是车、马，线条简洁明快，动态和神韵都刻画得惟妙惟肖。壁画色彩浓厚，气氛隆重，富有生活气息。

　　其中有一匹缓步前行的红马，体形彪悍雄健。由于当时的制作者巧妙地运用了散点透视和焦点透视的构图方法，又适当考虑到人在仰视中的错觉关系，即每当人们从不同的位置和不同的角度来看，它都有不同的走向和动势。说明我国古代画师已掌握了透视原理及高超的技艺。（张萍）

Mural Paintings of *Carriage and Horses Outing*

Copy by Feng Zhongnian
Northern Zhou Dynasty
Length: 117 cm, Width: 93 cm
Cave 4
Art Institute of Maijishan Cave-Temple Complex

The original mural is located in the first grid from the inside to the outside in the second row from the right at the top of the seventh niche in Cave 4. Most of the edge frames are damaged, and the edges of the mural are mostly worn (though they have been repaired). The mural depicts a scene of a noble lady's outing.

In the mural of the Carriage and Horses on an Outing, a carriage is pulled by four horses. A noble lady sits solemnly inside, adorned with a flower crown and wearing a high-collared robe. In front of her, attendants lead the way, while around the carriage are riding attendants wearing headscarves and guards dressed in round-necked, narrow-sleeved, waist-tight short robes typical of minority clothing. Some attendants are on horseback, while others walk beside the carriage. The lines depicting the figures, carriages, or horses are simple and crisp. The mural features rich colors and conveys a solemn atmosphere. The movements and expressions are vividly captured, exuding a lively essence.

Among them is a red horse moving slowly, strong and majestic. The creators of that time cleverly used the composition techniques of both scattered perspective and focal perspective, and properly considered the illusion created by the upward gaze of viewers. When people observe the mural from various positions and angles, they perceive different directions and movements. This demonstrates that ancient Chinese painters had mastered the principles of perspective and superb skills. (By Zhang Ping)

《车马出行图》壁画现状
Current Condition of the *Carriage and Horses on an Outing* Mural

　　麦积山石窟群中最宏伟、最壮丽的一座建筑是第4窟上七佛龛，又称"散花楼"，位于东崖大佛上方，距地面约80米，为七间八柱庑殿式结构，高约9米，面阔30米，进深8米，分前廊后室两部分。立柱为八棱大柱，覆莲瓣形柱础，建筑构件无不精雕细琢，体现了北周时期建筑技术的日臻成熟。后室由7个并列四角攒尖式帐形龛组成，帐幔层层重叠，龛内柱、梁等建筑构件均以浮雕表现。麦积山第4窟的建筑是全国各石窟中最大的一座模仿中国传统建筑形式的洞窟，是研究北朝木构建筑的重要资料，如实地表现了南北朝后期已经中国化的佛殿的外部和内部面貌，在石窟发展史上具有重要的意义。

第 4 窟外景图
Exterior View of Cave 4

The most magnificent and splendid building in Maijishan Grottoes group is the Upper Seven-Buddha Niche in Cave 4, also known as the "Scattering Flowers Pagoda". This structure is located above the Giant Buddha on the eastern cliff, approximately 80 meters above the ground. It features a hip-roofed design with seven bays and eight columns, standing about 9 meters high, 30 meters wide, and 8 meters deep. The cave is divided into two sections: a front porch and a back chamber. The columns are large octagonal columns with lotus petal-shaped column bases, and all architectural components are exquisitely carved, reflecting the increasingly refined architectural techniques of the Northern Zhou Dynasty. The back chamber consists of seven parallel niches, each with a four-sided pyramidal roof and overlapping layers resembling curtains. The architectural components such as columns and beams in the niche are represented through reliefs. The architecture of Cave 4 at Maijishan is the largest example of a cave imitating traditional Chinese architectural form among all grottoes in China. It serves as a vital reference for studying wooden structures from the Northern Dynasties and authentically represents the exterior and interior designs of Buddhist halls that had adapted to Chinese styles during the late Southern and Northern Dynasties. This cave holds great significance in the history of grotto development.

《供养飞天》薄肉塑壁画

48

李西民临摹
北周
长 289 厘米　宽 144 厘米
第 4 窟第 2 龛
麦积山石窟艺术研究所藏

　　北周艺术家巧妙地采用了塑、绘相结合的表现形式，创绘了麦积山第 4 号窟的飞天作品，吴作人先生对这种手法提出了"薄肉塑"之说，此后专家学者一直沿用至今。飞天的面部、五官、颈、胸、胳膊、手、足等裸露在外的部位采用薄塑的方式来表现，浮塑极薄，立体效果毕现，使飞天形象有脱壁欲出的感觉。飞天的其他部分，如衣裙、飘带、臂钏、项圈、璎珞、流云、天花等则采用绘画的语言来表现。"薄肉塑"绝非借古得来，而是北周艺术家的伟大创造。（王通玲、谈叶闻）

Mural Paintings of *Apsaras Attendents Named as Baorousu*

Copy by Li Ximin
Northern Zhou Dynasty
Lenght: 289 cm, Width: 144 cm
Niche 2 of Cave 4
Art Institute of Maijishan Cave-Temple Complex

Artists of the Northern Zhou Dynasty skillfully combined sculpture and painting techniques to create the flying apsara works in Cave 4 of Maijishan. Mr. Wu Zuoren introduced the concept of "thin-flesh sculpture" to describe this technique, which has since been adopted by experts and scholars. In this method, the exposed parts of the flying apsaras, including the face, facial features, neck, chest, arms, hands, and feet, are rendered using a thin sculpture technique. The sculpture is extremely delicate, achieving a three-dimensional effect that gives the impression of the flying apsaras about to emerge from the wall. Conversely, the non-exposed elements, such as the dresses, streamers, armlets, necklaces, pendants, flowing clouds, and ceiling flowers, are depicted using painting technique. The concept of "thin-flesh sculpture" is not a mere borrowing from antiquity but rather a remarkable innovation by artists of the Northern Zhou Dynasty. (By Wang Tongling and Tan Yewen)

《伎乐飞天》薄肉塑壁画

49

刘俊琪临摹
北周
长 342 厘米　宽 160 厘米
第 4 窟第 3 龛
麦积山石窟艺术研究所藏

　　四身伎乐飞天两两相对，分别演奏琴、笛、阮咸和笙。飞天头戴花冠，面形圆润，五官清晰。形象端庄，飞动自然，从天而降。

　　《旧唐书·音乐志》记载："阮咸，亦秦琵琶也，而项长过于今制，列十有三柱，武太后时，蜀人蒯朗于古墓中得之，晋《竹林七贤图》阮咸所弹与此类，因谓之阮咸。"阮咸是魏晋时期的名士，旷达放逸，为著名的竹林七贤之一，善于弹奏此种乐器。此乐器最初名称是秦琵琶，其形制和琵琶基本相似，或者就是琵琶的一种，最主要区别就是琵琶的共鸣腔是梨形、半球形底，而阮咸的共鸣腔是圆形、平底，其弹奏出的音色是有区别的。（王通玲、谈叶闻）

Mural Paintings of *Apsara Musicians Named as Baorousu*

Copy by Liu Junqi
Northern Zhou Dynasty
Lenght: 342 cm, Width: 160 cm
Niche 3 of Cave 4
Art Institute of Maijishan Cave-Temple Complex

Four flying apsara musicians are depicted in pairs, facing each other, as they play traditional instruments including the qin, flute, ruanxian, and sheng, all adorned with flower crowns. Their faces are round, and their facial features are distinctly rendered. The figures exude a dignified presence, appearing to float gracefully as if descending from the heavens.

According to the Old Book of Tang: Treatise on Music, "Ruanxian is also a Qin pipa, but its neck is longer than the current form. There are thirteen frets. During the time of Empress Wu Zetian, Jing Lang, a person from Shu, discovered it in an ancient tomb. The instrument depicted in the Picture of the Seven Sages of the Bamboo Grove from the Jin Dynasty is of this type, hence it is called ruanxian." Ruan Xian was originally the name of a renowned scholar during the Wei and Jin dynasties, celebrated for his broad-mindedness and unrestrained nature as one of the famous Seven Sages of the Bamboo Grove. He was skilled in playing a musical instrument that was originally called the Qin Pipa, which shares a similar shape to pipa, or is a kind of pipa. The primary distinction lies in their resonance cavities: the pipa has a pear-shaped, hemispherical bottom, while the resonance cavity of the ruanxian is round with a flat bottom, resulting in different timbres. (By Wang Tongling and Tan Yewen)

50 泥塑佛坐像

北周
高 75 厘米　宽 58 厘米　厚 50 厘米　重 56.25 千克
第 197 窟
麦积山石窟艺术研究所藏

　　坐佛磨光低平肉髻，面型方圆，弯眉细目，鼻隆且直，薄唇小口，嘴角内敛，长颈圆肩，身躯饱满。着圆领通肩袈裟，双肩浑圆。双手自然叠握抚于腹部，呈跏趺坐状。布满阴刻纹的袈裟紧贴身躯，有"曹衣出水"之状。造像端庄敦厚，温婉可亲，为典型北周代表作品。

　　原为麦积山第 197 窟（王子洞）造像，由于王子洞位置较偏僻，窟内造像已存无几，麦积山石窟艺术研究所在 20 世纪 90 年代将其移入文物库房妥善保存。（张萍）

第 197 窟泥塑佛坐像线描图
Line Drawing of Seated Buddha in Cave 197

Clay Sculpture of Seated Buddha

Northern Zhou Dynasty
Height: 75 cm, Width: 58 cm, Thickness: 50 cm, Weight: 56.25 kg
Cave 197
Art Institute of Maijishan Cave-Temple Complex

The seated Buddha features a polished, low, flat ushnisha and a roundish face with curved eyebrows and thin eyes. His nose is high and straight, while his lips are thin and his mouth small, with restrained corners. He has a long neck and rounded shoulders, giving his full body a robust appearance. His hands are naturally folded on his abdomen, positioned in a cross-legged sitting posture. He wears a round-collared, through-shoulder kasaya that clings closely to his form, adorned with incised lines. The kasaya's design resembles "Cao's clothes emerging from water". The statue exudes dignity, sincerity, gentleness, and approachability, making it a typical representative work of the Northern Zhou Dynasty.

It was originally a statue in Cave 197 (Prince's Cave) of Maijishan. Due to the cave's relatively remote location and the few remaining statues within it, the Maijishan Grottoes Art Research Institute moved the statue to the cultural relics warehouse for proper preservation in the 1990s. (By Zhang Ping)

王子洞区域

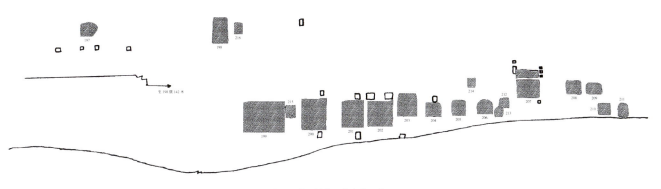

王子洞窟区新编洞窟分布示意图
New Diagram of Cave Distribution in the Prince's Cave Area

51 泥塑弟子立像

Clay Sculpture of Standing Disciple

北周
高 50.5 厘米　宽 15.1 厘米　厚 9.8 厘米　重 5.086 千克
第 129 窟
麦积山石窟艺术研究所藏

Northern Zhou Dynasty
Height: 50.5 cm, Width: 15.1 cm, Thickness: 9.8 cm, Weight: 5.086 kg
Cave 129
Art Institute of Maijishan Cave-Temple Complex

　　弟子面型方圆，弯眉细目，高鼻阔口，鼻梁直通额际，唇薄且棱角分明，嘴角内敛，下颌微翘，双耳垂肩紧贴两侧，短颈圆肩，身躯浑圆，内着僧祇衼，外穿垂领式袈裟，阴刻线清晰流畅，衣纹线条简洁，双臂屈肘、双手合抱笼袖拱手于胸前，隐于外翻下摆的袈裟内，双足穿云头鞋立于圆形台基之上。体态饱满端庄，神情恬静，俨然一副眉慈目善的俊秀少年模样。

　　20世纪80年代麦积山石窟山体加固工程期间从129窟移入文物库房保存。（张萍）

　　The disciple has a roundish face, curved eyebrows, thin eyes, a high nose and a wide mouth. The bridge of his nose extends straight to the forehead, and his lips are thin with distinct edges. The corners of his mouth are restrained, with a slightly raised jaw. Two ears hang down to the shoulders and are close to the sides of his head, complemented by a short neck and rounded shoulders. The body is plump, dressed in a sanghati underneath and a hanging-collar kasaya on the outside, featuring clear and smooth incised lines. The design of the clothing lines is simple, and his arms are bent at the elbows with hands clasped together, the sleeves held in front of the chest, concealed in the kasaya with turned-out hem. He wears cloud-pattern shoes, standing on a circular pedestal. His posture is full and dignified, with a serene expression, resembling a handsome young man with kind brows and gentle eyes.

　　During the mountain reinforcement project of the Maijishan Grottoes in the 1980s, the statue was relocated from Cave 129 and stored in the cultural relics warehouse. (By Zhang Ping)

52 泥塑菩萨立像

Clay-Sculpture of Standing Bodhisattva

北周
高 73 厘米　宽 24.2 厘米　厚 11.3 厘米　重 11.63 千克
第 100 窟
麦积山石窟艺术研究所藏

Northern Zhou Dynasty
Height: 73 cm, Width: 24.2 cm, Thickness: 11.3 cm, Weight: 11.63 kg
Cave 100
Art Institute of Maijishan Cave-Temple Complex

　　菩萨头戴花冠，面型长圆，长眉细目，短颈溜肩，身躯浑圆。着羊肠大裙，紧贴于身。左手提巾，右手屈肘置于肩。容貌清雅娟秀，体态端庄秀美，表现出温婉秀丽、宁静谦和的形象。衣纹线条自然流畅、简洁贴体，朴素无华。在整体造型上比例准确，姿态生动；在服饰的处理上采用概括简练的手法，主次分明，体现出轻纱裹体、质感娴静之美。有麦积山石窟典型的北周造像特征。

　　20 世纪 60 年代麦积山石窟山体加固工程前从 100 窟移入文物库房保存。（张萍）

　　The Bodhisattva wears a flower crown and has a long, round face with long eyebrows and narrow eyes. She has a short neck, sloping shoulders, and a plump body. She wears a large bodycon skirt that follows the form of her body. The left hand holds a handkerchief, while the right hand is bent at the elbow and placed on the shoulder. With an elegant and delicate appearance, the statue has a dignified and beautiful posture, conveying a gentle, serene and modest image. The clothing lines are natural, smooth, simple and close-fitting, without ornamentation. In terms of overall modeling, the proportions are accurate and the posture is vivid. The treatment of the clothing employs a concise, generalized approach, with clear distinction between primary and secondary elements, reflecting the beauty of a light gauze wrapping the body and a refined texture. This statue exhibits the typical features of statues from the Northern Zhou Dynasty at the Maijishan Grottoes.

　　Before the mountain reinforcement project of the Maijishan Grottoes in the 1960s, the statue was relocated from Cave 100 and stored in the cultural relics warehouse. (By Zhang Ping)

53 石雕菩萨立像

北周
高 145 厘米　宽 38 厘米　厚 24 厘米　重 72 千克
第 47 窟
麦积山石窟艺术研究所藏

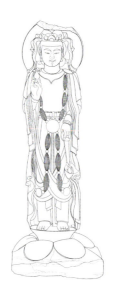

第 47 窟石雕菩萨立像线描图
Line Drawing of Standing Bodhisattva in Cave 47

　　菩萨有莲瓣形头光。头戴宝冠，面型方圆，上额略宽，双目微睁，棱鼻，唇略厚，面部可见彩绘眉线、眼珠、口红等，嘴两边及下颌彩绘一束小胡，大耳平贴，短颈端肩，平胸鼓腹，颈戴桃形宽边项圈。披帛左侧外搭，右侧自双肩穿肘下垂，上身祖露，下着翻边束腰羊肠大裙，璎珞自腹部穿环顺双腿下垂至膝后上卷回环。身体修长匀称，左手提环，环内饰带自然下垂，右臂屈肘手掌外翻持莲，赤足于跣台之上。

　　立像姿态优美，衣纹线条自然流畅、简洁贴体，体现出娴静之美。

　　20 世纪 80 年代麦积山石窟山体加固工程期间从 47 窟移入文物库房保存。（张萍）

Stone Carving of Standing Bodhisattva

Northern Zhou Dynasty
Height: 145 cm, Width: 38 cm, Thickness: 24 cm, Weight: 72 kg
Cave 47
Art Institute of Maijishan Cave-Temple Complex

The Bodhisattva has a lotus petal-shaped halo and wears a precious crown. His face is roundish, with a slightly wider upper forehead. His eyes are slightly open, his nose is angular, and his lips are slightly thick. Painted details such as eyebrow lines, eyes, and lipstick are visible on the face, along with small beards painted on both sides of the mouth and chin. His large ears are flat against the head, and he has a short neck and square shoulders, with a flat chest and bulging abdomen. Around his neck is a peach-shaped, wide-rimmed necklace. The scarf drapes over the left side, with the right side passing through the shoulders and hanging down from the elbows. The upper body is exposed, while the lower body is clad in a turned-up, waist-tightening bodycon skirt. Pendants pass through a ring on the abdomen and hang down along the legs, curling up and looping back after reaching the knees. The whole body is slender and well-proportioned, with the left hand holding a ring, within which a belt hangs down naturally. With the right arm bent at the elbow, the palm is turned outward and holding a lotus. The Bodhisattva stands barefoot on the pedestal.

The standing statue exhibits a graceful posture, with clothing lines that are natural, smooth, simple and close-fitting, embodying a sense of refined beauty.

During the mountain reinforcement project of the Maijishan Grottoes in the 1980s, the statue was relocated from Cave 47 and stored in the cultural relics warehouse. (By Zhang Ping)

第 47 窟主佛
Main Buddha of Cave 47

第 47 窟立佛像
Standing Buddha of Cave 47

54 泥塑菩萨立像

段一鸣临摹
隋
高 105 厘米　宽 36 厘米　厚 26 厘米
第 60 窟
麦积山石窟艺术研究所藏

　　第 60 窟位于西崖西侧，因塑造精美、彩绘富丽，又是浅龛，宜于观赏，故备受瞩目。龛内正壁塑一佛，结跏趺坐，身躯为西魏原作，造型扁平，着通肩大衣，衣褶用阴刻线；头部经补塑，轮廓圆润，肉髻低平，补塑时间当在北周至隋代之间。左、右壁各塑一胁侍菩萨。

　　此即右胁侍菩萨，为隋代重塑，发髻已残，头发中分，颈部细长，面形方圆，上额较宽，嘴角微翘，面带微笑。着天衣、僧祇衼，颈戴项圈，发辫下垂，披巾垂于两侧。左手下垂托摩尼宝珠，右手上举于胸前，掌心向外持莲蕾。身体微微前倾，立于半圆形坛基上，是隋代的优秀作品。

　　　　　　　　　　　（王通玲、谈叶闻）

第 60 窟菩萨
Seated Buddha of Cave 60

Clay Sculpture of Standing Bodhisattva

Copy by Duan Yiming
Sui Dynasty
Height: 105 cm, Width: 36 cm, Thickness: 26 cm
Cave 60
Art Institute of Maijishan Cave-Temple Complex

Cave 60 is located on the west of the western cliff. It attracts significant attention due to its exquisitely sculpted and richly painted figures in a shallow niche, making it well-suited for viewing. On the main wall inside the niche, there is a Buddha seated in a lotus position. The body is an original work from the Western Wei Dynasty, with a flat form and wearing a through-shoulder robe, folds of which are rendered in incised lines. The head has been remodeled, resulting in a rounded outline and a low, flat ushnisha. The remodeling likely occurred between the Northern Zhou Dynasty and the Sui Dynasty. On the left and right walls, there is a bodhisattva attendant figure on each side.

This is the right attendant bodhisattva, remolded in the Sui Dynasty. The hair bun is partially damaged, with hair parted in the middle. The neck is slender, and the face is rounded in shape. The upper forehead is relatively wide, and the corners of the mouth are slightly upturned, giving the figure a gentle smile. The bodhisattva is dressed in celestial garment and a sanghati, adorned with a necklace around the neck. Braids hang down, and a scarf drapes on both sides. The left hand hangs down, holding a mani pearl, while the right hand is raised in front of the chest, palm facing outward, holding a lotus bud. The body leans slightly forward, standing on a semicircular altar base. This piece is an outstanding example of the Sui Dynasty. (By Wang Tongling and Tan Yewen)

第 60 窟坐佛
Cave 60, Seated Buddha

第 60 窟左壁菩萨线描图
Line Drawing of a Bodhisattva on the Left Wall in Cave 60

第 60 窟左壁菩萨
the Bodhisattva on the Left Wall in Cave 60

第 60 龛 西壁下部西侧
Niche 60. West Side of the Lower Part of the Western Cliff

泥塑弟子立像

55

Clay Sculpture of Standing Disciple

段一鸣临摹
北周
高 93 厘米　宽 26 厘米　厚 18 厘米
第 12 窟
麦积山石窟艺术研究所藏

Copy by Duan Yiming
Northern Zhou Dynasty
Height: 93 cm, Width: 26 cm, Thickness: 18 cm
Cave 12
Art Institute of Maijishan Cave-Temple Complex

　　第 12 窟位于东崖中部，是第 13 龛摩崖大像左下方的一个小窟，平面方形，四角攒尖顶。此窟虽小，却极精致，造像保存完整，虽经明代妆彩，但都保持着原作风格。

　　此为第 12 窟前壁右侧弟子像，面庞丰圆，浓眉弯目，双眼微睁下视，高鼻梁，红唇小嘴。着偏袒右肩僧衣，衣饰质地厚重，衣纹简洁流畅。双手相握从衣袖中伸出，形象生动地展现了一位满怀虔敬、一心向佛的少年弟子。（王通玲、谈叶闻）

Cave 12 is situated in the middle of the Eastern cliff, positioned below the left side of the large cliffside statue in Niche 13. The cave has a square plan and a four-sided pyramidal roof. Despite its small size, this cave is remarkably exquisite, with the statues fully preserved. Although they were adorned with colors during the Ming Dynasty, they retain the original artistic style.

This is the disciple statue on the right side of the front wall of Cave 12. The statue features a plump and round face, curved eyebrows and eyes that are slightly open and looking downward. It has a high nose and small, red lips. The figure is dressed in a monk's robe that exposes the right shoulder, made of thick fabric. The clothing lines are simple and smooth. His hands are clasped and extended from the sleeves, vividly portraying a young disciple filled with piety and devotion to the Buddha. (By Wang Tongling and Tan Yewen)

第 12 窟全景
Panoramic View of Cave 12

56 泥塑菩萨立像

Clay Sculpture of Standing Bodhisattva

董晴野临摹
北周
高 106 厘米　宽 36 厘米　厚 28 厘米
第 12 窟
麦积山石窟艺术研究所藏

Copy by Dong Qingye
Northern Zhou Dynasty
Height: 106 cm, Width: 36 cm, Thickness: 28 cm
Cave 12
Art Institute of Maijishan Cave-Temple Complex

　　第12窟正壁主佛左侧菩萨像，头戴三珠宝冠，面部丰满圆润，头部略向左侧倾斜，目光下视。宝缯及飘带自双肩处下垂，胸腹间饰璎珞。裸露的手臂佩戴臂钏、手镯，双手于胸前捧宝瓶。腿部有动态扭动姿势，赤足立于莲台之上。

（王通玲）

　　The Bodhisattva statue on the left side of the main Buddha on the front wall of Cave 12 wears a three-jeweled crown. The statue features a plump and round face, with the head slightly tilted to the left and the eyes looking downward. Precious ribbons and streamers cascade from the shoulders, and decorative pendants adorn the area between the chest and abdomen. The bare arms are embellished with armlets and bracelets. The hands hold a vase in front of the chest, while the legs exhibit a dynamic twisting posture, standing barefoot on a lotus pedestal. (By Wang Tongling)

57　泥塑佛坐像

Clay Sculpture of Seated Buddha

中央美院翻模
北周
高 93 厘米　宽 64 厘米　厚 32 厘米
第 141 窟
麦积山石窟艺术研究所藏

Remolded by the Central Academy of Fine Arts
Northern Zhou Dynasty
Height: 93 cm, Width: 64 cm, Thickness: 32 cm
Cave 141
Art Institute of Maijishan Cave-Temple Complex

　　此为 141 窟右壁后部坐佛，着通肩袈裟，手施禅定印，结跏趺坐。

　　141 窟位于西崖东侧上层，窟内平面方形，覆斗顶，天井浮塑莲花，梁、枋、脊檩均塑出，仿木构帐形。（谈叶闻）

This is a seated Buddha located at the back of the right wall of Cave 141. The buddha is adorned in a through-shoulder kasaya, and is seated in a full lotus position. The hands are in the meditation mudra.

Cave 141 is located on the upper level of the east side of the Western Cliff. The cave has a square floor plan and features a bucket-shaped ceiling adorned with floating lotus motifs. Its beams, purlins, and ridge poles are all molded to imitate a wooden tent-shaped structure. (By Tan Yewen)

第 141 窟右壁坐佛（局部）
Seated Buddha (Detail) on the Right Wall of Cave 141

第 141 窟正壁及窟顶
Main Wall and Ceiling of Cave 141

第127窟壁画整体复原窟

58

Mural Restored Cave 127

127窟是北魏晚期开凿的一个平面横长方形帐形顶窟，窟宽8米、深4米、高4米。前壁开门，正、左、右三壁各开一龛，供三佛，其余壁面均绘满壁画，是麦积山石窟壁画最丰富的洞窟，也是麦积山北朝时期壁画保存最为丰富和完整的窟龛。

窟内各壁及其窟顶分别绘制了西方净土经变、维摩经变、涅槃经变、地狱变、睒子本生、十善十恶、帝释天出行、七佛等佛经内容，均场面宏大，内容丰富。进入其中，仿佛置身于北朝时期中国绘画的艺术殿堂。这些经变故事画是国内最早、最大的经变故事画（敦煌同类的经变画最早出现于隋代），同时，画面中所表现出的人物画、山水画、建筑画等的技法已经相当成熟，在现存同时期的各类绘画作品中，尚未有在构图、技法、艺术成就等方面超越于此的。因此，麦积山石窟127窟壁画在中国佛教史和绘画史的研究中都占有很高地位。

Cave 127 features a flat, horizontal rectangular tent-shaped ceiling, carved during the late Northern Wei Dynasty. The cave measures 8 meters in width, 4 meters in depth and 4 meters in height. The front wall includes a door, while niches are carved into the front, left, and right walls to enshrine the Three Buddhas. The remaining wall surfaces are adorned with murals, making this cave the richest in mural content within the Maijishan Grottoes. It is also notable for having the most abundant and well-preserved murals from the Northern Dynasties period.

The walls and ceiling of cave 127 are adorned with extensive murals depicting various Buddhist scriptures, including the Illustration of the Western Pure Land, the Vimalakirti Sutra Illustration, the Nirvana Sutra Illustration, the Illustration of Hell, the Jataka of Syama, the Ten Virtues and Ten Evils, the Departure of Sakra, and the Seven Buddhas. These artworks are grand in scale and rich in content, immersing visitors in the artistic realm of Chinese painting from the Northern Dynasties. These narrative paintings represent some of the earliest and largest examples of sutra illustrations in China. In contrast, similar narrative paintings of sutra illustrations in Dunhuang first appeared in the Sui Dynasty. The techniques employed in the figure painting, landscape painting, and architectural painting within these murals are already quite advanced. Among the existing artworks from the same period, none surpasses Cave 127 in terms of composition, technique, and artistic achievement. As a result, the murals in Cave 127 of the Maijishan Grottoes hold a significant position in the study of both Chinese Buddhist history and the history of painting.

窟内顶部正中
The central area of the cave's ceiling

右披
The Right Ceiling

The C

右壁上方绘《西方净土变》，下方不明
The right wall features the *Illustration of the Western Pure Land*
at the top, while the lower section is unclear

窟内正壁上方绘《涅
On the central wall, the up
Illustration, with a symm

前披绘《睒子本生故事》
The front ceiling is adorned with the *Syama Jataka*

前壁上方通壁绘《七佛图》，下方甬门左侧绘《地狱变》，右侧绘《十善十恶图》
The upper section of the front wall showcases a continuous painting of the *Seven Buddhas*. Below, the left side of
the entrance features the *Illustration of Hell*, while the right side illustrates the *Ten Virtues and Ten Evils*

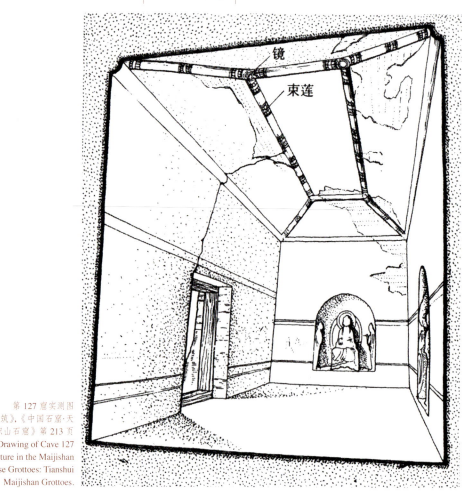

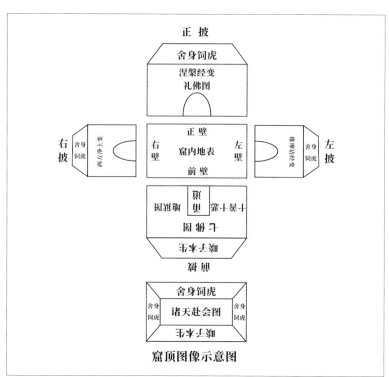

正、左、右披连续绘《萨埵那太子本生故事》
The central, left, and right Ceilings present a continuous
depiction of the *Jataka Tale of Prince Sattva*

合图》

th the *Assembly of the Devas*

左披
The Left Ceiling

方对称绘《礼佛图》

epicts the *Nirvana Sutra*

na *Worship Scene* below

左壁上方绘《维摩诘经变》，下方绘《听法信众》
The left wall displays the *Vimalakirti Sutra Illustration* at the top,
with *Audience of the Faithful Listening to the Dharma* depicted below

《西方净土变》壁画

59

杨晓东临摹
西魏
长 508 厘米　宽 232 厘米
第 127 窟
麦积山石窟艺术研究所藏

原作绘制于第 127 窟右壁佛龛上部，是中国北朝时期保存最完整的大型经变画之一。画面正中殿内为一佛二菩萨组成的说法图，台基之下，两阙之间有一支由 12 名舞乐伎组成的乐队正在表演。两侧各 4 名乐伎，呈八字形分别跽坐于地毯上，演奏着各种乐器。不仅场面壮观、人物众多、动静结合，而且构图严谨、错落有序，相得益彰。

画面虽有剥落和模糊之处，但所绘人物建筑、花卉树木等都清晰可辨。绘画技法成熟，线描极其流畅，施以石青、石绿等色，浓淡相宜，增加了画面庄重雅致和清淡秀丽的气氛。

《西方净土变》是根据《阿弥陀佛经》所画的，故又叫作《阿弥陀经变》。（张萍）

Mural Paintings of *Illustration of the Western Pure Land*

Copy by Yang Xiaodong
Western Wei Dynasty
Length: 508 cm, Width: 232 cm
Cave 127
Art Institute of Maijishan Cave-Temple Complex

The original painting was situated on the upper part of the Buddha niche on the right wall of Cave 127, and is one of the most well-preserved large-scale sutra illustrations from the Northern Dynasties in China. At the center of the mural, within the hall is a preaching scene featuring one Buddha and two bodhisattvas. Below the platform and between the two watchtowers, a band of 12 musicians and dancers performs, with four musicians on each side, arranged in a herringbone pattern, kneeling on the carpet and playing various instruments. The scene is not only spectacular, with a multitude of figures combining movement and stillness, but also meticulously composed, with elements scattered but orderly, complementing each other harmoniously. Despite some peeling and blurring, the figures, architecture, flowers, and trees remain clearly discernible. The technique is mature, with exceptionally smooth line work. The use of azurite, malachite green, and other colors, in balanced shades, enhances the mural's solemn, elegant, and serene beauty.

The Illustration of the Western Pure Land was painted according to the Sutra of Amitabha Buddha, and is therefore also known as the *Illustration of the Amitabha Sutra*. (By Zhang Ping)

《萨埵那太子舍身饲虎》壁画（局部）

60

李光霖临摹
西魏
长 335 厘米　宽 154 厘米
第 127 窟
麦积山石窟艺术研究所藏

　　"舍身饲虎"是广为流传的本生故事，讲述了佛祖释迦牟尼前世萨埵那太子为拯救老虎生命甘愿牺牲自己肉身的故事情节。

　　127 窟窟顶正、左、右三披通壁绘萨埵那太子舍身饲虎本生故事，采用中国长卷式构图，场面生

动自然，将人物情节、山水及自然景观融为一体，构图采用平远、高远不同的表现手法，既是一幅长卷故事画，又是一幅山水人物画。画面以连续多情节从左到右按顺序展开：左披内三太子出游、回宫报信等内容。正披壁画内由于泥皮剥落仅存三块互

不相连的壁画，即车马人物行进图像，当为表现国王闻讯后率众前往三太子舍身饲虎之地的情景。右披绘萨埵那太子舍身饲虎内容。

本铺壁画位于第127窟窟顶右斜坡，呈梯形结构。上画一座大山，山崖之下是群虎啖食太子尸体、

饥饿觅食的情景。图中故事内容与环境景物紧密结合，构图巧妙，描绘生动，具有强烈的悲剧气氛，只因剥落、漫漶，未见最后因其起塔供养的场面。

（张萍）

Mural of *Prince Sattva's Self-Sacrifice to Feed Tigers* (Detail)

Copy by Li Guanglin
Western Wei Dynasty
Length: 335 cm, Width: 154 cm
Cave 127
Art Institute of Maijishan Cave-Temple Complex

"The Self-Sacrifice to Feed Tigers" is a widely known Jataka tale that recounts the story of Prince Sattva, the previous incarnation of Sakyamuni Buddha, who willingly sacrificed his own body to save the lives of tigers.

In Cave 127, the ceiling's central, left, and right sections are adorned with a continuous mural illustrating the Jataka tale of Prince Sattva's self-sacrifice to feed tigers. It employs the long-scroll composition style of traditional Chinese painting. The scenes are vivid and natural, seamlessly integrating character narratives with landscapes and natural elements. The composition employs various techniques to depict both flat and high perspectives, making it both a long-scroll narrative painting and a landscape figure painting. The narrative unfolds sequentially from left to right, depicting multiple scenes. The left section portrays events such as the three princes' excursion and their return to the palace to deliver the news. In the central section of the mural, due

to the peeling of the plaster, only three disconnected fragments remain. These fragments depict images of a procession with chariots and figures, likely illustrating the scene where the king, upon hearing the news, leads his entourage to the site where Prince Sattva sacrificed himself to feed tigers. The right section of the mural illustrates the tale of Prince Sattva's self-sacrifice to feed the tiger.

This mural is located on the right slope of the ceiling in Cave 127 and features a trapezoidal structure, showcasing a large mountain. Below the cliff, a group of tigers are depicted eating the prince's body, illustrating the scene of hungry tigers searching for food. The story is intricately linked with the surrounding environment, featuring clever composition and vivid depiction, creating a strong sense of tragedy. Due to peeling and blurring, the final scene of the pagoda built for worship is not visible. (By Zhang Ping)

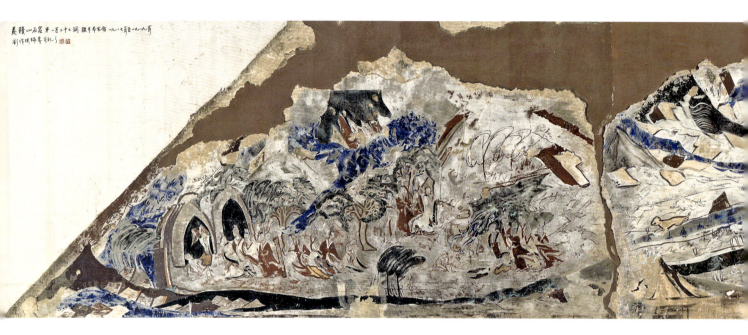

61 《睒子本生》壁画

刘俊琪临摹
西魏
长 805 厘米　宽 164 厘米
第 127 窟
麦积山石窟艺术研究所藏

本生故事讲述释迦牟尼前世的经历，显示其为了积行善业和功德，不惜牺牲一切的精神。

"睒子本生"讲述孝子睒子被国王误射身亡，后因善行被复活的故事。这一题材符合中国传统的孝道思想，在南北朝时期曾广为流传。壁画由国王出行、射猎、误射、睒子倾诉、探望盲父母、盲父母哭诉、天神相救等画面组成，以连环画的形式，将不同的情节连续地展现开来。画面上的山川河流、树林巨石的构图及技法在中国早期山水画中独树一帜，具有极高的艺术欣赏和研究价值。（王通玲）

Mural Painting of *the Syama Jataka*

Copy by Liu Junqi
Western Wei Dynasty
Length: 805 cm, Width: 164 cm
Cave 127
Art Institute of Maijishan Cave-Temple Complex

The Jataka tales recount the experiences of Sakyamuni in his previous lives, illustrating his spirit of accumulating good deeds and merits, as well as his willingness to sacrifice everything.

The Jataka of Syama tells the story of the filial son Syama, who was accidentally shot and killed by the king and was later revived due to his good deeds. This theme aligns with traditional Chinese values of filial piety and was widely disseminated during the Northern and Southern Dynasties. The mural consists of scenes such as the king's outing, hunting, the accidental shooting, Syama's appeal, his visits to his blind parents, their sorrowful cries, and his rescue by the gods. Presented in a comic strip format, these various plots are displayed in succession. The composition and techniques used to depict mountains, rivers, forests, and large rocks in the mural are distinctive in early Chinese landscape painting, providing significant artistic appreciation and research value. (By Wang Tongling)

Stone Carvings of One Buddha with Two Bodhisattvas

62 石雕一佛二菩萨

Copy by Duan Yiming and Sun Jing
Western Wei Dynasty
Main Buddha: Height: 208 cm, Width: 86 cm, Thickness: 40 cm
Bodhisattva on the Right: Height: 163 cm, Width: 35 cm, Thickness: 25 cm
Bodhisattva on the Left: The same as above
Cave 127
Art Institute of Maijishan Cave-Temple Complex

段一鸣、孙靖临摹
西魏
主佛：高 208 厘米　宽 86 厘米　厚 40 厘米
右菩萨：高 163 厘米　宽 35 厘米　厚 25 厘米
左菩萨：同上
第 127 窟
麦积山石窟艺术研究所藏

　　组像取材于"阿弥陀经"，主佛为阿弥陀佛，佛像为背屏式坐佛、头部作旋涡纹高肉髻，微微俯视，佛结跏趺坐，脸形长方，双眉弯曲向外扬起，两眼正视。长颈溜肩，双手作无畏与愿印，结跏趺坐于须弥座上。身穿通肩袈裟，内着僧祇支，中衣于胸前打结自然下垂，衣摆分三瓣自然下垂，衣纹流畅。造像神情端庄，衣着繁缛华丽，仪态雍容典雅。两侧观音和大势至菩萨，左右侧胁侍菩萨身后为舟形背光，上有莲花图案。菩萨束发戴冠，面容清秀，双目半睁，面容清俊，微微俯视，露出笑意，与主佛产生呼应之美，身躯扁平，戴桃形项圈，下垂花卉。内着僧祇支，腰系长裙。双肩有圆形饰物，帔帛覆盖双肩，胸佩璎珞。菩萨一手屈二指举于胸前，一手提桃形玉璧，置于腹侧。造像简洁明快，技法细腻精湛，动态优美自然，堪称北魏石雕造像的精品之作。背光浮雕十二身伎乐飞天，两侧各六身，花卉、流云点缀其间，或手持供品，或弹奏乐器，气氛欢快祥和，飞天的衣带向外飘扬，使画面充满了一种跳动的韵律。飞天的帔帛和裙摆向外飘扬，巧妙地构成背光边缘常见的火焰纹图形，整体效果完美和谐。（张萍）

The group of sculptures is inspired by the "Amitabha Sutra", with the central figure being Amitabha Buddha. The depiction is a seated Buddha with a screen-like backdrop. The head features a high usnisa with spiral patterns and is slightly inclined downwards. The Buddha is in the lotus position, with an elongated rectangular face, eyebrows arcing outward, and eyes gazing directly forward. The Buddha possesses a long neck and graceful shoulders, with both hands forming the "gesture of Abhaya" and the "gesture of granting wishes," while seated in the lotus position on a tiered base. The figure is adorned with a robe draped over both shoulders, with the inner garment tied at the chest and falling naturally. The hem splits into three sections, cascading smoothly with elegant folds. The sculpture exudes an aura of solemnity and grace, with attire that is ornate and luxurious, embodying a dignified and elegant demeanor. Flanking the central figure are Avalokiteshvara (Guanyin) and Mahasthamaprapta Bodhisattvas, each positioned as attendant bodhisattvas. Behind them is a boat-shaped halo adorned with lotus motifs, enhancing their divine presence. The bodhisattvas are depicted with hair bound and crowned. Their faces exude a delicate beauty, their eyes are half-open, and their expressions are refined and serene, with a gentle downward gaze and a subtle smile that harmonizes with the central Buddha figure. The figure features a flat torso adorned with a peach-shaped necklace, from which floral motifs elegantly hang. Underneath, the bodhisattva wears a traditional monk's inner garment (samghati) and a long skirt cinched at the waist. Circular ornaments embellish both shoulders, while a draped shawl (patta) covers them. The chest is adorned with a bejeweled necklace (mala), adding to the figure's opulence. One hand is gracefully positioned with two fingers bent and raised in front of the chest, while the other hand holds a peach-shaped jade disc, resting at the side of the abdomen. The sculpture is characterized by its simplicity and clarity, with exquisite and meticulous craftsmanship. Its graceful and natural dynamism makes it a masterpiece of Northern Wei stone sculpture. The halo features a relief of twelve apsaras musicians, six on each side, interspersed with floral motifs and flowing clouds. Some figures hold offerings, while others play musical instruments, creating a joyful and harmonious atmosphere. The garments of the apsaras billow outward, infusing the scene with a rhythmic vitality. The flowing scarves and skirts of the apsaras cleverly form flame-like patterns along the halo's edge, resulting in a perfectly harmonious overall effect. (By Zhang Ping)

保护

Part Two: Preservation

"要十分珍惜祖先留给我们的这份珍贵文化遗产，坚持保护优先的理念，加强石窟建筑、彩绘、壁画的保护，运用先进科学技术提高保护水平，将这一世界文化遗产代代相传。"几次考察石窟，习近平总书记格外强调遗产保护的重要价值。亿万年的地球沧桑，雕刻出麦积山灵秀俊朗的身姿；千百年人类的智慧，将自然奇景打造成文化艺术的殿堂；一代代石窟保护者的前赴后继，将这一自然与人文完美结合的典范更长久地留存于世。

"We must highly cherish the precious cultural heritage left by our ancestors, uphold the principle of prioritizing preservation, enhance the protection of grotto architecture, paintings, and murals, and utilize advanced scientific technologies to improve preservation standards, ensuring this world cultural heritage is passed down through generations." During several inspections of the grottoes, General Secretary Xi Jinping has particularly emphasized the significant value of heritage preservation. The Earth's transformations over hundreds of millions of years sculpted the graceful and striking form of Maijishan; the wisdom of humanity over the centuries has transformed this natural wonder into a hall of cultural and artistic achievement; and generations of grotto protectors have ensured the lasting preservation of this perfect blend of nature and culture.

63 「大魏洛阳法生」造像碑

Stone Tablet of Fasheng from Luoyang
in the Great Wei Dynasty

北魏
长 43 厘米　宽 37 厘米　厚 6 厘米
第 127 窟
麦积山石窟艺术研究所藏

Northern Wei Dynasty
Length: 43 cm, Width: 37 cm, Thickness: 6 cm
Cave 127
Art Institute of Maijishan Cave-Temple Complex

　　1953 年 8 月，中央勘察团在麦积山石窟进行考察时，在西崖第 12 层的龛架之间的第 127 洞窟中发现此碑。据僧人讲此碑非本窟之物，是从邻窟移来，但邻窟是哪一个、何时移来，没有可靠的依据，因此难以说明其出处。该造像碑时代约在北魏景明至熙平（500—518）年间，洛阳沙弥法生刻于麦积山（此法生是否是洛阳法生待考）。

　　单面刻碑，上有一字排开五个莲花瓣浅佛龛，每龛高 8 厘米、宽 5 厘米、深 1 厘米，内凿浮雕坐佛像各一身，其中五佛左端一身残缺。佛像面目已模糊不清。无碑题，下刻碑文已残缺。字迹共 12 行，满行 12 字。其中"大魏"依稀可见。碑文记录北魏景明年间洛阳沙弥法生开窟造像一事。

（张萍）

In August 1953, during an inspection by the Central Survey Team at the Maijishan Grottoes, this stele was found in Cave 127, located between the niche frames on the 12th floor of the western cliff. According to some monks, this stele does not belong to this cave, but was relocated from a neighboring cave. However, there is no reliable evidence which neighboring cave it came from or when it was relocated, making its origin difficult to ascertain. The stele dates to the Jingming to Xiping period (500—518) of the Northern Wei Dynasty, and was engraved by Fasheng, a novice monk from Luoyang. Its remains to be determined whether this Fasheng is indeed the same individual from Luoyang.

This is a single-sided engraved stele featuring five shallow niches, each adorned with lotus petals arranged in a row. Each niche measures 8.0 cm in height, 5.0 cm in width, and 1.0 cm in depth. Inside each niche is a relief sculpture of a seated Buddha. Notably, the Buddha statue on the left end of the five is incomplete, and the faces of the statues have become blurred over time. The stele lacks an inscription of the title, and the engraved text is partially damaged. There are twelve lines of characters in total, with twelve characters per line, among which, "Da Wei (Great Wei)" can be faintly discerned. The inscription records the activities of Fasheng, a novice monk from Luoyang, who created these statues during the Jingming period of the Northern Wei Dynasty. (By Zhang Ping)

64 『大魏洛阳法生造像碑』拓片

Rubbing of the *"Stone Tablet of Fasheng from Luoyang in the Great Wei Dynasty"*

1953 年
长 209 厘米　宽 75.5 厘米
冯国瑞捐赠
麦积山石窟艺术研究所藏

1953
Length: 209 cm, Width: 75.5 cm
Donated by Feng Guorui
Art Institute of Maijishan Cave-Temple Complex

　　蝉翼拓本，20 世纪 50 年代冯国瑞邀请我国著名的学者和专家为此拓片作题跋，永久保存。其中有名家郭沫若、吴作人、马衡、谢国桢、叶恭绰、丁希农以及天水籍著名爱国民主人士、时任甘肃省省长、民革中央副主席邓宝珊和甘肃学术文化史上一位颇多建树的学者、诗人冯国瑞本人考证题跋。原悬挂于瑞应寺院麦积山馆，由僧人收藏。（张萍）

　　This is a cicada-wing rubbing. In the 1950s, Feng Guorui invited prominent scholars and experts in China to write postscripts for this rubbing. This effort aimed to ensure its permanent preservation. Among those who contributed are renowned scholars such as Guo Moruo, Wu Zuoren, Ma Heng, Xie Guozhen, Ye Gongchuo, Ding Xinong, and Deng Baoshan, a notable patriotic figure from Tianshui, who served as the governor of Gansu Province, and vice chairman of the Central Committee of the Revolutionary Committee of the Chinese Kuomintang. Feng Guorui himself, a distinguished scholar and poet with significant contributions to the academic and cultural history of Gansu, also provided textual research. The rubbing was originally displayed in the Maijishan Pavilion of Ruiying Temple and was collected by monks. (By Zhang Ping)

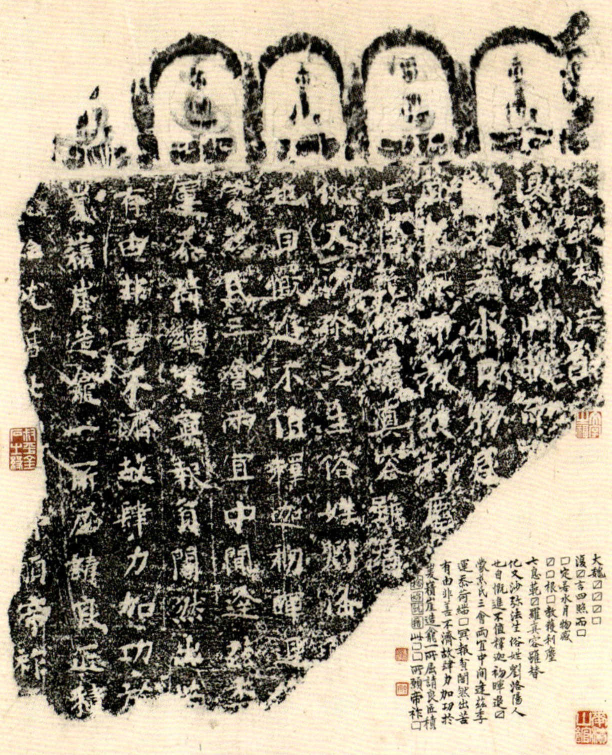

65 泥塑坐佛

Clay Sculpture of Seated Buddha

隋
长 80 厘米　宽 70 厘米　厚 60 厘米
第 135 窟
麦积山石窟艺术研究所藏

Sui Dynasty
Length: 80 cm, Width: 70 cm, Thickness: 60 cm
Cave 135
Art Institute of Maijishan Cave-Temple Complex

　　冯国瑞先生 1941 年考察麦积山，在木匠文得权的帮助下，首次到达第 135 窟，通过历史文献推测 135 窟就是王仁裕笔下的"天堂洞"。五代诗人王仁裕登临此窟，慨叹"空中倚一独梯，攀缘而上，至此，则万中无一人敢登者"。

　　坐佛低平发髻，面型方圆丰满，颧骨略高，眼角细长，双目微微下视，目光柔和亲切，一双稚嫩丰腴的双手，轻轻地抚慰在胸前，似冰清玉洁一般。袈裟线条简洁明快，手法洗练概括。古代工匠通过高超的艺术手法，表现出一位安详而蕴含着青春朝气的少年之形象，达到"以形写神、形神兼备"的人性化特征，是麦积山北周向隋代过渡时期具有代表性的泥塑造像。隋代艺术是在北周基础上发展起来的，它继承和发展了北周造型的特点，又使艺术表现手法更为丰富和成熟。隋工朝统一了全国，实现了南、北方文化艺术的融合，从而为唐代艺术辉煌时期的到来拉开了序幕。

　　20 世纪 90 年代从 135 窟移入文物库房保存。

（张萍、谈叶闻）

In 1941, Mr. Feng Guorui conducted an inspection of Maijishan. With the assistance of the carpenter Wen Dequan, he reached Cave 135 for the first time. Based on historical documents, he speculated that Cave 135 was the "Paradise Cave" described by Wang Renyu. The poet Wang Renyu of the Five Dynasties ascended this cave and sighed, "There is only a single ladder leaning in the air. Climbing up, there is no one among ten thousand people who dares to ascend."

The seated Buddha features a low, flat bun and a round, full face with slightly high cheekbones. The eyes are long and narrow, gazing softly downward, exuding a gentle and kind demeanor. His tender, plump hands rest lightly on his chest, as pure as ice and jade. The lines of his kasaya are simple yet lively, reflecting a concise and refined technique. Ancient craftsmen skillfully captured the image of a serene young man imbued with youthful vitality, achieving the humanized characteristics of "depicting the spirit through form and combining both spirit and form". This clay-covered sculpture is representative of the transitional period from the Northern Zhou Dynasty to the Sui Dynasty in Maijishan. Sui Dynasty art evolved from the Northern Zhou Dynasty, inheriting its stylistic features while enriching artistic expression techniques. The Sui Dynasty unified China, facilitating the integration of southern and northern cultures and arts, thus paving the way for the flourishing artistic achievements of the Tang Dynasty.

In the 1990s, the statue was relocated from Cave 135 and preserved in the cultural relics warehouse. (By Zhang Ping and Tan Yewen)

泥塑菩萨头像

66

宋
高 39.5 厘米　宽 16.0 厘米　厚 18.1 厘米
第 135 窟
麦积山石窟艺术研究所藏

　　菩萨束环状高发髻，戴莲花瓣华冠，发丝中分外翻到两侧，有清晰的发际线，一缕一缕的发丝非常写实。面型圆润，宽额，眉间有白毫，双眉如新月，微睁下视。悬胆鼻，丹凤立眼，四瓣小口，嘴角内敛，如樱桃一般。双耳下垂紧贴于两颊，下颌有阴刻线。颈部两道横纹。面部施彩，泥质细腻光滑，比例准确、技法熟练高超。容貌端庄秀美，神态肃穆安详，是麦积山宋塑精品，有唐代丰满圆润之遗风。

　　原为麦积山石窟第 135 窟宋人在北魏菩萨造像上重新安装的头像，由于材质和时代极不相称，1997 年被取下移入文物库房存放。（张萍）

第 135 窟泥塑菩萨头像线描图
Line Drawing of Head of Bodhisattva in Cave 135

Clay Sculpture of Bodhisattva Head

Song Dynasty
Height: 39.5 cm, Width: 16.0 cm, Thickness: 18.1 cm
Cave 135
Art Institute of Maijishan Cave-Temple Complex

The Bodhisattva features a high, ring-shaped bun, adorned with a flower crown of lotus petals. The hair is parted in the middle and turned out to both sides, showcasing a clear hairline, with the strands rendered in a highly realistic manner. His face is round with a broad forehead, featuring an urna between the eyebrows. The eyebrows resemble crescent moons, and the eyes are slightly open, gazing downward. His nose is shaped like a hanging gallbladder, while his upright phoenix-like eyes are striking. The small mouth resembles four petals, with the corners gently curved inward, reminiscent of cherries. His ears droop closely against his cheeks, and there is an engraved line on his jaw. Two horizontal lines adorn his neck. His face is painted on fine, smooth clay, with accurate proportions and highly skilled techniques. The Bodhisattva's appearance is dignified and beautiful, exuding a solemn and serene expression. This sculpture is a fine work of Song Dynasty artistry within the Maijishan Grottoes, reflecting the legacy of the plump and rounded style characteristic of the Tang Dynasty.

Originally, this statue features a head that was reattached by artisans of the Song Dynasty to the Bodhisattva statue from the Northern Wei Dynasty in Cave 135 of the Maijishan Grottoes. Due to the significant mismatch in material and era, the head was removed in 1997 and relocated to the cultural relics warehouse for storage. (By Zhang Ping)

第 135 窟 窟内正佛及菩萨
Central Buddha and Bodhisattvas, Cave 135

第 135 窟 窟内立佛西侧菩萨
Bodhisattva on the West Side of the Standing Buddha, Cave 135

67

《八王争舍利》壁画

Mural Paintings of *The Eight Kings Contending for the Sarira*

高兴旺临摹
西魏
长 160 厘米　宽 150 厘米
第 135 窟
麦积山石窟艺术研究所藏

Copy by Gao Xingwang
Western Wei Dynasty
Length: 160 cm, Width: 150 cm
Cave 135
Art Institute of Maijishan Cave-Temple Complex

　　"八王争舍利"是《大般涅槃经》中的一个情节：释迦牟尼在拘尸那城外的双树林涅槃之后于荼毗场火化为舍利子，拘尸那国人视为珍宝，准备起塔供奉。其余七国来拘尸那国争舍利。一位婆罗门长者说明争斗违背佛教精神，各国便偃旗息鼓，将舍利分装八个宝瓶，由众国王带回起塔供养。

　　画面中，矫健的战马纵横驰骋；身着铠甲的武士挥刀举盾，奋勇冲杀；四周观战的士兵抽刀出鞘，战马昂首扬蹄，跃跃欲上。画面上方，荼毗台之上并列放置 8 个宝瓶，是最后平分舍利的场景。长期生活在战乱中的匠师们，发挥了高超绘画技巧，如身临其境般成功地绘制了军队的征战场面；同时通过分舍利平息事端，结局圆满，寄托了老百姓对和平生活的渴望。整个画面构图严谨，绘画技法高超，特别是战马的绘制，继承了汉代马的画法，奔放、矫健，具有很高的艺术造诣。

　　135 窟保留了约 50 平方米的壁画精品，色彩和谐，线条流畅，人物形象清秀潇洒。

（张萍、谈叶闻）

"The Eight Kings Contending for the Sarira" is a narrative found in the Mahaparinirvana Sutra: After Sakyamuni attained parinirvana in the twin groves outside Kusinagara, he was cremated at the cremation ground and transformed into sarira. The people of Kusinagara regarded these relics as treasures and prepared to build a stupa for worship. The other seven kingdoms came to Kusinagara to contend for the sarira. An elder Brahmin pointed out that such contention was contrary to the Buddhist spirit, so the kingdoms ceased their fighting. The sarira was then divided into eight portions, placed into vases, and taken back by the kings to build stupas for worship.

In the mural, athletic war horses gallop freely, while armored warriors brandish swords and hold up shields, charging bravely into battle. Soldiers watching from all around draw their swords from their sheaths, and the war horses raise their heads and stamp their hooves, eager to charge. Above the scene, eight vases are placed side by side on the cremation platform, depicting the moment of dividing the sarira equally. The craftsmen, having lived through prolonged warfare, demonstrated exceptional skills, successfully capturing the battlefield scenes as if they were present. The resolution of the conflict through the division of the sarira conveys a perfect ending, embodying the common people's longing for a peaceful life. The entire mural features a rigorous composition and superb painting techniques. Notably, the depiction of the war horses draws from the painting style of the Han Dynasty, showcasing their unrestrained vigor and robustness, reflecting a high level of artistic achievement.

Cave 135 has preserved approximately 50 square meters of exquisite murals, characterized by harmonious colors, smooth lines, and elegant, unrestrained figures. (By Zhang Ping and Tan Yewen)

68 石雕造像塔

Stone-Carved Pagoda

北魏
长 35.8 厘米　宽 21.5 厘米　厚 21.1 厘米
西崖
麦积山石窟艺术研究所藏

Northern Wei Dynasty
Length: 35.8 cm, Width: 21.5 cm, Thickness: 21.1 cm
Western cliff
Art Institute of Maijishan Cave-Temple Complex

麦积山石窟加固工程前，在西崖堆积层清理发掘而出。造像塔分塔顶、塔身、塔座三层。上层塔顶为四面坡仿木构建筑形式，塔身四面雕有方形佛龛，龛内各雕一佛二菩萨，下层塔基雕刻供养人像。

其中塔顶为以圆形球状为中心四面呈放射状挑檐屋脊形，虽然边缘有磨损，但瓦楞及椽脊清晰可见。檐下四面分别雕四个兽头，气势威猛犹如下山之虎，既是护法又有较强的装饰性。塔身四面各一佛龛，龛楣上方中部一力士双手托举屋脊兽头，左右两侧各一飞天，体型纤细，呈对称形式相向飞往力士。长方形龛内雕一禅定印坐佛，高肉髻，面型长方，双耳垂肩，端肩细腰，袈裟下摆分三瓣，结跏趺坐于坛基之上，左右两侧各一站立胁侍菩萨，四根立柱敦实厚重，柱头上分别雕有力士作托举状，覆莲柱础硕大。塔基部分四面，其中有两面中间各一佛龛，两侧分别有一供养菩萨；另两面各不相同，一面中间立柱上方有一力士双手作托举状，两侧已模糊不清，另一面也是中间一立柱、有一力士双手作托举状，两侧不同的是各雕一前腿跃起、威猛咆哮状之虎扑向立柱，有不可阻挡之气势。画面静中有动，动中有静，布局和谐，结构完整，整体造型敦厚稳定。

（张萍）

Before the reinforcement project of the Maijishan Grottoes, the stone-carved pagoda was unearthed from the accumulation layer on the western cliff. The pagoda consists of three layers: the pagoda top, pagoda body, and pagoda base. The upper section features a four-sided sloped roof designed to resemble wooden architecture, while the pagoda body is adorned with square niches on all sides, each housing a Buddha and two bodhisattvas. The lower pagoda base is carved with figures of patrons.

The pagoda top features a circular sphere at its center, with eaves radiating outward in four directions. Despite some wear, the corrugated tiles and rafters are clearly visible. Each side under the eaves is adorned with a carved beast head, exuding an imposing presence reminiscent of a tiger descending from the mountain. These figures serve both as protectors of the Dharma and as striking decorative elements. The pagoda body contains a Buddha niche on each of its four sides. Above each niche, a Warrior is depicted holding up the roof beast head with both hands, flanked on either side by slender flying apsaras that symmetrically soar toward the Warrior. Inside the rectangular niche, a seated Buddha in meditation mudra is carved. He features a high ushnisha, a rectangular face, and drooping ears reaching the shoulders. With broad shoulders and a slender waist, the hem of his robe is divided into three flaps as he sits in full lotus position on the altar base. On either side of him stands a Bodhisattva attendant. The four pillars are solid and thick, each topped with carvings of Warriors in a lifting posture. The large lotus pedestal beneath them is thick and stable. On the base of the pagoda, two of the four sides feature a Buddha niche in the center, with patron Bodhisattvas on either side. The other two sides differ: One side has a Warrior above the central pillar in a lifting pose, while the other side also features a Warrior but adds an intricately carved fierce tiger leaping forward with its front legs raised and roaring, pouncing towards the pillar with an irresistible momentum. The image captures stillness within motion and motion within stillness, creating a harmonious layout with complete structural integrity. The overall shape is thick and stable. (By Zhang Ping)

石雕造像碑线描图
Line Drawing of Stone-Carved Tablet

69 石雕造像碑

Stone-Carved Tablet

北魏
长 47 厘米　宽 37.5 厘米　厚 10 厘米
西崖
麦积山石窟艺术研究所藏

Northern Wei Dynasty
Length: 47 cm, Width: 37.5 cm, Thickness: 10 cm
Western cliff
Art Institute of Maijishan Cave-Temple Complex

　　石雕造像碑（弥勒下生经碑），是麦积山加固工程前，在西崖堆积层清理发掘出土。

　　此碑是根据《弥勒下生经》绘制而成。画面分上下两部分，上部中间描绘雕交脚弥勒菩萨从兜率天下生阎浮提、于龙华树下成佛、弥勒菩萨在兜率天宫说法，左侧龙华树下的成佛，右侧对天人说法；下部中间造弥勒三尊，左右两侧护法天王造像。整个造像碑将兜率天宫、弥勒三尊、对天人的说法、龙华树下的弥勒成佛等场面组合在一起，表现《弥勒下生经》的内容。用高浮雕完成人物及背光雕刻，合理地运用了阴刻线和阳刻线，布局严谨，构思巧妙。（张萍）

　　Stone-carved tablet (The tablet of the Sutra on the Descent of Maitreya) was unearthed from the accumulation layer on the western cliff before the reinforcement project of Maijishan.

　　This stele is based on the *Sutra on the Descent of Maitreya* and is composed of two parts: The upper section depicts the Maitreya Bodhisattva, seated with crossed legs, descending from the Tusita Heaven to Jambudvipa and attaining Buddhahood under the Longhua tree. In this section, the Maitreya Bodhisattva preaches in Tusita Heaven. On the left, we see the scene of Maitreya becoming a Buddha under the Longhua tree, while on the right, he is preaching to the gods and humans. The lower part features three Maitreya statues in the center, flanked by the statues of Dharma-protecting heavenly kings on both sides. The entire statue stele combines scenes from the Tusita Heaven, the three Maitreya statues, the preaching to the gods and humans, and Maitreya's attainment of Buddhahood under the Longhua tree, effectively conveying the content of the *Sutra on the Descent of Maitreya*. The figures and backlighting are executed in high relief, skillfully employing both incised and raised lines. The layout is meticulous, and the conception is ingenious. (By Zhang Ping)

70

《火头明王》壁画

Mural Painting of Ucchusman

隋
长 60 厘米　宽 40 厘米
第 78 窟
麦积山石窟艺术研究所藏

Sui Dynasty
Length: 60 cm, Width: 40 cm
Cave 78
Art Institute of Maijishan Cave-Temple Complex

　　此壁画残块在 1978 年于麦积山石窟第 78 窟主佛台座四周的泥土和碎石中发现，泥土的掩埋使壁画仍保留着强烈而鲜艳的色彩和清晰的笔触。

　　火头明王头上和双手都燃烧着橘红色的火焰。深目高鼻，八字须，山羊胡，横眉怒目张口呵斥。上身赤裸，通身青黑，胸部隆起，肚腹突出，双肩披蓝紫色披巾，戴橘红色项圈、手镯，下身穿红色卷边束腰羊肠大裙。右下方两身弟子，绘圆形项光。右上侧残存供养人上半身，披发戴巾。左下方残存两身供养人，手持莲蓬。这幅火头明王是唐以前唯一可见的汉地火头明王像，与其他石窟寺明王相比显得文儒多了，它为研究佛教密宗经典在中原的传播与翻译，以及火头金刚的演变过程提供了宝贵的实物资料。

　　火头明王作为佛教密宗护法神之一，又称大威德焰发德迦明王，也是佛教十大明王之一，是妙吉祥菩萨的化身，曾发愿成就火光三昧作如来力士，为如来降伏魔怨，唵尽秽迹，故又称"火头金刚""秽迹金刚"。（张萍）

This mural fragment was discovered in 1978 among the soil and gravel surrounding the main Buddha pedestal in Cave 78 of the Maijishan Grottoes. Being buried in the soil has allowed the mural to retain its strong, vivid colors and clear brushstrokes.

The Fire-Headed King (Ucchusman) is depicted with orange-red flames burning on his head and both hands. He has deep-set eyes, a prominent nose, a mustache shaped like the Chinese character "八", a goatee, and an angry glare with his mouth open as if shouting. His upper body is bare and bluish-black, featuring a bulging chest and protruding abdomen. He wears a blue-purple shawl draped over his shoulders, along with an orange-red necklace and bracelets. His lower body is adorned with a red turned-up bodycon skirt that is tightly cinched at the waist. In the lower right, two disciples are depicted with circular halos around their heads. In the upper right, the upper body of a patron is visible, characterized by loose hair and a scarf. In the lower left, two additional patrons are shown holding lotus pods. This Ucchusman mural is the only known representation of the Fire-Headed King in Han regions prior to the Tang Dynasty. Compared to the depictions of Ucchusman in other grotto temples, this image appears much more refined and scholarly. It provides invaluable materials for studying the spread and translation of Buddhist tantric scriptures in the Central Plains, as well as the evolution process of Ucchusman.

As one of the protector deities of Buddhist tantra, the Fire-Headed King, also known as Mahabala Yamari Vajra, is one of the ten great kings in Buddhism and is considered the incarnation of Manjusri Bodhisattva. He once made a vow to attain the Samadhi of Firelight and become the Warrior of the Tathagata, subduing demons and resentments on behalf of Tathagata while devouring defilements. For this reason, he is also referred to as the "Fire-Headed Vajra" and "Vajra of Defilement". (By Zhang Ping)

71 颜料碗

Painting Pigment Bowls

口径 9 厘米—11.5 厘米
第 74 窟
麦积山石窟艺术研究所藏

Caliber: 9 cm—11.5 cm
Cave 74
Art Institute of Maijishan Cave-Temple Complex

　　这批画具于 1987 年夏季在麦积山石窟西崖第 74 号窟正壁主佛左侧的倒凹型高坛基座上，意外发现于残破的碎石与沙土堆积层中，并经过抢救性发掘出土。是工匠绘制完壁画和塑像之后，将其埋在佛座旁的。

　　出土时两个木质大碗内有 10 个陶质小碗依次重叠倒扣其中，它们最大的碗口径 11.5 厘米，最小的碗口径 9 厘米。10 只陶碗中均残留有当年彩画完毕后所剩下的各色颜料，有红、黄、绿、蓝等，保存良好，色彩鲜艳如新，这是麦积山石窟目前出土的唯一一套完整的古代彩画颜料盛放器具，更是研究古代石窟彩画制作工艺的珍贵实物资料。（张萍）

　　This batch of painting tools was unexpectedly discovered in the summer of 1987 within the accumulation layer of broken gravel and sand on the inverted concave-shaped high altar base, located on the left side of the main Buddha on the main wall of Cave 74 on the western cliff of the Maijishan Grottoes. They were unearthed through emergency excavation. It is believed that the craftsmen buried these tools beside the Buddha pedestal after completing the murals and statues.

　　When unearthed, two large wooden bowls contained ten small pottery bowls, which were overlapping and inverted within them. The largest bowl has a diameter of 11.5 cm, while the smallest measures 9 cm in diameter. Each of the ten pottery bowls retains various pigments left over after the completion of the colorful paintings, including red, yellow, green, and blue. These pigments are well preserved, with colors that remain as vibrant as new. This discovery represents the only complete set of ancient pigment containers for holding paints unearthed to date in the Maijishan Grottoes. It served as a valuable physical resource for studying the production techniques of ancient grotto paintings. (By Zhang Ping)

72 《伎乐飞天》壁画

隋
长 58 厘米　宽 50 厘米
第 78 窟
麦积山石窟艺术研究所藏

　　1978 年于第 78 窟主佛台座周围的泥土和碎石中发现，壁画色新如故。

　　壁画内容为上下两身反向飞翔的伎乐飞天、飘带、流云等。下方伎乐飞天束高髻，面型方圆秀丽，长眉细目，上穿蓝色短袖，下着束腰长裙，手持弦乐器作弹奏状。上方伎乐飞天上身着绿色短袖，下着白色束腰长裙，飘带穿肘外，做飞行状。手持弦乐器作弹奏势。伎乐面部及祖露的肌肤部分均施白粉，增加了肌肤的柔和细腻之感。（张萍）

Mural Painting of *Apsaras Musicians*

Sui Dynasty
Length: 58 cm, Width: 50 cm
Cave 78
Art Institute of Maijishan Cave-Temple Complex

In 1978, the mural was discovered in the soil and gravel surrounding the main Buddha pedestal in Cave 78, and its colors remain as vibrant as ever.

The mural depicts two apsaras musicians flying in opposite directions, accompanied by ribbons and flowing clouds. The lower apsara has a high bun, with a round and beautiful face, long eyebrows, and slender eyes. She wears a blue short-sleeved top and a long, fitted skirt, holding a stringed instrument as she plays. The upper apsara is dressed in a green short-sleeved top and a white long skirt, with ribbons flowing outside her elbows, creating a sense of flight. She also holds a stringed instrument in a playing gesture. Both apsaras have their faces and exposed skin dusted with white powder, enhancing the softness and delicacy of their skin. (By Zhang Ping)

第 78 窟全景图
Panoramic View of Cave 78

73 金光明经卷第四

唐
长 740 厘米　高 25 厘米
第 13 窟
麦积山石窟艺术研究所藏

　　麦积山存卷四首残尾全，唐末写本，卷轴装，"装藏"品。其上有手写的经文，卷首有《金光明经卷第四》字样，竹质卷轴高 28 厘米，两端朱底墨漆。经卷用黄麻纸裱褙。楷书，每行 15—17 字不等，共 424 行。于 1982 年修复东崖 13 窟大佛时从主佛右脸颊内取出。

　　《金光明经》共有四卷，不知何因，其余三卷佚失，仅存《金光明经》卷四，包括第十六、第十七、第十八、第十九等四部分。其中第十六首部略有残损，其余完好，字迹工整，是麦积山现存最早的珍贵卷轴装写佛经。2000 年经甘肃省文物局组织专家鉴定为国家一级文物。此本于 2008 年 4 月入选第一批《国家珍贵古籍名录》（编号 00141），并获得中华人民共和国文化部颁发的国家珍贵古籍名录证书。

　　《金光明经》为北凉昙三藏法师昙无谶译，是大乘佛教中有着重要影响力的经典之一。由于经中所说的诵持本经能够带来不可思议的护国利民功德，能使饥馑、疾疫、战乱得以平息，国土丰饶，人民欢乐，故历代以来《金光明经》被视为护国之经，在大乘佛教流行的所有地区都受到了广泛重视。（张萍）

天水麦积山石窟外景
Exterior View of Maijishan Grottoes

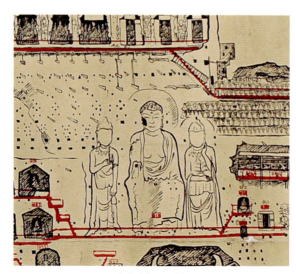

石窟编号简图（局部）
Simplified Map of Grotto Numbers (Detail)

神等常當隨侍擁衛隱蔽其身是說法
者背惡消滅諸惡人令得安隱顧不有慮
介時釋迦牟尼佛現大神力十方無量世
界皆六動震動是時諸佛皆大歡喜嗟
累是經故讚美文持法者現无量神力其是
無量無邊阿僧祇菩薩摩訶薩大眾及
信相菩薩金光金藏常悲法上等及四天大
王十千天子與道場菩提樹神堅牢等及
一切世間天人阿修羅等聞佛所說皆發无

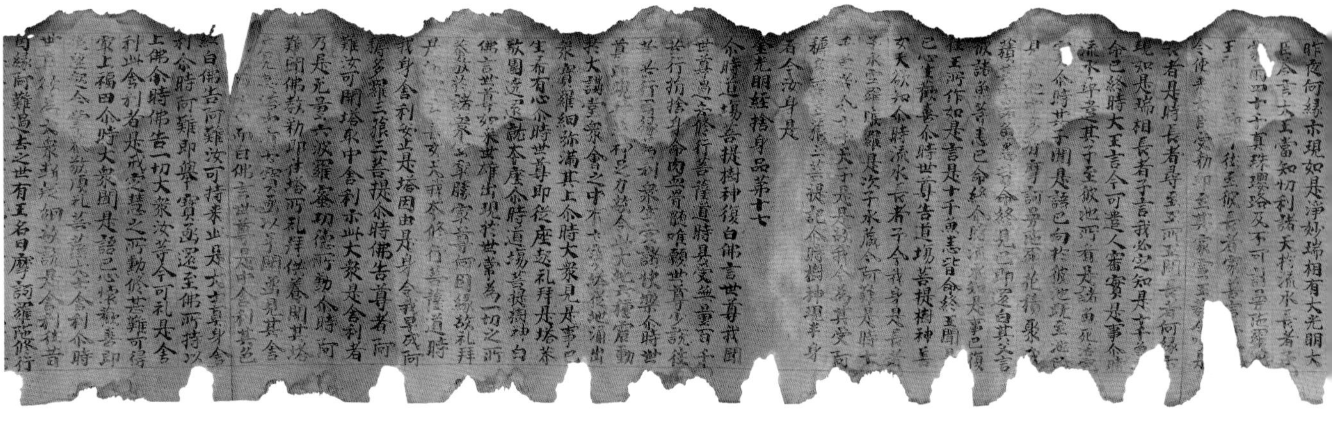

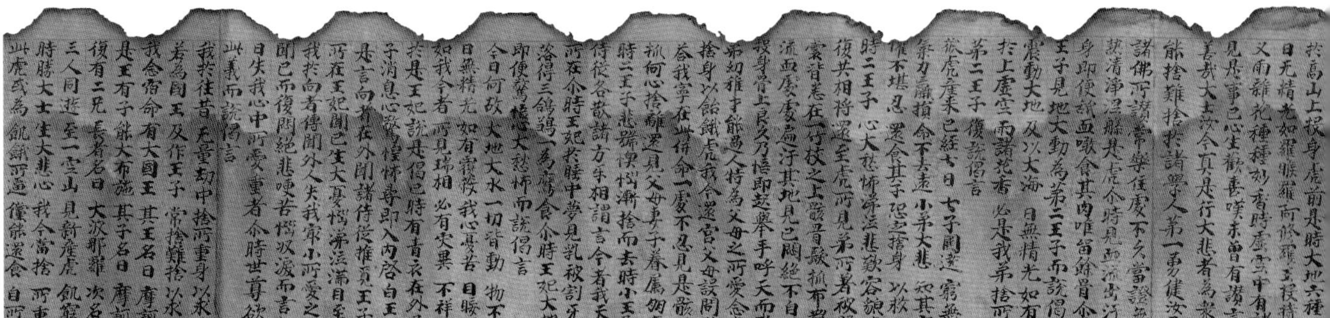

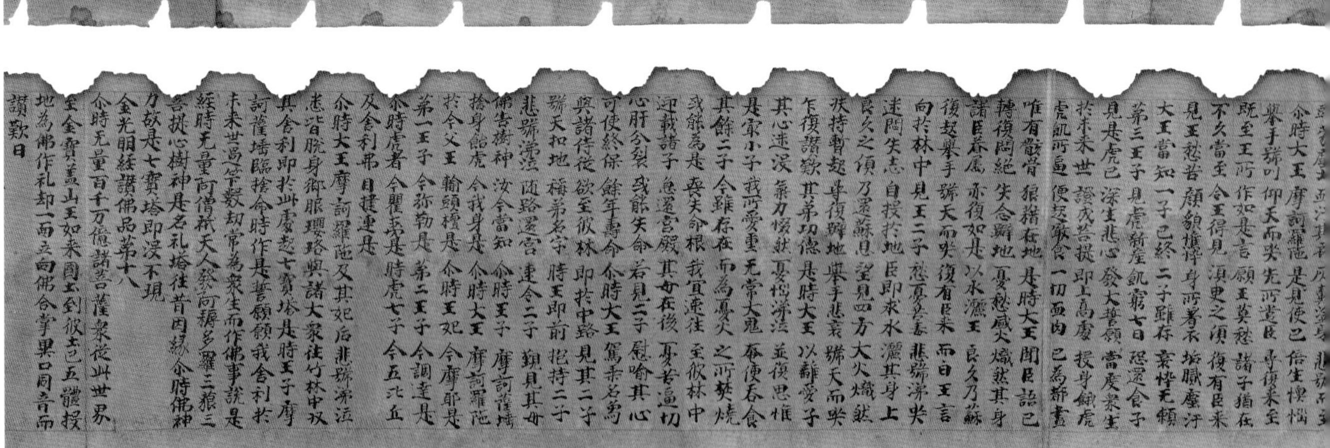

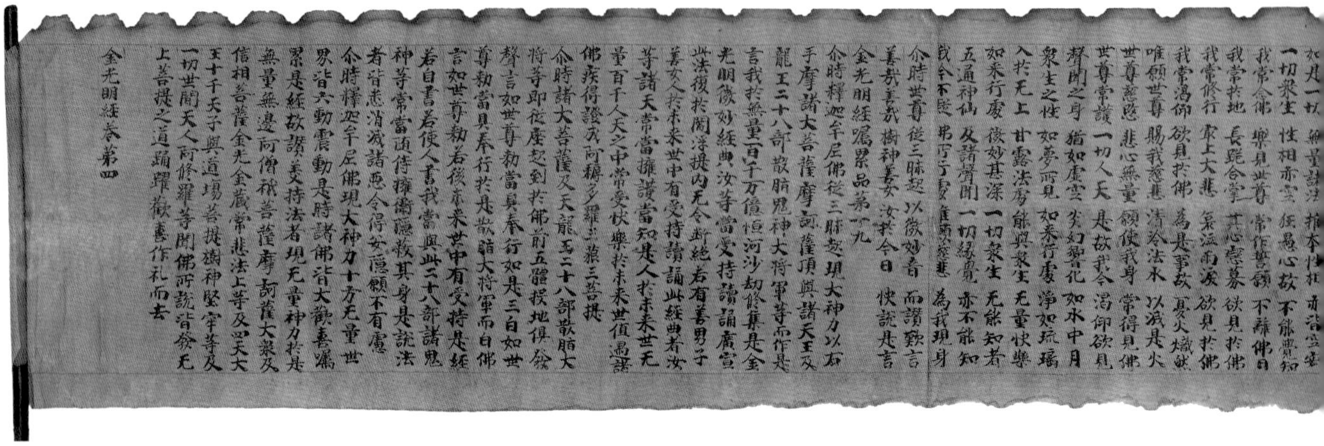

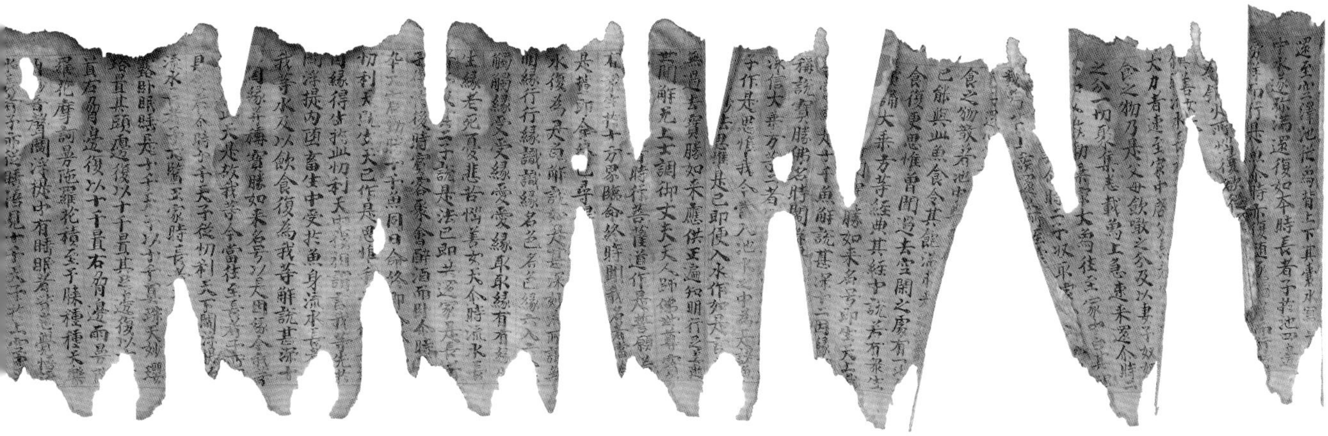

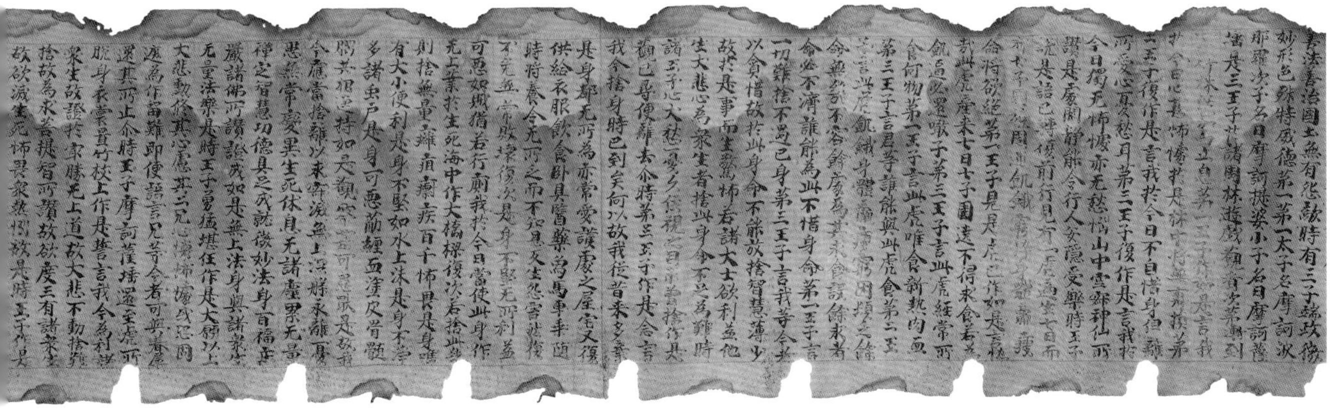

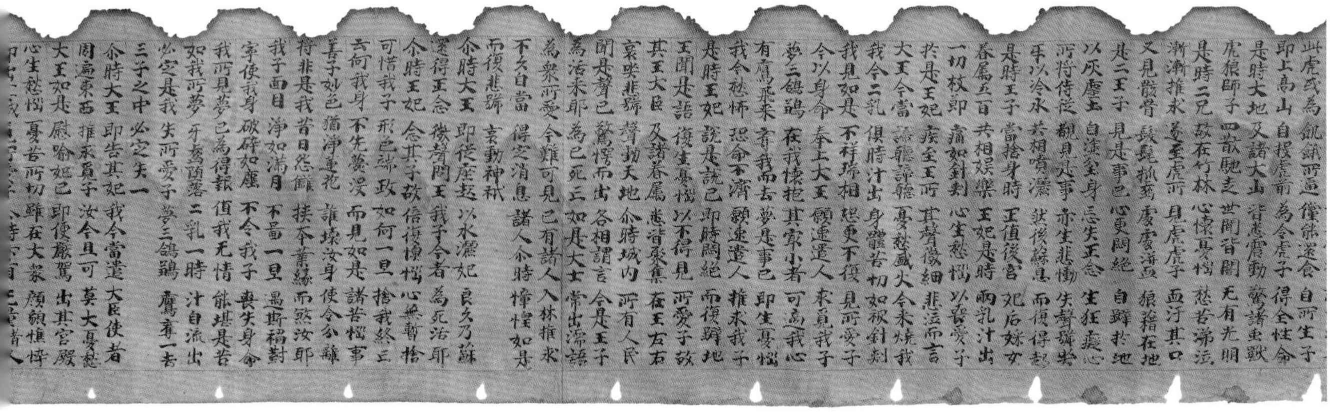

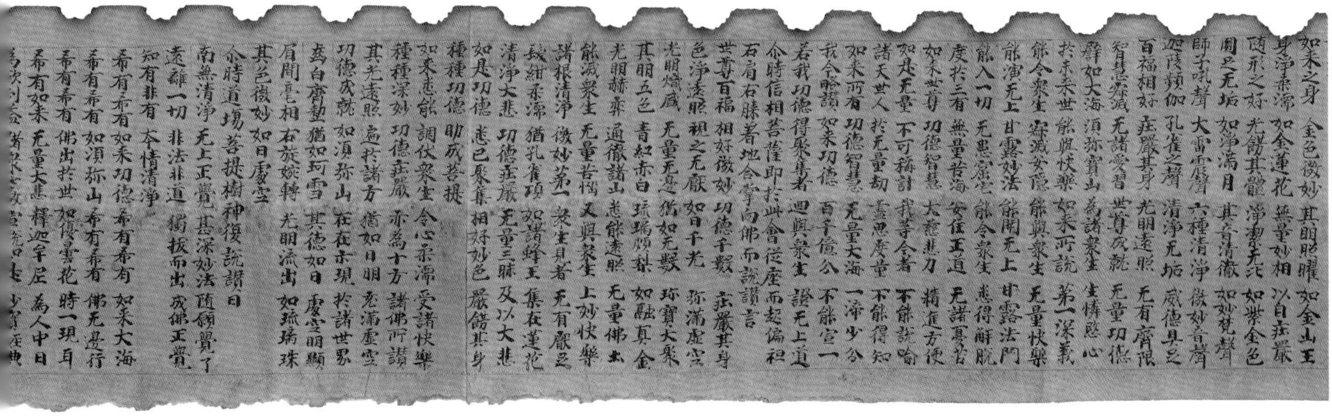

Volume IV of the *Golden Light Sutra*

Length: 740 cm, Height: 25 cm
Cave 13
Art Institute of Maijishan Cave-Temple Complex

At Maijishan, there exists Volume IV of the *Golden Light Sutra*, which has an incomplete beginning but an intact ending. This manuscript dates back to the late Tang Dynasty and is bound in scroll format, referred to as a "concealed treasure". The scroll features handwritten scripture, and at the beginning, it is labeled with the words *Volume IV of the Golden Light Sutra*. The bamboo scroll measures 28 cm in height, with both ends painted in black lacquer on a vermilion background. The sutra scroll is backed with jute paper. Written in regular script, it contains 15 to 17 characters per line, totaling 424 lines. The scroll was extracted from the right cheek of the main Buddha in Cave 13 on the eastern cliff in 1982.

The Golden Light Sutra originally consists of four volumes; however, for unknown reason, the other three volumes are lost, leaving only Volume IV. This volume includes four parts: parts 16, 17, 18, and 19. The beginning of part 16 is slightly damaged, while the rest is intact, with neat handwriting. It is the earliest extant scroll-bound Buddhist scripture in Maijishan. In 2000, it was appraised as a National Grade I Cultural Relic by experts organized by the Gansu Provincial Cultural Relics Bureau. In April 2008, this scroll was included in the first batch of the *National List of Rare Ancient Books* (No. 00141) and was awarded the certificate of the National List of Rare Ancient Books issued by the Ministry of Culture of the People's Republic of China.

The *Golden Light Sutra* was translated by Dharmacarya Tanwu Chen of the Northern Liang Dynasty and is considered one of the influential classics in Mahayana Buddhism. According to the sutra, reciting and upholding this text can bring incredible merits and virtues for protecting the country and benefiting the people. It is said to have the power to quell famine, epidemics, and wars in the land, leading to prosperity and happiness for the people. As a result, throughout the ages, the *Golden Light Sutra* has been regarded as a sutra for protecting the country and has received widespread reverence in all regions where Mahayana Buddhism has flourished. (By Zhang Ping)

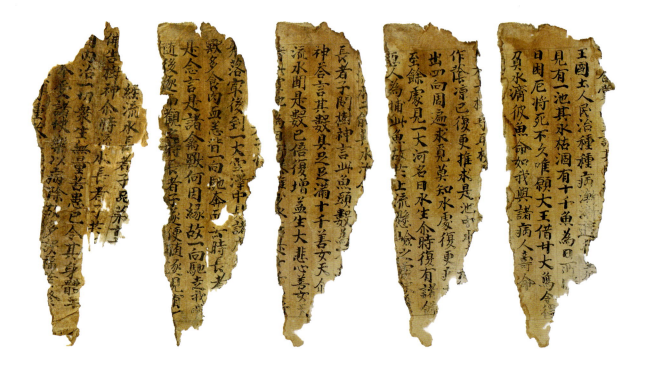

74 宋代定窑白瓷碗

Ding Kiln White Porcelain Bowl from the Song Dynasty

宋
口径 16.4 厘米　底径 6.4 厘米　通高 5.4 厘米
第 13 窟
麦积山石窟艺术研究所藏

Song Dynasty
Caliber: 16.4 cm, Bottom diameter: 6.4 cm, Total height: 5.4 cm
Cave 13
Art Institute of Maijishan Cave-Temple Complex

　　在 1981 年麦积山石窟加固东崖 13 窟大佛时，从大佛的眉间白毫中发现并取出。白毫源自佛教经典《法华经》"菩萨摩诃萨，若有人能持戒斋戒，身心清净，如白毫无瑕"，意思是如果一个人能够持戒斋戒，保持身心的纯净，就像白色的绒毛一样没有瑕疵。《法华经句解·序品》："佛放眉间白毫相光。"亦称作"白毫"。"白毫相"是如来三十二相之一。眉间有白色毫毛，右旋宛转，如日正中，放之则有光明。

　　此碗内壁有一道旋纹，外壁有"绍兴二十七年"即公元 1157 年墨书题记："秦州甘谷城塑题高振同□□是绍兴二十七年八月廿五日□□高振□"。字体为行书楷体。由此可看，此件白瓷碗至少为宋代绍兴二十七年的器物，器形质地及工艺具有宋代定窑光素无纹白瓷的特征，为敞口斜腹圈足底，通体施白釉，釉色白里泛黄，且厚薄不均，光素无纹饰，足内亦施白釉。碗底圈足露胎，胎釉相容一体，无明显的界线，露胎圈足细密有致。该器白中泛黄，有油脂的光泽。此碗对麦积山石窟的修造与分期断代，提供了重要的实物例证。（张萍）

The white porcelain bowl was discovered and retrieved from the urna (the white curl between the eyebrows) of the giant Buddha in Cave 13 on the eastern cliff of Maijishan Grottoes during the reinforcement work in 1981. The urna originates from the Buddhist scripture The Lotus Sutra, which states, "For a Bodhisattva Mahasattva, if someone can observe precepts and fasts and keep the body and mind pure, it is like a white down without blemish." It means that if a person can uphold the precepts, maintain purity of body and mind, they are like a flawless white down. In the Annotations on Sentences of the Lotus Sutra - Preface, it is written: "The Buddha emits the light of the urna between the eyebrows." The "appearance of urna" is also known as one of the thirty-two major marks of Tathagata. There is a white hair tuft between the eyebrows, spiraling to the right, like the sun at high noon, and when emitted, it radiates light.

There is a spiral pattern on the inside wall of this bowl, while the outside wall bears an ink inscription from the 27th year of Shaoxing era, corresponding to 1157 AD. The inscription reads: "Plastered and inscribed in Gangu City, Qinzhou, Gao Zhentong...was on August 25th, the 27th year of Shaoxing; Gao Zhen..." The calligraphy combines running (xingshu) and regular (kaishu) scripts. From this inscription, it is evident that this white porcelain bowl dates back to at least the 17th year of Shaoxing in the Song Dynasty. Its shape, texture, and craftsmanship exhibit the characteristic of plain white porcelain from the Ding Kiln. It has an open mouth, inclined abdomen, and ring foot, all uniformly coated in white glaze. The glaze exhibits a yellowish tint and is uneven in thickness, with no decorative patterns. The interior of the foot is also glazed in white. The ring foot at the bottom of the bowl reveals the body, with the body and glaze blending seamlessly without clear demarcation. The exposed ring foot is finely detailed and orderly. This bowl, with its yellowish-white hue and greasy luster, provides an important physical example for understanding the construction and chronological context of the Maijishan Grottoes. (By Zhang Ping)

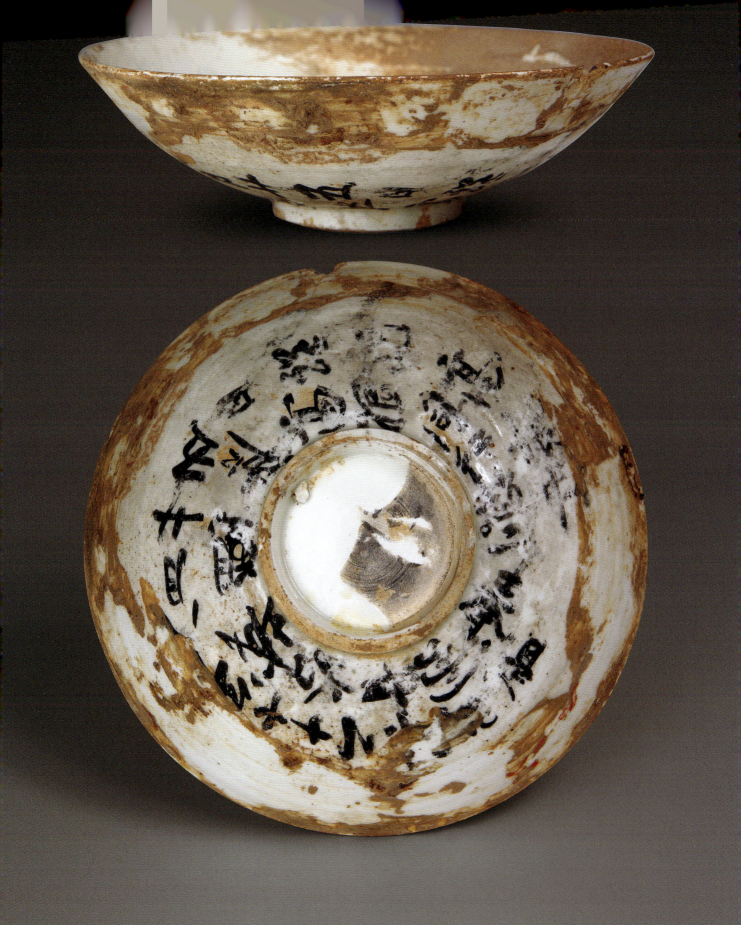

75 钱币幡

Coin Streamer

元
长 108 厘米　宽 25 厘米　重 1.235 千克
第 98 窟
麦积山石窟艺术研究所藏

Yuan Dynasty
Length: 108 cm, Width: 25 cm, Weight: 1.235 kg
Cave 98
Art Institute of Maijishan Cave-Temple Complex

　　该钱币幡是在 1981 年修复第 98 窟西崖大佛时从主佛胸部泥层中取出，体现了麦积山石窟大佛装藏之功用。

　　由 287 枚钱币用棉线串成，最上部由 55 枚钱币串成一个等腰三角形，下部两串分左右两侧下垂，中部自上而下呈倒三角形、菱形、圆形、方形组成的图案，其下部 4 行流苏状下垂，末端有象征莲台的六边形图案相连。钱币有十余种，多为唐宋时期，其中宋代钱币最多，早至秦代，晚为元代，除少量钱币破损外，其余均保存完整。它是一个由铜钱币相串而成幡的形状，有幡头、幡手、幡足、幡身等，符合佛教礼仪中的"金铜幡"形象，组成的图形结构复杂富于变化，装饰性强。具有较高的历史、艺术研究价值。

　　用钱币做成幡的形状，与"幢"同为供养佛菩萨的庄严法具，用以象征佛菩萨之威德。在经典中多用为降魔的象征。《华严经》亦常谓造立幡，能得福德，避苦难，往生诸佛净土，又说供养幡可得菩提及其功德，故寺院、道场常加使用，因而成为庄严之法具。（张萍）

This coin streamer was extracted from the mud layer on the chest of the main Buddha during the restoration of the giant Buddha on the western cliff of Cave 98 in 1981. It reflects the function of enshrining in the giant Buddha of the Maijishan Grottoes.

This streamer is composed of 287 coins strung together with cotton thread. The uppermost part forms an isosceles triangle made up of 55 coins, while the two lower strings hang down on the left and right sides. The middle section features a pattern consisting of an inverted triangle, rhombus, circle, and square. The lower part has four rows of tassel-like pendants, with a hexagonal pattern symbolizing the lotus pedestal at the end. The coins include more than ten varieties, primarily from the Tang and Song dynasties, with the majority being from the Song Dynasty. They date as early as the Qin Dynasty and as late as the Yuan Dynasty. Except for a small number of damaged coins, the rest are intact. The streamer has the shape of a traditional banner made of copper coins, complete with a streamer head, handles, feet, and body. It aligns with the "golden and copper streamer" used in Buddhist rituals. The graphic structure is complex and varied, showing strong decorative quantities. This artifact holds significant historical and artistic value for research.

Creating a streamer from coins serves, like a "banner", as a solemn object for making offerings to Buddhas and Bodhisattvas, symbolizing their dignity and power. In Buddhist text, it is frequently associated with the subjugation of demons. The Avatamsaka Sutra states that making and erecting a streamer can bring blessings, help avoid hardships, and facilitate rebirth in the pure lands of the Buddhas. It also says that offering to a streamer can lead to the attainment of Bodhi and its associated merits. Therefore, such streamers are commonly used in temples and religious venues, becoming solemn religious implements. (By Zhang Ping)

76

石雕弟子跪像

Stone Carving of Kneeling Disciple

北周
长 65 厘米　宽 28 厘米　厚 28 厘米
舍利塔出土
麦积山石窟艺术研究所藏

Northern Zhou Dynasty
Length: 65 cm, Width: 28 cm, Thickness: 28 cm
Unearthed from the stupa
Art Institute of Maijishan Cave-Temple Complex

　　2009 年 4 月麦积山石窟维修舍利塔时，在地宫考古发掘出土 11 件北朝瘞埋的石雕造像。佛像在佛教中有着特殊的意义，被视为圣物，具有灵性的象征，应该受到崇敬和尊重，不能随意抛弃。因此人们将要残损或已经残损的塑像埋入地中。这些造像出土时相对较完整，这是为了躲避战争的灾难还是有意保护而进行的瘞埋活动，有待考证。

　　此件为 11 件出土造像的其中之一，清理后存入文物库房。此造像呈跪拜状弟子像，头部缺失，身躯浑圆，端肩。内着僧祇袄，外披偏右袒袈裟，衣巾自右侧外搭于左臂自然下垂，双手合十，双膝跪于正方形台座之上。阴刻线清晰可见，衣纹错落有致、流畅自如。造型敦厚稳重，体态端庄。其身材比例适中，有北周"珠圆玉润"造像之风格。

（张萍）

In April 2009, during the repair of the stupa at the Maijishan Grottoes, 11 stone-carved statues from the Northern Dynasties were unearthed through archaeological excavation in the underground palace. Buddha statues hold special significance in Buddhism, regarded as sacred objects and symbols of spirituality. They should be respected and revered, and cannot be discarded carelessly. Therefore, statues that were nearly damaged or already damaged were buried underground. These statues that were unearthed are relatively intact. Whether this burial was intended to avoid the calamities of war or was a deliberate act of preservation remains to be verified.

This statue is one of the 11 unearthed pieces. After cleaning, it was stored in the cultural relics warehouse. This statue depicts a kneeling disciple. Although his head is missing, the body is rounded with broad shoulders. It is dressed in a sanghati underneath and a right-slanting kasaya on top, with the clothing draping from the right side and hanging naturally over the left arm. The hands are clasped together, and the knees rest on a square pedestal. The intaglio lines are clearly visible, and the patterns of the clothing are well-arranged, smooth, and natural. The modelling is robust and stable, and the posture is dignified. His body proportions are moderate, reflecting the style of the plump statues from the Northern Zhou Dynasty. (By Zhang Ping)

舍利塔

77 石雕力士头像

Stone Carving of Warrior Head

高 27 厘米　宽 17.6 厘米　厚 14.4 厘米
舍利塔出土
麦积山石窟艺术研究所藏

Height: 27 cm, Width: 17.6cm, Thickness: 14.4 cm
Unearthed from the stupa
Art Institute of Maijishan Cave-Temple Complex

　　2009 年 4 月麦积山石窟维修舍利塔时，在此塔地宫考古发掘出土，同样也是瘗埋的 11 件北朝石雕造像之一。力士与佛、菩萨、弟子等佛教造像同样都可以进行瘗埋，以示尊重。出土时头与躯体断开分离，清理后存入文物库房。

　　力士束低平发髻，戴冠，宽额，面型方圆，突眉，眼球突出似蝌蚪状，高鼻、宽鼻翼，张口露齿，呈怒吼状。颈部清晰可见暴露的筋骨。从造像风格上看有北周丰润之特点。（张萍）

In April 2009, during the repair of this pagoda at the Maijishan Grottoes, the statue was unearthed through archaeological excavation in the underground palace of the stupa. It is also one of the 11 stone-carved statues buried in the Northern Dynasties. Similar to the statues of Buddhas, Bodhisattvas, and disciples, warriors can also be buried as a sign of respect. Upon excavation, the head was found disconnected from the body. After cleaning, it was stored in the cultural relics warehouse.

The warrior features a low and flat bun, wears a crown, has a wide forehead and a round face. Its prominent eyebrows and protruding eyeballs resemble tadpoles, complemented by a high nose and wide nostrils. The mouth is open, revealing teeth, and the expression conveys a roaring demeanor. The exposed tendons and bones on the neck are clearly visible. Based on the style of the statue, it exhibits the plump characteristics typical of the Northern Zhou Dynasty. (By Zhang Ping)

78 宋白釉瓷瓶

Song Dynasty White Glazed Porcelain Vase

宋
高 9.2 厘米　口径 2.2 厘米　底径 2.9 厘米
舍利塔天宫
麦积山石窟艺术研究所藏

Song Dynasty
Height: 9.2 cm, Mouth Diameter: 2.2 cm, Base Diameter: 2.9 cm
The Celestial Chamber of the Stupa
Art Institute of Maijishan Cave-Temple Complex

　　舍利塔是佛塔中的一种塔，在塔刹的下面，有的还设置了天宫，专门用来珍藏和供奉舍利、供养物品等。一般舍利塔中供奉的物品是佛祖释迦牟尼或者其他高僧的舍利子。

　　2009 年 4 月麦积山石窟维修山顶舍利塔时被发现，出土时被放置在舍利塔顶部用砖堆砌的立方体空间天宫中的一个灰黑色陶罐内，罐内填充有五谷、砂金、铜钱等装藏物品，其中就有这个被白色布封口的白瓷瓶，内有黏稠状液体渗出，呈黄色。此瓶是否装舍利，有待考证。（张萍）

A relic stupa is a type of Buddhist pagoda. Beneath its pinnacle, some stupas feature a celestial chamber, specifically designed to house and venerate sacred relics and offerings. Typically, the relics enshrined within a stupa are those of the Buddha, Shakyamuni, or other revered Buddhist monks.

In April 2009, during the restoration of the stupa atop the Maijishan Grottoes, a grey-black ceramic jar was discovered within a brick-encased cubic space known as the celestial chamber. This jar contained various offerings, including grains, gold dust, and copper coins. Among these items was a white porcelain bottle, sealed with white cloth, from which a viscous yellow liquid had seeped. The contents of this bottle, potentially relics, are yet to be confirmed.(By Zhang Ping)

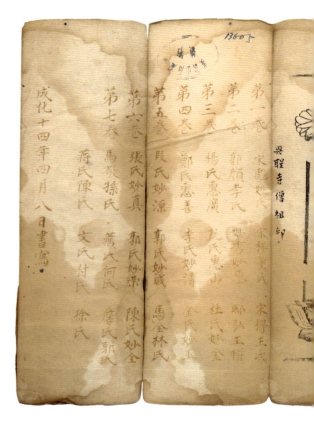

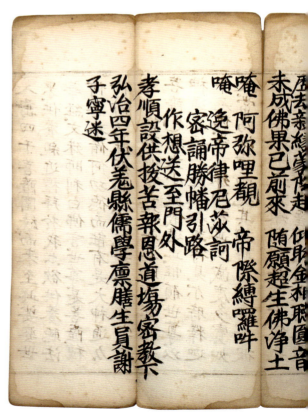

《大乘妙法莲华经》卷七

79

明
单开长 26.6 厘米　宽 9 厘米
瑞应寺旧藏
麦积山石窟艺术研究所藏

　　《大乘妙法莲华经》简称《法华经》，是佛陀释迦牟尼晚年所说的教法，属于开权显实的圆融教法，大小无异，显示人人皆可成佛之一乘了义。因经中宣讲内容至高无上，明示不分贫富贵贱，只要依循佛法，人人皆可成佛，而其他经典尚有阶级上下之分，所以《法华经》也被誉为"经中之王"。麦积山藏此经卷 7 卷，为明代经折刻写本《血书》，姚秦三藏法师鸠摩罗什译。此本系两面书，正面为血书《大乘妙法莲华经》，背面为写本《报恩科仪》。其中《大乘妙法莲华经卷》第七有发愿文："比丘恭能发心刺血书写」大乘妙法莲华经一部专祈保佑」信官宋」四恩念报三有均资」法界有情同缘种智"，尾题"成化十四年四月八日书写"。卷尾通列每卷本施主姓名。此本前六卷字迹血色较浅，后被人加墨描润，第七卷未描润，保存较好。此卷本系木刻板本印制，未墨印，后系人用血描润，做法较罕见。（张萍）

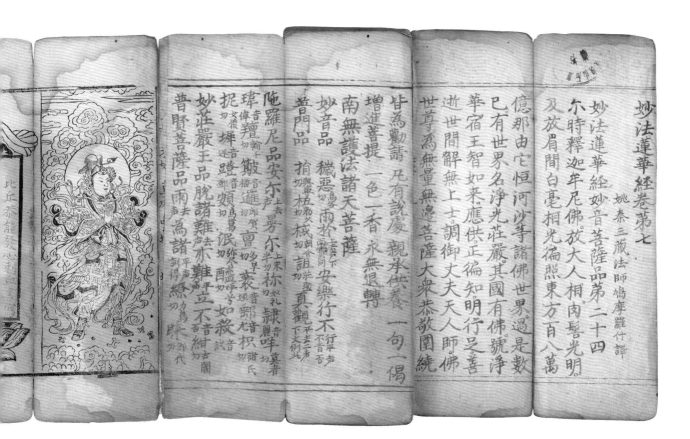

妙法蓮華經卷第七

姚秦三藏法師鳩摩羅什譯

妙法蓮華經妙音菩薩品第二十四

尔時釋迦牟尼佛放大人相肉髻光明。及放眉間白毫相光徧照東方百八萬

億那由佗恒河沙等諸佛世界過是數已有世界名淨光莊嚴其國有佛號淨華宿王智如來。應供正徧知明行足善逝世間解無上士調御丈夫天人師。佛世尊為無量無邊菩薩大衆恭敬圍繞

普賢菩薩勸發品

妙莊嚴王品

陀羅尼品

普門品

妙音品

南無護法諸天菩薩

增進菩提一色一香永無退轉

昔為勤請尼有誠慶親承供養

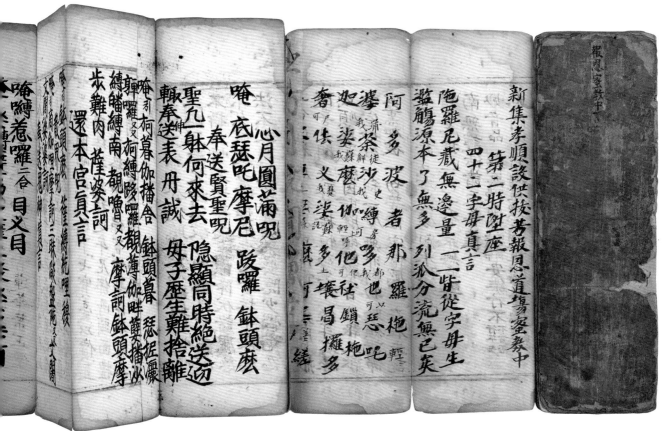

新集孝順設供報恩道場蜜教中

陀羅尼藏無邊量　一一皆從字母生

監龍源本了無多　列派分流無巳矣

第二時陛座　四十二字母真言

阿　多　波　者　那　邏　拕　者

婆　迦　娑　磨　迦　娑

奢

唵　底瑟吒摩尼　跋囉　鉢頭麼

心月圓芒蒲咒

聖九一躰何來去　隱顯同時絕送迎

奉送賢聖呪

輙奉送表冊誠　母子歷生難捨離

唵引　阿暮伽播合　鉢頭暮

縛日囉　阿縛嚕枳羝　阿

步難肉　南　觀嚕

此難肉　南　薩埵嚩

還本宮真言

摩訶鉢頭摩

Seventh Scroll of the *Lotus Sutra*

Ming Dynasty
Height: 26.6 cm, Width: 9 cm
Formerly in the collection of Ruiying Temple
Art Institute of Maijishan Cave-Temple Complex

The *Lotus Sutra*, also known as the *Sutra* on the White Lotus of the Sublime Dharma, is a pivotal teaching attributed to Buddha Shakyamuni during the later years of his life. This sutra embodies a doctrine of perfect harmony, transcending distinctions between greater and lesser teachings, and reveals the profound truth that all individuals have the potential to attain Buddhahood through a singular, definitive path. Renowned as the "King of Sutras," the *Lotus Sutra* is celebrated for its supreme teachings, which assert that enlightenment is accessible to everyone, irrespective of social status or wealth. Unlike other scriptures that may suggest hierarchical distinctions, the *Lotus Sutra* proclaims that by adhering to the Dharma, all beings can achieve enlightenment. Seven scrolls of this sutra are preserved at Maijishan. This artifact is a Ming Dynasty folded scripture, known as a *Blood Scripture*, translated by the renowned Tripitaka Master Kumarajiva during the Yao Qin period. The manuscript is double-sided, with the front featuring the "Blood Scripture" version of the *Lotus Sutra*

and the back containing the text *Rituals for Repaying Kindness*. Within the seventh scroll of the *Lotus Sutra*, a vow inscription reads: "Monk Gongneng, with a devoted heart, inscribed the entire Great Vehicle Lotus Sutra using his own blood, praying for the protection of the faithful official Song. May the four great kindnesses be repaid, and may all sentient beings in the Dharma realm equally attain wisdom." This inscription is dated to the eighth day of the fourth month in the fourteenth year of the Chenghua era. At the end of the scroll, the names of the patrons for each volume are meticulously listed. The initial six scrolls of this manuscript display lighter blood-colored script, which was subsequently reinforced with ink. In contrast, the seventh scroll remains untouched by ink enhancement and is exceptionally well-preserved. Originally produced using woodblock printing without ink, this scroll was later traced over with blood—a rare and unique practice for manuscripts of this kind. (By Zhang Ping)

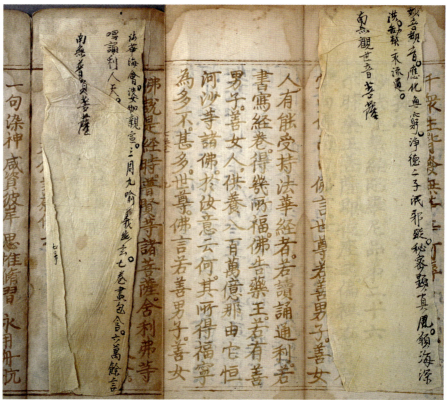

明行

佛號

大智

第三部分

麦积奇观

Part Three:
Marvel of Maijishan

丝路遗珍、麦积烟雨、十二联架、绝壁崖阁、神秘微笑……究竟是什么吸引他们奔赴麦积山，并为之栉风沐雨、披荆斩棘？

Silk Road treasures, Maijishan in misty rain, twelve connected Plank Roads, cliffside pavilions, mysterious smiles... What draws people to Maijishan, compelling them to brave the elements and overcome obstacles?

133 窟
Cave 133

　　北魏洞窟，俗称万佛洞、碑洞。窟内复室重叠，大小高深各异，结构特殊复杂，在中国佛窟中较为罕见。四壁原满贴影塑千佛，现大多剥落。宋代大型泥塑释迦会子以及第 9 龛北魏泥塑小沙弥为麦积山泥塑中的上乘之作。现存北朝石刻造像碑 18 通。尤以第 1、10、11、16 号碑最为精美，10 号碑以连环画的形式雕刻佛传故事，为佛教造像碑中的精品。窟顶彩绘乘龙骑凤仙人及散花飞天、羽人，右侧藻井内绘千佛、忍冬等。

Created during the Northern Wei Dynasty, Cave 133 is commonly known as Ten Thousand Buddhas Cave or Stele Cave. Inside, the cave features overlapping chambers of varying sizes and depths, characterized by a unique and complex structure that is rare among Chinese Buddhist caves. Its four walls were originally adorned with clay-molded sculptures of the Thousand Buddhas, although most have now peeled away. The large clay sculpture of Meeting of Sakyamuni and His Son in the Song Dynasty and the small novice monk clay sculpture from the Northern Wei Dynasty in the ninth niche are excellent works among the clay sculptures of Maijishan. There are currently eighteen stone-carved statue steles from the Northern Dynasties, with steles 1, 10, 11, and 16 being particularly exquisite. Stele 10 is especially remarkable, depicting the story of the Buddha's life in the form of a comic strip, making it a masterpiece among Buddhist statue steles. On the ceiling of the cave are painted immortals riding dragons and phoenixes, along with flower-scattering apsaras and feathered spirits. Inside the caisson on the right, images of the Thousand Buddhas, and honeysuckle motifs are depicted.

第 121 窟　　　第 123 窟　　　第 60 窟　　　第 128 窟　　　第 76 窟　　　第 141 窟　　　第 142 窟

第 155 窟　　　第 78 窟

第 44 窟

第 15 窟

第 27 窟

第 12 窟

80 第62窟整体复原窟

北周
高 240 厘米　宽 276 厘米　深 225 厘米

　　麦积山第 62 窟为平面方形四角攒尖顶窟，是北周洞窟中保存最好而又未经后代重修的洞窟，为麦积山石窟特级保护洞窟。

　　窟内三壁开凿三龛供三佛，外立胁侍菩萨和弟子，这是北周洞窟中唯一供奉三佛的洞窟。窟内佛造像低平肉髻、面型方圆，弯眉细目，高鼻、薄唇、短颈端肩，头及躯体微微向前倾斜，结跏趺坐于高佛座之上，着紧贴躯体的袈裟，繁简适度的阴刻线体现出"曹衣出水"之状，衣裾采用变化多样的曲线，层层叠叠，变化多样，富于装饰趣味。菩萨珠圆玉润、眼眉低垂、嘴角上翘、头戴化佛冠、宝缯下垂、斜披络腋、颈佩项圈，帔带自双肩沿双臂自然垂下，又饰以手镯、璎珞，下身系贴体大裙，衣纹舒朗，衣饰精致华丽。

　　此外，该窟前后双室，前部分塌毁，留一力士造像，为麦积山现存北周孤例。（张萍、谈叶闻）

Restored Cave 62

Northern Zhou Dynasty
Height: 240 cm, Width: 276 cm, Depth: 225 cm

Cave 62 is a square grotto with a four-sided pyramidal roof. This cave is recognized as the best-preserved example from the Northern Zhou Dynasty that has not undergone renovations by later generations. It is classified as a top-grade protected cave within the Maijishan Grottoes.

Inside the cave, three niches are carved into three walls to enshrine the Three Buddhas, accompanied by standing attendant bodhisattvas and disciples. This cave is unique among those from the Northern Zhou Dynasty caves for its enshrinement of the Three Buddhas. The Buddha statues feature low, flat ushnishas, with faces that are roundish, curved eyebrows, and slender eyes, complemented by high noses and thin lips. Their necks are short, and their shoulders are square, with heads and bodies slightly inclined forward. They are seated in full lotus position on elevated Buddha pedestals, adorned in kasayas that cling closely to their forms. The moderately elaborate incised lines evoke the appearance of "Cao's clothes emerging from water", while the hems of their garments display a variety of curves, layered and rich in decorative detail. The Bodhisattvas are depicted with round, pearl-like faces and smooth, jade-like skin. Their eyes and eyebrows are gently drooping, and the corners of their mouths are uplifted. They wear crowns featuring transformed Buddhas, with precious ribbons cascading down. Draped diagonally across their bodies are shawls, and they wear necklaces around their necks, with sashes that naturally hang down from their shoulders along their arms. Additionally, they are adorned with bracelets and pendants, while their lower bodies are clad in close-fitting, large skirts. The lines of their clothing are clear, and the decorations are exquisite and gorgeous.

In addition, this cave consists of front and back chambers. The front section has collapsed, leaving behind a statue of a Warrior, which stands as a unique example of the Northern Zhou Dynasty artistry remaining in the Maijishan Grottoes. (By Zhang Ping and Tan Yewen)

正壁

左壁

右壁

前壁

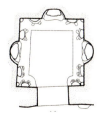

平面

窟顶

①　②　③

①泥塑弟子像（Clay Sculpture of Disciple）
张北平临摹（Copy by Zhang Beiping）
北周（Northern Zhou Dynasty）
高 105 厘米　宽 30 厘米　厚 20 厘米
（Height: 105 cm　Width: 30 cm　Thickness: 20 cm）
第 62 窟（Cave 62）
麦积山石窟艺术研究所藏（Art Institute of Maijishan Cave-Temple Complex）

②泥塑菩萨立像（Clay Sculpture of Standing Bodhisattva）
张北平临摹（Copy by Zhang Beiping）
北周（Northern Zhou Dynasty）
高 116 厘米　宽 54 厘米　厚 30 厘米
（Height: 116 cm　Width: 54 cm　Thickness: 30 cm）
第 62 窟（Cave 62）
麦积山石窟艺术研究所藏（Art Institute of Maijishan Cave-Temple Complex）

⑨泥塑佛坐像（Clay Sculpture of Seated Buddha）
化雷临摹（Copy by Hua Lei）
北周（Northern Zhou Dynasty）
高 115 厘米　宽 80 厘米　厚 40 厘米
（Height: 115 cm　Width: 80 cm　Thickness: 40 cm）
第 62 窟（Cave 62）
麦积山石窟艺术研究所藏（Art Institute of Maijishan Cave-Temple Complex）

⑩泥塑菩萨立像（Clay Sculpture of Standing Bodhisattva）
张北平临摹（Copy by Zhang Beiping）
北周（Northern Zhou Dynasty）
高 120 厘米　宽 47 厘米　厚 31 厘米
（Height: 120cm　Width: 47cm　Thickness: 31cn）
第 62 窟（Cave 62）
麦积山石窟艺术研究所藏（Art Institute of Maijishan Cave-Temple Complex）

⑦

⑧

⑤泥塑菩萨立像（Clay Sculpture of Standing Bodhisattva）
张北平临摹（Copy by Zhang Beiping）
北周（Northern Zhou Dynasty）
高 120 厘米　宽 45 厘米　厚 35 厘米
（Height: 120 cm　Width: 45 cm　Thickness: 35 cm）
第 62 窟（Cave 62）
麦积山石窟艺术研究所藏（Art Institute of Maijishan Cave-Temple Complex）

⑥泥塑佛坐像（Clay Sculpture of Seated Buddha）
化雷临摹（Copy by Hua Lei）
高 100 厘米　宽 62 厘米　厚 36 厘米
（Height: 100 cm　Width: 62 cm　Thickness: 36 cm）
第 62 窟（Cave 62）
麦积山石窟艺术研究所藏（Art Institute of Maijishan Cave-Temple Complex）

⑨ ⑩ ⑪ ⑫

⑦泥塑菩萨立像（Clay Sculpture of Standing Bodhisattva）
张北平临摹（Copy by Zhang Beiping）
北周（Northern Zhou Dynasty）
高 127 厘米　宽 31 厘米　厚 58 厘米
（Height: 127 cm　Width: 31 cm　Thickness: 58 cm）
第 62 窟（Cave 62）
麦积山石窟艺术研究所藏（Art Institute of Maijishan Cave-Temple Complex）

⑧泥塑菩萨立像（Clay Sculpture of Standing Bodhisattva）
张北平临摹（Copy by Zhang Beiping）
北周（Northern Zhou Dynasty）
高 121 厘米　宽 40 厘米　厚 30 厘米
（Height: 121 cm　Width: 40 cm　Thickness: 30 cm）
第 62 窟（Cave 62）
麦积山石窟艺术研究所藏（Art Institute of Maijishan Cave-Temple Complex）

④

⑤

⑥

③泥塑佛坐像（Clay Sculpture of Seated Buddha）
化雷临摹（Copy by Hua Lei）
北周（Northern Zhou Dynasty）
高 115 厘米　宽 80 厘米　厚 40 厘米
（Height: 115 cm　Width: 80 cm　Thickness: 40 cm）
第 62 窟（Cave 62）
麦积山石窟艺术研究所藏（Art Institute of Maijishan Cave-Temple Complex）

④泥塑菩萨立像（Clay Sculpture of Standing Bodhisattva）
张北平临摹（Copy by Zhang Beiping）
北周（Northern Zhou Dynasty）
高 120 厘米　宽 47 厘米　厚 31 厘米
（Height: 120 cm　Width: 47 cm　Thickness: 31 cm）
第 62 窟（Cave 62）
麦积山石窟艺术研究所藏（Art Institute of Maijishan Cave-Temple Complex）

⑪泥塑弟子像（Clay Sculpture of Disciple）
张北平临摹（Copy by Zhang Beiping）
北周（Northern Zhou Dynasty）
高 96 厘米　宽 25 厘米　厚 16 厘米
（Height: 96 cm　Width: 25 cm　Thickness: 16 cm）
第 62 窟（Cave 62）
麦积山石窟艺术研究所藏（Art Institute of Maijishan Cave-Temple Complex）

⑫泥塑力士像（Clay Sculpture of Warrior）
化雷临摹（Copy by Hua Lei）
北周（Northern Zhou Dynasty）
高 90 厘米　宽 27 厘米　厚 20 厘米
（Height: 90 cm　Width: 27 cm　Thickness: 20 cm）
第 62 窟（Cave 62）
麦积山石窟艺术研究所藏（Art Institute of Maijishan Cave-Temple Complex）

81 | 第
123
窟
整
体
复
原
窟

第 123 窟是麦积山石窟西魏保存最完整的窟
龛之一，且未受后世修缮扰动。

窟内造像生动秀美，引起艺术家的广泛注意，
尤以窟内前部两侧的一对少年侍者为盛。

Restored Cave 123

Cave 123 is one of the most well-preserved caves and
niches from the Western Wei Dynasty in the Maijishan Grottoes.
Remarkably, it has remained untouched by later renovations,
maintaining its historical integrity.

The statues in the cave are vivid and beautiful, attracting
widespread attention from artists, especially a group of young
attendants on both sides of the front of the cave.

①

②

①泥塑童女立像（Clay Sculpture of Standing Girl）
段一鸣临摹（Copy by Duan Yiming）
高 100 厘米　宽 25 厘米　厚 24 厘米
（Height: 100 cm　Width: 25 cm　Thickness: 24 cm）
第 123 窟（Cave 123）
麦积山石窟艺术研究所藏
（Art Institute of Maijishan Cave-Temple Complex）

②泥塑文殊菩萨坐像（Clay Sculpture of Seated Manjusri Bodhisattva）
段一鸣临摹（Copy by Duan Yiming）
西魏（Western Wei Dynasty）
高 118 厘米　宽 93 厘米　厚 60 厘米
（Height: 118 cm　Width: 93 cm　Thickness: 60 cm）
第 123 窟（Cave 123）
麦积山石窟艺术研究所藏
（Art Institute of Maijishan Cave-Temple Complex）

⑤

⑥

⑦

lpture of Seated Buddha）

uan Yiming）

sty）

厚 48 厘米

110 cm　Thickness: 48 cm）

Cave-Temple Complex）

⑥泥塑菩萨立像（Clay Sculpture of Standing Bodhisattva）
段一鸣临摹（Copy by Duan Yiming）
西魏（Western Wei Dynasty）
高 123 厘米　宽 49 厘米　厚 28 厘米
（Height: 123 cm　Width: 49 cm　Thickness: 28 cm）
第 123 窟（Cave 123）
麦积山石窟艺术研究所藏
（Art Institute of Maijishan Cave-Temple Complex）

⑦泥塑阿难弟子立像（Clay Sculpture of Disciple Ananda）
段一鸣临摹（Copy by Duan Yiming）
高 98 厘米　宽 33 厘米　厚 22 厘米
（Height: 98 cm　Width: 33 cm　Thickness: 22 cm）
第 123 窟（Cave 123）
麦积山石窟艺术研究所藏
（Art Institute of Maijishan Cave-Temple Complex）

⑧

⑨

⑧泥塑维摩诘居士坐像（Clay Sculpture of Seated Vimalakirti）
段一鸣临摹（Copy by Duan Yiming）
高 121 厘米　宽 98 厘米　厚 64 厘米
（Height: 121 cm　Width: 98 cm　Thickness: 64 cm）
第 123 窟（Cave 123）
麦积山石窟艺术研究所藏
（Art Institute of Maijishan Cave-Temple Complex）

⑨泥塑童男立像（Clay Sculpture of Standing Boy）
段一鸣临摹（Copy by Duan Yiming）
高 100 厘米　宽 25 厘米　厚 24 厘米
（Height: 100 cm　Width: 25 cm　Thickness: 24 cm）
第 123 窟（Cave 123）
麦积山石窟艺术研究所藏
（Art Institute of Maijishan Cave-Temple Complex）

③  ④

③泥塑迦叶弟子立像（Clay Sculpture of Disciple Kasyapa）
段一鸣临摹（Copy by Duan Yiming）
西魏（Western Wei Dynasty）
高 96 厘米　宽 36 厘米　厚 23 厘米
（Height: 96 cm　Width: 36 cm　Thickness: 23 cm）
第 123 窟（Cave 123）
麦积山石窟艺术研究所藏
（Art Institute of Maijishan Cave-Temple Complex）

④泥塑菩萨立像（Clay Sculpture of Standing Bodhisattva）
段一鸣临摹（Copy by Duan Yiming）
西魏（Western Wei Dynasty）
高 124 厘米　宽 48 厘米　厚 28 厘米
（Height: 124 cm　Width: 48 cm　Thickness: 28 cm）
第 123 窟（Cave 123）
麦积山石窟艺术研究所藏
（Art Institute of Maijishan Cave-Temple Complex）

⑤泥塑佛坐像（Clay Scu
段一鸣临摹（Copy by D
西魏（Western Wei Dyna
高 130 厘米　宽 110 厘米
（Height: 130 cm　Width:
第 123 窟（Cave 123）
麦积山石窟艺术研究所
（Art Institute of Maijisha

82

民国罗家伦行书对联

Running Script Couplet by Luo Jialun

民国
各纵 115 厘米　横 30.5 厘米
麦积山石窟艺术研究所藏
对联："行经千折水，来看六朝山。"
题："麦积山瑞应寺"
落款："罗家伦"

the period of the Republic of China
Vertical: 115cm, Horizontal: 30.5 cm
Art Institute of Maijishan Cave-Temple Complex
Couplet: "After navigating a thousand bends, we come to view the
mountains of six dynasties."
Title: "Ruiying Temple on Maijishan"
Inscription: "Luo Jialun"

　　1945 年 12 月，曾任国立清华大学校长的罗家伦先生游览麦积山石窟，即兴为麦积山瑞应寺撰写此诗联，表达了在跋山涉水、历经千山万水之后看到麦积山石窟后的喜悦之情。

　　这里的"六朝山"指的是麦积山石窟。原悬挂于麦积山瑞应寺僧人下榻的麦积山馆，后存入库房。在瑞应寺山门的左右门柱上用木板刻的就是此对联。（张萍）

　　In December 1945, Mr. Luo Jialun, who had served as the president of National Tsinghua University, visited the Maijishan Grottoes. Inspired by the visit, he spontaneously composed this couplet for the Ruiying Temple at Maijishan, expressing his joy upon seeing the Maijishan Grottoes after a long journey through numerous landscapes.

　　The phrase "mountains of six dynasties" refers to the Maijishan Grottoes. Originally, the couplet was hung in the Maijishan Hostel, where the monks of the Ruiying Temple stayed, and later stored in a warehouse. This couplet was carved on wooden boards on the left and right doorposts of the mountain gate of the Ruiying Temple. (By Zhang Ping)

行经千折水，

未看六朝山

李积山瑞应寺

罗家伦

论 文

麦积山石窟及其价值

魏文斌

（兰州大学考古学及博物馆学研究所）

丝绸之路陇右段南道，从宝鸡向西沿渭河河谷或从陇县越陇山抵古代秦州（天水），再向西过陇西、临洮至临夏，渡黄河入青海。古秦州境内，是丝绸之路甘肃段石窟寺分布较集中的区域。天水、甘谷、武山等在渭河河谷或秦岭余脉小陇山区域，分布有天水麦积山、仙人崖，甘谷大像山、华盖寺，武山水帘洞和木梯寺等著名的石窟寺。其中规模最大、价值最高的是麦积山石窟。

古代秦州地区的石窟寺，根据文献记载，以麦积山石窟为最早，开凿于十六国后秦时期，之后北朝至隋唐时期兴盛，逐渐形成了一些以石窟寺为中心的大型佛教聚落，以麦积山、仙人崖、水帘洞、大像山为代表。宋代仍处于发展的阶段，明清时期更多地与寺院相结合，石窟寺的开凿逐渐进入尾声。作为丝绸之路的重要地段，北魏早期较多接受外来艺术风格的影响，以麦积山北魏早期洞窟为主。北魏太和之后，佛教石窟艺术在中原北方地区形成新的模式如云冈、龙门等之后，受中心地区的影响，逐渐中国化，并承担着回向传播的任务。隋唐时期，两京地区佛教及佛教艺术发达，麦积山石窟艺术更多受两京地区的影响。

2014 年 6 月，麦积山石窟作为丝绸之路沿线最为重要的一处石窟寺类文化遗产之一，以其突出的价值，成为"丝绸之路：长安—天山廊道的路网"遗产项目成功进入世界文化遗产的行列。使得这处优秀文化遗产的价值得以进一步地被认知，并更广泛地为世人所知。

一、麦积山石窟遗产构成

麦积山石窟是由崖面（崖面遗迹包括洞窟及其造像、壁画、摩崖题刻等）、寺院、舍利塔等其他建筑及馆藏文物、古代文书等组成的综合体文化遗产；麦积山山体及周围景观是佛教遗存及佛教活动依托的载体（图1）。由洞窟开凿活动产生的技术、佛教信仰而形成的思想、景观而产生的文学作品等构成麦积山石窟无形的遗产。

1. 洞窟

现存洞窟由麦积崖本体和东面的王子洞窟区组成。现编号窟龛 221 个，西崖 142 个，东崖 56 个，王子洞窟区 20 个。另外，2007 年在中区崖根外部塌落的堆积中清理出三个残空窟，分别编号为第 219、220、221 号（图2）。

2. 造像

麦积山石窟各时代洞窟内均由造像（包括泥塑和石雕、石胎泥塑）、壁画构成其内容和艺术形式。据统计，现存各类造像 3938 件 10632 身，壁

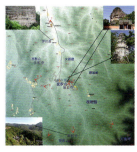

图 1　麦积山及周围
佛教聚落和景观

图 2　麦积山洞窟
（东崖和西崖）

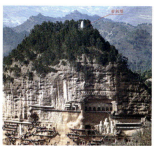

图 3　麦积山顶舍利塔

画面积约979.54平方米。其中造像多为北朝（北魏、西魏、北周）作品，并反映了北朝各个阶段的造像艺术特点，全面展示了北朝泥塑造像发展演变的过程，被誉为"北朝雕塑陈列馆"。隋唐时期的造像较少，宋代对北朝洞窟和造像大量重修，多数洞窟都可见宋代重修的痕迹。元明清时期仅对部分洞窟进行重修重绘，并有极少量的泥塑造像。

3. 壁画

由于麦积山处于比较潮湿的环境，洞窟内壁画大多脱落，少量洞窟保存壁画。较重要的有北朝晚期的第127、133、26、27、4等窟，其中一些经变画和本生故事画保存相对完整，尤其是第127、135、26、27等窟的大型经变画如西方净土变、维摩变、涅槃变、法华变等是国内石窟现存最早、最为完整的大型经变画，对研究中国经变画的发展演变具有十分重要的价值。

4. 建筑

洞窟内壁画所反映的北朝建筑、洞窟内部空间建筑结构以及现存的崖面崖阁建筑是麦积山石窟的重要组成部分或载体。第4、127、140、26等窟内的壁画中有一些北朝建筑的形象资料。西魏、北周以及隋代等洞窟内部的构造如帐形洞窟多反映了古代室内建筑的形式，如第15、141、4、12等洞窟。而第1、2、3、4、5、43、49、28—30等洞窟外部的崖阁建筑形式是北朝时期的仿木构建筑遗存，是研究北朝建筑的珍贵形象实物资料。

附属于麦积山石窟的寺院建筑和舍利塔等建筑也是构成麦积山整体的重要内容。根据南宋嘉定十五年（1222年）《四川制置使司给田公据碑》记载："自东晋起迹，敕赐无忧（寺）□□□给田供瞻，次七国重修，敕赐石岩寺，大隋敕赐净念寺，大唐敕赐应乾寺，圣朝大观元年（1107年）……敕改赐瑞应寺。"麦积山的寺院东晋时期始建，称"无忧寺"，北朝时期称"石岩寺"，隋称"净念寺"，唐为"应乾寺"，至北宋大观元年起称为"瑞应寺"，其名称沿用至今。寺院东晋起迹与其他碑刻文献所载麦积山石窟始凿于姚秦时期大体一致。现存的瑞应寺建筑为明清重修，中轴线上依次为山门、天王殿、大雄宝殿，天王殿两侧有钟鼓楼，殿内两侧有厢房。

麦积山山顶的舍利塔为砖结构，清康熙八年（1669年）圆惠和尚等重建，通高9米（图3）。其最初可能是隋文帝仁寿元年（601年）敕建的佛舍利塔。2009年对舍利塔重修，在塔基内发现十余件北朝石雕造像，是麦积山石窟多年来的

图 4　隋　麦积山第 78 窟出土绘制壁画调色碗

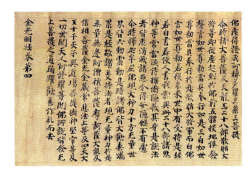

图 5　唐　麦积山藏《金光明经》写卷

重要发现。

5. 碑刻及其他附属文物

洞窟及崖面碑刻、题刻也是麦积山重要的组成部分，多反映麦积山石窟的营建历史等。第 4 窟外壁以及东崖第 168 窟廊道上以及崖面上有宋代以后的一些摩崖题刻和碑刻，都是记录麦积山石窟的重要文献资料，如《瑞应寺再藏佛舍利碑》（北宋靖康元年，1126 年）、《四川制置使司给田公据碑》（南宋嘉定十五年，1222 年）、《麦积山开除常住地粮碑》（明崇祯十五年，1642 年）、《秦州天水郡麦积崖佛龛铭并序》（明嘉靖四十三年重刻，1564 年）等。它们也是珍贵的书法作品和文学作品，具有重要的历史价值、书法价值和景观文学价值。

麦积山石窟历代保存下来的单体文物包括陶器、瓷器、铜器、碑刻、书画、古文书、拓本以及泥塑造像等 2450 余件，都是研究麦积山石窟必不可少的珍贵资料（图 4）。其中古代文书 1500 余件，时代最早的为唐代，大部分为明清时期。除多数为佛教经典外，也有少量的道教、社会文书等，具有极高的史料价值。其中部分已被列入国家珍贵古籍名录（图 5）。

二、麦积山石窟特征与价值

麦积山石窟及其景观特征，大体体现在以下几方面。

1. 秦地林泉之冠——极致的景观

麦积山，又名麦积崖，位于甘肃省天水市东南 45 公里秦岭山脉西段北麓，地理坐标北纬 34°21′09″，东经 106°00′10″，海拔 1671.4 米，山高 142 米。山顶呈棱锥形，其南面与西南面中腰突出，山根凹进。四周环绕香积山、天池坪、豆积山、罗汉崖、小献山、蜂儿崖等大小群山，麦积居中一峰突起，奇特别致。

《太平广记》卷三百九十七引《玉堂闲话》谈到了"麦积山"名称的由来及其形胜：

麦积山者，北跨清渭，南渐两当，五百里岗峦，麦积处其半。崛起一石块，高百万寻，望之团团，如民间积麦之状，故有此名。其青云之半，峭壁之间，镌石成佛，石龛千室，虽自人力，疑其神功。[1]

因山形酷似农家所积麦垛之状，故名。"麦积烟雨"被称为秦州八景之一。清代诗人吴西

1.（宋）李昉等《太平广记》，人民文学出版社，1995 年，第 3181 页。

川曾以秦州十景之一诗咏《麦积烟雨》："麦积峰千丈，凭空欲上天。最宜秋雨后，兼爱暮时烟。境胜端由险，梯危若未连。钟声落何处，遥想在层颠。"

2. 秦州四塞之道关陇重镇
——交通承载文化交流

古代秦州具有十分重要的交通地理优势。

乾隆二十八年（1763 年）钟兰村《秦州志序》："秦州四塞之道，关西一大都会也，山川灵秀之气,磅礴蜿蜒。"顾祖禹《读史方舆纪要》曰："当关陇之会，介雍梁之间，屹为重镇。"足见秦州在古代丝绸之路上的重要性。

汉唐之际长安至凉州的南道驿程必经天水，这条道路在汉晋南北朝时期非常繁荣，是丝绸之路陇右道的南道。法显西行即走此道。

交通地理位置的重要和优越，也往往是文化交流的重要条件。佛教的传播基本上沿着古代丝绸之路沿线传播，丝绸之路沿线的重要城镇，则很容易接受这种外来文化。古代石窟寺的分布，也遵循这一规律，基本选择于既适合于佛教徒清净修行又离大的市镇或交通要道不太远的地方开凿，麦积山石窟也符合这样的条件。

3. 著名的禅修之地
——佛教思想与修行的途径

僧人习禅需有安静的环境。从 5 世纪初，麦积山便成为陇右著名的禅修之地，并进而发展为石窟的开凿胜地。

庾信《秦州天水郡麦积崖佛龛铭并序》曰："麦积崖者，乃陇坻之名山，河西之灵岳，高峰寻云，深谷无量。方之鹫岛，迹遁三禅；譬彼鹤

鸣，虚飞六甲。"[2] 庾信的文章中，对麦积山石窟所在的环境适宜禅观修行描述精准。麦积山为"秦地林泉之冠"，所处的环境正是适宜修禅的理想之地。

《高僧传》卷十一《释玄高》详述玄高的禅修历程和境界，玄高到麦积山时，从其修禅者百余人，并且在其来之前已有来自长安的禅僧昙弘在此隐居修禅，可见麦积山的禅事早已有之，止玄高时达到极盛。

麦积山第 148 窟正壁佛背光两侧所绘的树下禅修图，即裹着禅巾的修行僧人，说明这个洞窟的禅观功能非常明显，进而可知麦积山早期洞窟表现的强烈禅观思想。第 114、115 窟也可看到壁画的禅修图像。这种禅修图像，本身就意味着该洞窟中对禅观实践的重视。麦积山初期洞窟中的佛像有 50%—80% 以上都作禅定印，相当可观，充分说明了这个时期对于禅定的重视，表现了非常明显的禅观意味。麦积山初期洞窟的造像题材比较单一，主要有释迦牟尼佛、三世佛、释迦多宝佛、弥勒、千佛等，这些造像内容正是禅观的主要对象。早期洞窟中的第 76、89、115、156 窟等都是面积不大仅能容一人安坐的方形洞窟，正适于坐禅、观想、修行。

建造石窟、窟居禅观、配合适宜禅观的一系列造像，共同构成了麦积山石窟的禅观体系。

4. 绝壁栈道与北朝崖阁建筑
——建造技术与科学

麦积山崖面的各种大小窟龛和摩崖造像通过纵横交错、上下多达 14 层的栈道相连，其间又点缀多座崖阁，远眺极为壮观，令人叹为观止，堪称古代人类建筑艺术的杰出范例。

2.张锦秀编撰《麦积山石窟志》第六章《碑碣·铭文·匾额》，甘肃人民出版社，2002 年 4 月第一版，第 177 页。

麦积山岩壁陡直，部分崖面甚至呈倾斜角，当年开凿的难度可想而知。"古记云：六国共修，自平地积薪，至于岩巅，从上镌雕龛室神像，功毕，旋旋拆薪而下，然后梯空架险而上。"《玉堂闲话》描述出了麦积山石窟洞窟开凿的施工技术。

对麦积山石窟的开凿，民间有"砍完南山柴，修起麦积崖"的传言，形象地反映了麦积山石窟在开凿过程中所用木材的量非常大，这与麦积山所处的秦岭山区相当丰富的木材资源的实际相符合。木材是麦积山石窟开凿首先要大量利用的材料。麦积山既为"秦地林泉之冠"，有着很茂密的森林，为麦积山石窟的开凿、栈道的修建以及塑像的制作等提供了可资利用的丰富资源。

《麦积山勘察团工作日记》对1953年勘察团勘察时木工文得全小组架设栈道的方法作了详细的描述，应与古代方法是一样。

麦积山最初的洞窟开凿，应该是按照洞窟开凿的次第，逐渐向上向东、西两侧方向架设栈道。

由于木质栈道长期暴露在外，容易风化糟朽，更加之易遭火灾，因此，保存至20世纪七八十年代的栈道，历史上曾经过多次的维修更换，远不是最初开凿洞窟时的样子。但历代维修并未改变历史上栈道的走向和位置。虽然现在全部改建为水泥栈道，但基本上保持了历史上的格局，仍然具有很高的研究价值和观赏价值。

崖阁建筑是麦积山石窟的重要建筑形式，现存崖阁建筑有第1、2、3、4、5、28、30、43、49等窟外的石雕立体建筑实体，是研究北朝建筑史的珍贵遗存。现全部集中于麦积山东崖。这些崖阁建筑的年代应始自西魏时期，"大统元年，再修崖阁，重兴寺宇"（麦积山现存《秦州雄武军陇城县第六保瑞应寺再葬佛舍利记》）所言不

虚。北周至隋达到鼎盛。

第43窟为西魏文帝乙弗氏的影窟，称"寂陵"。外观作附崖的仿木结构建筑三间，有单檐庑殿顶式殿堂，前檐三间四柱，檐柱内有廊，廊后凿一平面马蹄形穹窿顶敞口大龛。本窟为麦积山石窟中最特殊和最有代表性的西魏崖阁式建筑（图6），[3] 又是仿地面陵墓建筑的成功范例。

第4窟又称散花楼或上七佛阁，北周大都督李允信为其亡父所建的"七佛龛"，北朝文学家庾信为之作铭。平面呈横长方形大型庑殿顶崖阁。上凿单檐庑殿顶，前开7间8柱窟廊，后列七龛。殿顶上部雕正脊，两端有鸱尾，均素平无线脚。屋面雕筒瓦瓦垄。廊顶各间原凿平棋6块，共计42块，现仅残存两稍间6块，平棋内绘制壁画。廊后并列7个四角攒尖顶佛帐式大龛。整个建筑气势雄伟壮丽，雕造技艺精湛（图7）。

图6　麦积山第43窟崖阁建筑

图7　麦积山第4窟外景

---

3. 董广强、魏文斌《陵墓与佛窟——麦积山石窟第43窟形制若干问题研究》，《敦煌学辑刊》2014年第2期。

麦积山各时代不同类型的洞窟内部建筑形制、保存完整的崖阁式外观建筑以及杰出栈道建筑，构成了麦积山石窟建筑的综合组成，成为古代石窟寺建筑的杰出典范。

5. 雕塑陈列馆

20 世纪 50 年代，中央文化部组织的麦积山勘察团对麦积山石窟进行了大规模的考察，参与者之一的雕塑家刘开渠把麦积山石窟誉为"我国历代的一个大雕塑馆"。

麦积山石窟同敦煌莫高窟等一样，是建筑、雕塑与壁画的结合体。但麦积山所处的潮湿环境使得大部分洞窟的壁画未能保存下来，而适合麦积山崖体状况的泥塑造像却大多完整地保留至今，时代序列清晰，成为麦积山石窟与众不同的独特魅力所在。

麦积山造像大部分为北朝的泥塑作品，既系统又完整，体现出当时中国佛教泥塑造像艺术的发展规律，代表了北朝造像艺术的高度成就。

6. 珍贵的北朝壁画

麦积山石窟壁画数量不多，但保存有中国最早的大型经变画，对中国佛教绘画艺术的传播产生了重要作用，并影响到包括敦煌在内河西走廊地区北朝晚期到隋唐时期经变画的发展。[4]

第 127 窟是保存壁画最多的一个洞窟。该窟正壁绘涅槃经变、左壁绘维摩诘经变（图8）、右壁绘西方净土变、前披绘睒子本生、正披及左右披绘舍身饲虎本生、前壁下部绘地狱变，窟顶绘帝释天，这些壁画是北朝时期的壁画精品，具有很高的艺术成就。第 26、27 窟的法华经变和涅槃经变也是北周时期重要的成熟的经变画。北

图 8 维摩诘经变局部 第 127 窟 西魏

周第 4 窟的"薄肉塑"伎乐飞天组画，绘塑结合，构思奇妙，是中西文化结合的典范，不见于其他石窟。

7. 古代中西文化交流的见证

麦积山石窟的佛教文化不是孤立的存在，与其他地区的佛教文化存在着密切的交流关系，这些交流直接或间接地反映在麦积山石窟的佛教文化中，如洞窟形制、雕塑、壁画等，这些雕塑、壁画等是麦积山石窟通过丝绸之路进行文化交流的重要见证。

麦积山初期的洞窟，无论是洞窟形制还是雕塑、壁画等受到了西域、犍陀罗、平城等地佛教文化的影响，首先是在洞窟形制上，第 78、74、90、57、165 等窟都是敞口、圆弧形的基本形制，和云冈初期昙曜五窟的形制基本相同，可以肯定两者之间有密切的联系。同时，佛像着偏袒右肩的方式来自凉州模式，并在局部的刻画上受到云冈石窟的影响。另外，这个时期在洞窟正壁上均有对称的小龛，应该来自于犍陀罗雕刻板；同时，佛发髻上图案化的水波纹，最初来源也是犍陀罗地区，两者的区别在于麦积山的更加图案化。

北魏早期的菩萨在头冠上有一种仰月冠和三珠冠，这种冠饰来源于古波斯萨珊王朝的装饰。

4. 张宝玺《麦积山石窟壁画叙要》，麦积山石窟艺术研究所编《中国石窟·天水麦积山》，文物出版社，1998 年。

现存克孜尔等地石窟壁画中，菩萨头冠大多流行三珠冠饰。其最初的形式，可以追溯到印度早期的佛像雕刻，如 1—2 世纪的马土拉菩萨及药叉形象，在犍陀罗雕刻中仍然十分流行。西域龟兹接受这种装饰后加以发展，把在印度本为束发的形式改变为饰有圆珠形的头冠。现存龟兹、吐木休克一带的彩塑菩萨像以及壁画菩萨像中，有单珠的头冠，也有三珠的，还有极少数为二珠的。三珠冠也是云冈石窟菩萨像的主要冠饰之一。而在北魏时期直到唐代，敦煌的菩萨像在三珠冠上多表现为日月形装饰，形成了流行时间较长的三珠日月冠，是在西域式的三珠冠的基础上，接受了波斯萨珊王朝流行的日月形冠饰而形成的。

5 世纪末期及 6 世纪初，麦积山石窟接受的文化主要来自洛阳和西安等文化中心地区，这些地区产生的新的佛教艺术影响到麦积山石窟，第114 窟的影塑造像中就明显地可以看出这一点，其形式明显是来源于洛阳和长安地区。特别是北魏分裂为东、西魏以后，西魏迁至长安，大量的官僚贵族以及文人士大夫等来到长安，标志着当时的文化中心西移至长安，使麦积山石窟更快地接受那里的文化。这一时期的洞窟如 43、44、127 等窟，都可以明显地看出中原中心地区的影响。而这一时期出现的大型经变画，应该受长安地区佛寺壁画的影响，为隋唐以后如莫高窟大型经变画的繁荣奠定了基础。

北周时期，麦积山石窟的造像风格又受到了北齐的影响，这个时期山东半岛通过海上丝绸之路接受了印度本土的笈多佛教艺术，从而影响北齐佛教造像，进而影响到了麦积山石窟，第141、94、67 等窟则是北齐风格影响的直接产物。第 22、141、142 等窟壁画的同心圆头光，也是文化交流的见证。

隋唐时期，我们也可以看到丝绸之路交流的现象，天水出土的粟特人石棺床，其雕刻内容和风格属于粟特文化，另外这时期出土的波斯银币、凤首壶等都可以明显地看出中亚、西亚的文化通过丝绸之路对天水产生了影响。在麦积山石窟，这个时期壁画中突然大量出现了联珠纹图案（第 70、71、74、78 等窟隋代重绘的壁画），这种图案来源于波斯，隋朝时正值萨珊王朝盛世，而此时隋王朝大力经营河西，隋炀帝西巡，通过政治和军事手段使丝绸之路保持畅通，中亚、西亚等地区的艺术风格便通过丝绸之路影响了麦积山石窟。

两宋时期，由于天水的地理位置，天水和南方地区的文化交流也进一步密切起来，南方地区的茶叶通过多条道路输入秦州，而秦州地区的马匹等也输入内地，天水成为茶马古道必经的重镇之一。当时政府在秦州地区设置了催场和茶马司，在麦积山 4 窟、26 窟等处都可以看见和茶马贸易相关的题记，见证了当时的道路交通和贸易。

元代，随着藏传佛教逐渐影响到内地，麦积山也出现了藏传佛教的造像，如第 35 窟、第 48窟带有密教色彩的造像，就是藏传佛教传播到这一地区的见证。

总之，麦积山石窟所处的交通位置，决定了其在丝绸之路上西来东往文化交流上的桥梁与纽带作用。这种作用使麦积山的佛教艺术融汇了多种文化，在此基础上，形成了显著的本地域地方性特征。

麦积山石窟以其精美的泥塑造像、杰出壮观的洞窟建筑以及自然与人文景观的完美结合，成为享誉海内外的著名佛教圣地，具有突出的价值。由于其反映了多方面的文化交流以及在丝绸之路上的重要作用，使之成为古代丝绸之路沿线最为辉煌的佛教艺术宝库，并成为 5—18 世纪最为杰出的石窟类文化遗产之一。

"丝绸之路：长安—天山廊道的路网"申遗文本对麦积山石窟的价值特征做了如下描述：

麦积山石窟开凿于 5—13 世纪，是河西走廊及其周边地区仅次于敦煌莫高窟的大型石窟寺。是中国石窟遗产中西魏、北周石窟的代表窟群之一，也是中国佛教石窟群经云冈石窟汉化的进一步延续与发展。以其位居当时东西南北交通的要冲的地理位置，麦积山石窟既受到中原北方云冈、龙门等主流石窟的影响，也受到南方和西方文化的冲击。麦积山石窟以其明显地反映中国佛殿建筑形象的石窟形式、最早期的经变画等遗迹，影响广泛，成为丝绸之路佛教艺术自东向西影响的转折性阶段重要遗迹。[5]

麦积山石窟具有独特的自然文化景观，并产生了大量文学作品，成为文学渊薮。

麦积山石窟人文景观与奇特的自然景观完美结合，与其他石窟相比，麦积山四周群山环抱、树木掩映，四季分明，景色秀丽，自古就有"秦地林泉之冠"的美誉，东汉以来就被称为"陇右名山"，历史上备受达官显贵和文人墨客的青睐。而山形奇特的麦积崖在绵延起伏的群山中突兀挺立，颇得大自然"鬼斧神工"之韵，配以崖面上历代开凿的宏伟壮观的窟龛建筑群，堪称是人类与自然和谐相处的绝妙组合。崖面上的窟龛建筑群与周边自然风光浑然一体，是文化与自然完美结合的典范。[6]

由于优美的自然人文景观，孕育出了丰富的文学作品，一些写实或夸张的文学作品成为研究麦积山各方面十分重要的遗产，具有很高的价值。

现存最早最优美描写麦积山景观的当属北朝文学家庾信的《秦州麦积崖佛龛铭并序》，赋中将麦积山比喻为鹫岛、须弥山、忉利天。五代王仁裕的《玉堂闲话》是第一次将麦积山比喻成农家积麦之状的文献，其中还提到了麦积山一些洞窟的名称，价值极高。唐代诗圣杜甫游览麦积山，写下了流传千古的"山寺"诗。清代诗人吴西川直接以秦州十景之一"麦积烟雨"为题，描写了"最宜秋雨后，兼爱暮时烟"的极致景色。民国时期于右任留下了"文传庾子山，艺并莫高窟"的佳句。麦积山崖面上还保留着宋、明、清时期的石刻诗作，均具有极高的书法与文学价值。

麦积山的突出价值大致可概括为：麦积山石窟是中国石窟艺术的重要组成部分，规模宏大、内容丰富、保存完好、景观优美，具有极高的历史、艺术和科学价值，可与敦煌、云冈、龙门等石窟媲美。麦积山石窟的北朝泥塑造像特色鲜明，独树一帜，具有同时期最高的艺术造诣，吸收了西域、中原以及南朝佛教艺术因素，形成了民族化、民间化和世俗化风格，成为中原佛教艺术向西传播的中继站，并对周边及川北、河西诸石窟产生了重要影响。映射出随着丝绸之路而来的印度佛教艺术传入中原后，在不同历史时期的发展变化脉络，对于全面了解和掌握佛教艺术中国化的历史进程具有至关重要的作用。麦积山独特的山形，崖面上宏伟壮观的窟龛建筑群，与周边秀丽旖旎的自然景观完美地融为一体，是人类在追求精神信仰的历史进程所创造的一个奇迹，也是中国乃至世界宗教文化景观的典范之一。

5.《丝绸之路：长安至天山廊道的路网》申遗文本，2014 年。

6. 傅晶《麦积山石窟寺环境景观价值及保护策略》，《天津大学学报》(社会科学版) 2003 年第 1 期。

作为方法的文化景观

——麦积山石窟的价值认知过程与思考

杜晓帆　王军

在一般公众的视野里，石窟寺往往被视为对壁画和雕塑等精美艺术品的收藏馆，而石窟的管理和宣传往往也以此为重点，使得到访游客过于侧重重点洞窟及艺术品的欣赏，对孕育石窟寺产生的自然地理环境却不甚措意。对于麦积山而言，自20世纪50年代大规模考察以来，既往麦积山的保护管理与宣传重心仍较为侧重麦积山窟龛造像作为"东方雕塑馆"的杰作价值。并且由于考古部门设立相对较晚，对于历史信息的挖掘与研究尚不足备，因而对于包括山崖植被、地质地貌等自然环境的价值也存在认知不足。

从这层意义上看，当前对麦积山的价值挖掘与只是从其动态延展的历史进程中剥落一层断面加以审视，这使得麦积山展示内容和游径组织上至少存在两大局限：一是忽视整体环境，将石窟寺欣赏等同于雕塑和壁画的欣赏；二是过于强调视觉，将观看作为进入石窟寺欣赏的唯一方式。第一个局限使得麦积山的文化内涵拘囿于洞窟之内，麦积山石窟文化缩减为佛教艺术的表象，剥离了石窟赖以建成的历史地理环境；第二个局限使得麦积山的价值被"剪裁"为访客目光中呈现的艺术品形象，忽略了石窟欣赏同样需要依赖的听觉、味觉等多感官体验形成的环境氛围。就此，我们可以追问：除了对艺术作品的视觉欣赏之外，

石窟寺是否还有其余认知的可能性？我们应如何转换一种"见木不见林"的视野，转向对一种全面价值的探寻？这一问题值得从认知方法与研究方式等层面进行思考与研究。

文化景观理论的提出标志着自然物研究的"文化转向"[1]，同时该理论强调人地互动、时空发展与整体关联，能够更清晰地挖掘出遗产与其周边环境的关联，展现文化遗产的动态发展历程与人地关系，对于石窟寺这类特殊遗产的价值阐释具有启发意义。麦积山石窟的价值产生于不同历史时期人们情感、价值的投射以及人地关系的层叠演变，是一个长期变化的过程。本文试以文化景观作为方法指导，以动态、整体的研究视野分析麦积山的独特价值，进而了解麦积山在长达千年营建史中不同群体思想、文化和技术的交错环流和互动。

一、"文化景观"的内涵与应用特征

近年来，"文化景观"成为国内外学者们十分关注的话题，然而当前研究对这个概念的应用远多于对其理论本身的认识和阐述。面对"文化景观"这一舶来词汇及其理论体系，如何发掘其视野内涵并正确应用，仍然仰赖对其理论发展与

词义拓展的理解和认知。

在学科视野下，作为"景观"的延伸概念，"文化景观"是受到广泛社会背景和文化思潮影响的发展结果。回溯"景观"一词，自文艺复兴以来，其词义一直处于不断地嬗变与演化之中：从最开始的文学、艺术维度的风景概念，逐步被引入地理学科，成为描述地理形态与地貌构成的地学术语[2]。随着人类日益活动广泛，自然物的人文化程度不断加深，景观的地学意义逐渐被文化意义所取代，对于文化与自然物之间互塑关系的研究成为地理学的重要议题[3]，"文化景观"概念由此诞生并得到凸显。20 世纪初，索尔（C. O. Sauer）及其伯克利学派首次明确提出了"文化景观"（cultural landscape）概念——"文化景观由文化族群对自然的塑造而成。文化是动因，自然地域是媒介，文化景观是结果[4]。"这种主张不仅延续了"景观作为人类环境组成的一部分"的学科共识，更强调了人类以特定方式的活动所塑造的时空表达[5]，形象地揭示出文化景观是一个由自然载体、文化动因、时代变迁三个要素构成的复杂构造体。可以说，以伯克利学派为代表的经典理论建构出了文化景观最为关键的两个特征：一是具有漫长的时空演变过程，随时间发展而动态变化；二是由不同世代人群共同建构并具有层叠性和迭代性。

1992 年，联合国教科文组织世界遗产委员会将"文化景观"设立为世界遗产的一种类型，在其定义中强调"文化景观"是人类与自然共同的作品，旨在弥合世界遗产体系建构中长期存在的自然与文化的对立以及东西方文化差异的鸿沟[6]。

这一定义在肯定历时性演变和人类建构的基础上，进一步发展出文化景观的又一特征，即不仅包括人类创造的有形的物质作品，也包括人们的观念和行为等无形的或者动态的非物质的东西[7]，进而将物质与非物质的复合关系引入的文化遗产的构成要素分析。

由此可知文化景观是一个"复杂且完整的系统"，不仅包括在漫长历史进程中保留至今的物质遗产，也将各个历史断面的文化和社会背景、历史族群以及与物质形态遗存密切关联的非物质要素纳入范畴。并且，组成文化景观系统的各个子系统之间相互交织、有机组合，最终可以实现"整体大于部分之和"[8]。也就是说，文化景观还具备"整体性"特征，构成文化景观的每个要素既是局部，更是整体的一部分。

综上所述，无论是作为学科术语还是遗产类型的"文化景观"都涵盖了自然与文化两个面向。反过来，正因为"文化景观"搭建起了"文化"与"自然"的连接桥梁与阐释框架，超越了种族类别、物质形态和文化属性的藩篱，所以也为多元文化的具体阐释中提供了契合的理论依据与方法参考。因此，对于凝结了各民族独特文化与精神特质的文化遗产而言，文化景观除了作为一种认知工具，对其要素挖掘与价值阐释也生成了具有方法论意义的应用特征。可以简述如下：一是强调时空变化，文化遗产随着时间推移发生历时性、动态的演变；二是强调发展过程，文化遗产作为人类社会和聚居环境持续变化的见证，其形成经历了一个长期发展的过程；三是关注不同历史时期的人群，文化遗产经由不同人群的与环境的互动关系，是不同人群的文化作用于自然的结果；四是关注遗产要素构成，强调以整体性和系统性的思维去思考和理解人类利用和改造自然的不同态度与成就（或言"人地关系"），挖掘人类文化背后的空间差异，关注遗产系统中各个要素之间的有机互动。

二、作为文化景观的麦积山石窟

我国文化景观的研究源起于对乡村聚落、农业遗产的特征描述和价值挖掘[9]，乡村文化景观是人与自然共同作品的典型代表。尤其当2013年红河哈尼梯田被列为文化景观类型的世界遗产后，更是大为激励振奋学界，将之广为应用在乡村遗产的保护实践探索中。乡村作为"人与自然共同创作的作品"，是一个不断演进发展的过程。人的生产、生活以及在土地上持续不断的未来生活将成为景观空间构成的要素重点。

作为类比，石窟寺作为中古时期盛行的一种佛教营造工程，是古代信徒出于宗教信仰，不计时间精力挑战自然、改造山体的壮举之遗存。最重要的是，对于中古时代的僧侣、学士和道流来说，"自然"并不仅是物质世界的客观存在，而是充满了精神性和宗教性的主体，也是他们和超验的"道"进行交通的媒介[10]。尽管大多数中国北方石窟寺早在唐宋之后就停止了开窟砺石，但在此后漫长的时间段中，近古人群依然通过重妆、补塑、修建窟檐等手段，持续小规模地与山体保持改造互动，修补重塑前人之造像遗存。可以说，中古中国时期的石窟寺营建中并不存在一个"完成"时刻，营建工程必须经历了一个长久的历史过程才得以形成，其间各个时期的宗教自身发展变化、信众群体组成变化、绘画技巧、造像工艺、审美变化以及特殊历史事件都对石窟产生过影响[11]。换言

之，石窟寺的营建是不同的人群文化与观念在自然山水的投射，并由山崖、林泉、窟龛、造像、壁画共同反映并见证，是当之无愧的"人与自然共同杰作"。

如果按照联合国教科文的定义，乡村聚落和石窟寺都是"有机进化的景观"（organically evolved landscape）[1]，其中乡村属于持续性景观（continuing landscape），其自身仍处于活态演进的历史序列中，这种演化既是当下发展也是历史见证，因而更加关注其动态变化的人地关系；石窟寺作为遗迹性景观（relict [or fossil] landscape），其最为关键的人与自然合作的"作品"是一个早已完成的结果，其作为遗产的价值凝固在这些时空演进中最终遗留下的物质与非物质载体。因此，石窟寺作为文化景观，不仅需要关注时空演进与人地关系，更需要从中挖掘出石窟寺价值所依赖的空间格局与关联要素，实现一种整体性和系统性的保护。

麦积山石窟作为丝绸之路沿线重要的石窟寺遗址，拥有1600多年的营建史，是陇东南地区宗教文化景观的典型案例（图1）。以下从时空历程、人地关系和构成要素等层面分析麦积山石窟作为文化景观的特质。

从时空历程上角度分析，麦积山石窟始建于十六国的后秦，兴盛于北魏明元帝和太武帝时期，西魏文帝时期再修崖阁并将乙弗皇后安葬于此，北周武帝年间秦州大都督李允信造七佛阁，隋文

---

1. 世界遗产文化景观分为3类：（1）由人类有意设计和建筑的景观。包括出于美学原因建造的园林和公园景观，它们经常（但并不总是）与宗教或其他纪念性建筑物或建筑群有联系。（2）有机进化的景观。反映了组成要素和形式上的进化过程。它产生于最初始的一种社会、经济、行政以及宗教需要，并通过与周围自然环境的相联系或相适应而发展到目前的形式。它又包括2种次类别：一是残遗物（或化石）景观，反映一种过去某段时间已经完结的进化过程，不管是突发的或是渐进的。它们之所以具有突出、普遍价值，还在于显著特点依然体现在实物上。二是持续性景观，它在与传统生活方式相联系的当代社会中仍起到积极作用，而且其自身进化过程仍在进行，同时又是展示历史演变发展的物证。（3）关联性文化景观。这类景观列入《世界遗产名录》，以与自然因素具有强烈的宗教、艺术或文化相联系为特征，而不以不突出或缺失的文化物证为特征。详见：The World Heritage Committee. *The Operational Guidelines for the Implementation of the World Heritage Convention(2023)*[EB/OL]. (2023-09-24)[2024-07-23].http://whc.unesco.org/en/guidelines.

图1 麦积山石窟

年代	事件	发展历程
后秦 384—417	麦积山石窟初凿	麦积山石窟始凿于东晋十六国的后秦时期(公元384—417年),后秦姚苌、姚兴父子在位时,十分崇信佛教。在麦积山"凿山而修,千坐万象、转崖为阁",主要以敞口大龛为主要形制,内有"凹"字形高坛基,正壁左右有小龛。洞窟题材大多为三世佛;从第74、78窟可以看出受西域造像风格影响的特点。
北魏 386—534	麦积山石窟的大发展期 魏太武帝灭佛(446年) 文成复法(452年) 孝文帝汉化政策	公元446年,魏太武帝灭佛,焚烧洞窟,毁坏造像,对其造成较大破坏,文成复法(452年)后不但修复了残存塑像,同时掀起了前所未有的开窟造像热潮。孝文帝进行服饰改制,推行汉化政策,对石窟艺术有一定影响。
西魏 535—556	新的开窟高潮	西魏大统元年(535年)再镌崖阁,开窟造像活动再掀高潮。公元540年,魏文帝皇后乙弗氏 被赐死后。"凿麦积崖为龛而葬",第43号洞窟当为归葬乙弗氏之"寂陵",附近的王子洞即为武都王元戊为其母坐禅今瘗之处。
北周 557—581	军政力量扶持佛教发展 武帝灭佛(574年)	北周崇佛之风大盛,麦积山石窟又一次出现了开窟造像的高潮。随即在武帝灭佛(574年)中石窟受到很大破坏,但由于地方官员的庇护,仍然保存了大批北周造像。
隋代 581—618	延续前代渐革风气 建高僧智仙舍利塔(601年)	隋代弘佛,隋代使麦积山的开窟造像之风仍在延续,仁寿元年隋文帝敕造舍利塔。
唐代 618—907	开凿低落时期 公元708年大地震 公元734年大地震	唐初麦积山的开凿造像之风仍在延续。唐开元二十二年(734年)大地震,使麦积山中部崖壁,窟群遂分为东崖和西崖两部分。其后,唐武宗"会昌法难"(841年—846年)对佛教进行严厉打击,麦积山的佛教洞窟无一幸遭存,仅在前代洞窟中保存有少量唐代的塑像和壁画,数量虽然不多,却很有代表性。
五代 907—979	重修塑像时期	五代时重妆重塑像为主。沿袭了唐代风格。
宋代 960—1127	大规模重塑期 重妆东西山崖塑像 朝廷敕赐"瑞应寺"	宋代是麦积山石窟的大规模重塑时期。北宋景祐二年(1035年),重妆东西崖塑像。大观元年(1107年)山顶产灵芝,敬献朝廷敕赐"瑞应寺",寺名沿用至今。
元明清 1271—1911	逐渐衰落时期	元代及以后的历史时期,麦积山石窟进入衰落期,元、明、清各代仅有少量的塑像维护活动。这一时期,麦积山窟外界鲜有人知,也使其避免了战乱、盗窃等人为破坏活动,得以完好保存至今。

表1 麦积山石窟的历史沿革

帝年间于七佛阁下泥塑摩崖大佛三尊,后经唐、五代、宋、元、明、清各代不断开凿修建,逐渐形成现在的麦积山石窟的空间格局(表1)。

从人地关系层面,麦积山石窟是不同历史时期人类与自然互动的结果,其生成与发展、定型与延续经历了几个重要时代。通过对麦积山历史的梳理,可以勾勒出一幅不同历史时期人类改造麦积山的动态轨迹(图2)。具体划分为以下四个阶段:

1. 原始期:在5世纪之前,麦积山山形奇绝,周围丘陵环绕,溪水潺潺,在深林茂草中以绝壁挺立的孤峰统领着整个区域景观,这一时期人类活动尚未完全介入,但为后续的人地互动提供了必需的自然环境,人地互动以禅僧群体为代表的山林禅修为主。

2. 形成期:到了5—8世纪,这座山由高僧选址,工匠斫石,在险峻崖壁上营建了观像坐禅的绝佳环境。灵山开窟的加持效应,也让它成为西魏皇室与北周贵族为瘗埋和祭祀供奉先人选择的场所。这一时期在上一阶段基础上,形成由僧众、士官阶层和平民阶层为主的顶礼膜拜的人地互动关系。

3. 成熟期:到8—19世纪,开窟风气逐渐衰落后,麦积山又经历了不断重塑与供养。并且吸引了文人登临访古,早期的名家诗歌与文学创作,不断吸引唐、宋、明、清文人的怀古吟咏与登临观景。麦积烟雨也成为知名的秦地人文景观。这一时期人地互动主要由地方信众和文人群体形成的登临观景与地名景观建构。

4. 转折期:20世纪之后,北朝造像成就经由研究者深度挖掘,不断临摹,在诸多中国石窟寺中被推为"东方雕塑馆",引发现代游客对其中雕塑艺术杰作的珍赏。而丝绸之路世界文化遗

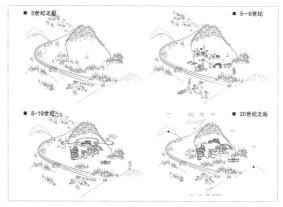

图2 麦积山石窟不同历史阶段的人地互动

产的评定，又带来了全球角度的重视和保护。这一时期人地互动可以概括为由保护单位、社会公众、遗产地居民等多个利益相关群体对麦积山的保护管理、艺术欣赏和活态利用等内容。

从构成要素来看，麦积山石窟文化景观的构成对象可以划分为三个层次。

第一层是自然景观环境与人文历史环境。自然景观环境主要包括体现麦积山石窟选址特征与地形地貌景观的重要的自然环境要素。包括麦积山石窟特殊的赋存山体与周边山形水系、构成"麦积烟雨"景观的区域气候与地形环境以及规划范围内的植被河流等要素，人文环境指在历史进程中与麦积山石窟的开凿、修葺、登临、观赏密切相关的人文景观要素，它们构成了文化景观所依托的地理基盘和文化特征。

第二层是石窟遗存与艺术作品。石窟遗存包括麦积山的全部洞窟遗存和建筑遗存；艺术作品包括221个洞窟及其雕塑、壁画、碑碣、建筑遗存在内的全部艺术载体，这些遗存是麦积山石窟历史、科学、艺术价值重要的物质载体。

第三层是形成上述空间格局的支撑体系和非物质要素。包括与麦积山石窟开凿、修葺、鉴赏密切相关的知识与技艺、代际延续的信仰习俗，还在持续的地方传统性相关活动以及受这些非物质要素影响所关联的人物群体等，这一构成是麦积山石窟"自然"与"文化"的连接桥梁与支撑体系。（图3）

三、文化景观视野下麦积山石窟价值分析

任何一个石窟寺在其兴建之初，从选址到洞窟的开凿，开窟者们除了考虑地理、地质环境和洞窟安全，无不充分地考虑了与周边环境的关系[12]。在这个基础上，我们需要认识到麦积山是一

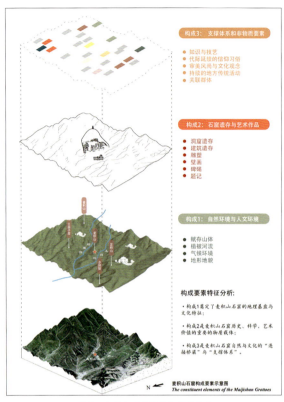

图3　麦积山石窟要素构成示意图

个广大的社会地理空间和综合的文化区域，而麦积山石窟的窟龛和艺术珍品只是构成这个整体的一小部分。通过对麦积山石窟构成要素的划分，可以初步提炼出麦积山石窟的历史、艺术、科学价值和景观价值（表2）。

根据上述的价值分析，笔者认为麦积山经由不同历史时期人类与自然互动建构完成的艺术珍品、整体空间格局与景观环境是其重要的价值组成部分，可以将其核心价值总结如下：

（一）麦积山石窟坐落于丝绸之路南来北往的交汇要点，是中国石窟遗产中西魏、北周石窟的代表窟群之一，也是中国佛教石窟群经云冈石窟汉化的进一步延续与发展。石窟选址的经营意趣、窟龛形制、造像风格、栈道营建等，不仅是对丝绸之路佛教艺术传播发展的重

表 2 麦积山石窟价值分析

价值类型		价值描述	价值载体	
历史价值		麦积山石窟真实反映了佛教中国化的过程，见证了河西陇东地区佛教自东向西的传播与发展。作为麦积山石窟是佛教遗址的重要类型，见证了不同时代的信仰变迁与社会风尚。	物质载体	壁画雕塑 窟龛建筑 建筑遗存 景观环境
			非物质载体	佛经教义
科学价值		麦积山现存的崖壁窟龛与栈道遗迹是古代石窟营造工程技术的典范。麦积山在离地面百米的悬崖上，完成了上下 14 层的开窟造像、崖阁建造与栈道工程。反映了古代关陇地区工匠高超的施工技艺。	物质载体	栈道遗迹 赋存山体 崖壁窟龛
			非物质载体	架栈技术
艺术价值		麦积山石窟是河西走廊及周边地区仅次于敦煌莫高窟的大型石窟，其中佛教造像数量众多，跨越时段长，题材广泛，是 5—13 世纪中国泥塑为代表的雕塑艺术杰作宝库。麦积山石窟造像是中国佛教艺术史在 5 世纪初至 6 世纪末艺术风格转变的突出代表。其中，"薄肉塑"技法结合了浅浮雕和壁画两种艺术形式，是麦积山石窟的独创技法。	物质载体	塑像 壁画
			非物质载体	造像技法 泥塑技艺
景观价值	自然面向	麦积山石窟的选址，既体现了 5—6 世纪盛行的禅修活动在石窟选址中依山傍水的共性特点，同时因地制宜，结合陇右地形地貌，选择了群山拱卫、奇峰耸立的麦积崖，反映了佛教传播过程中受中原文化影响形成的独特规划思想与审美意味。麦积山周围众山拱卫，树木丰美，溪水潺潺，形成了具有环境地势特征的独特地形小气候，自然景观与宗教文化互为衬托，融合一体。麦积山有典型的丹霞地质地貌，崖壁红色砂砾岩峭壁与山顶苍翠茂林共同构成具有美感的孤峰奇景，周围动、植物种类丰富，具备生物多样性特征。	物质载体	赋存山体 景观环境
			非物质载体	选址观念 佛经教义 时代信仰 禅修理念
	人文面向	自 5—13 世纪不断开凿、营建、重整的麦积山石窟，其错落的窟龛与山崖峭壁共同构成了景观杰作。作为古代秦州地区知名的景观遗迹，麦积山石窟不断有文人登临访古，早期的名家诗歌与文学创作不断吸引后世文人，逐渐将其塑造成为天水地区一处知名的人文史迹。	物质载体	题刻碑碣 赋存山体 景观环境
			非物质载体	诗歌词赋 文学传说 社会风尚 审美观念

注：本表中的价值阐述参考专著。《林泉积瑞：文化景观视野下的麦积山石窟价值阐释研究》[13]。

要表达，更是与天水地方的地形地貌、特殊气候、人文传统、造像技艺的完美结合，全面展现了佛教艺术中国化和世俗化的传播过程。

（二）麦积山石窟从 5 世纪以前的自然胜地，历经前期开凿、后期的修葺妆补以及明清

至近代的废弃与再发现，显示出麦积山作为重要地理要塞的文化传播功能，展现了在特定历史时期和生产力水平下，不同族群与阶层经营佛教圣地的文化想象与审美流变。由麦积山山崖、雕塑、壁画、建筑遗存与周围环境构成的

整体格局是人类与自然在长期持续互动中形成的杰作，是自然景观与宗教文化互为衬托，融合一体的典型例证，全景呈现了中古时期以来陇东南地区的信仰变迁与社会发展史。

系，在麦积山石窟保护与弘扬过程中同步构建加强相关社区文化。

总结地说，文化景观对麦积山石窟的价值阐释最大的启示在于将保护对象置于更宏大的时空背景中考量，使之重现自然与人文的互动关系，并借此拓宽石窟寺保护对象的认定，深化价值挖掘与阐释建构的多层次方向，使之符合新时期石窟寺整体保护、管理与展示利用的发展需要。

五、结论

文化景观同时关注自然环境与物质遗产的互动关系，关注时空演进的过程特征，因此逐渐从单一的遗产类型，转变为一种重视历时变化、时空演进与整体关系，兼顾过往遗存与人群未来发展的遗产研究的方法论[14]。

在文化景观方法论的应用下，拓展了欣赏与研究麦积山的时间维度和空间维度。对麦积山石窟的遗产构成认识不再局限于崖面窟龛以及窟龛内的雕塑与壁画，而是将保护目光扩大至与遗产密切相关的核心环境要素。这既包括与石窟直接相关的山体环境、地形地势、河流水系、村庄森林等自然环境要素，也包括构筑了麦积山人文历史的视点范围、登临游线与视觉景观等人文环境要素。与此同时，文化景观方法论在石窟寺价值阐释中的运用，尤其提出了一种整体保护与系统研究的宏观视野，加强了石窟本体结构与赋存崖面、栈道游线等功能上的联系性，更关注自然环境与遗产实存间的联系，还原了石窟寺作为一种中古佛教遗迹，在历史原境中对山林水体的选择与重视，进一步突出了自然景观中蕴含的宗教与文化意义。此外，通过文化景观的要素构成与特征分析，促使我们重新审视在麦积山石窟营造与保护过程中，物质和非物质文化遗产之间的互动与联

参考文献

[1] 唐晓峰. 文化转向与地理学 [J]. 读书，2005(6):8.
[2] 唐晓峰. 文化转向与地理学 [J]. 读书，2005(6):8.
[3] 俞孔坚. 景观的含义 [J]. 时代建筑，2002.
[4] 王恩涌，李贵才，黄石鼎. 文化地理 [M]. 南京：江苏教育出版社，1995.
[5] Sauer Carl O .*The morphology of landscape*[J]. University of California Publications in Geography, 1925, 2(1):19–53.
[6] Groth, P., Wilson, C. "1. The Polyphony of Cultural Landscape Study: An Introduction" [M]// Groth, P., Wilson, C. Everyday America: Cultural Landscape Studies after J. B. Jackson. Berkeley: University of California Press, 2003:1—22; 98—178.
[7] 陈瑞. 文化景观世界遗产突出普遍价值辨析 [J]. 故宫学刊，2015(2):14.
[8] 彭兆荣，秦红岭，郭旃，等. 笔谈：阐释与展示——文化遗产多重价值的时代建构与表达 [J]. 中国文化遗产，2023,(03):4—28.
[9] 王紫雯，叶青. 景观概念的拓展与跨学科景观研究的发展趋势 [J]. 自然辩证法通讯，2007,(03):90—95+112.
[10] 韩锋. 世界遗产文化景观及其国际新动向 [J]. 中国园林，2007,(11):18—21.
[11] (美) 巫鸿作. 空间的敦煌 走近莫高窟 [M]. 北京:生活·读书·新知三联书店，2022.01: 18.
[12] 杜晓帆著. 文化遗产价值论探微 [M]. 北京：知识产权出版社，2020.12: 191.
[13] 李天铭著. 林泉积瑞：文化景观视野下的麦积山石窟价值阐释研究 [M]. 北京：知识产权出版社，2023.09.
[14] 韩锋. 文化景观——填补自然和文化之间的空白 [J]. 中国园林，2010, 26(9): 7—11.

参考文献

史料文献：

[唐]李延寿：《北史》，北京：中华书局，1974 年

[宋]司马光著，[元]胡三省音注：《资治通鉴》，古籍出版社，1956 年

[宋]祝穆：《方舆胜览》，北京：中华书局，2003 年

专著：

天水麦积山文物保管所，麦积山艺术研究会.麦积山石窟资料汇编 [M]，1980

阎文儒主编.麦积山石窟 [M].甘肃：甘肃人民出版社，1983

建筑科学研究院建筑史编委会，刘敦桢主编：《中国古代建筑史》，中国建筑工业出版社，1984 年

天水麦积山石窟艺术研究所.石窟艺术 [M].陕西：陕西人民出版社，1990

国家文物局教育处.佛教石窟考古概要 [M].北京：文物出版社，1993

宿白.中国石窟寺研究 [M].北京：文物出版社，1996 年

张宝玺.甘肃石窟艺术壁画编 [M].甘肃：甘肃人民美术出版社，1997

花平宁编·中国古代壁画精华丛书·甘肃天水麦积山石窟壁画 [M].重庆：重庆出版社，2000

麦积山石窟志编撰委员会，张锦秀·麦积山石窟志 [M].甘肃：甘肃人民出版社，2002

圣辉法师.佛国麦积山.上海：上海辞书出版社，2003

唐冲.麦积山石窟线描集 [M].北京：人民美术出版社，2004

傅熹年.中国古代建筑十论 [M].上海：复旦大学出版社，2004

[日]名取洋之助.麦积山石窟 [M].日本：岩波书店

中国古代服饰研究 [M].沈从文编著.上海书店出版社，2005

郑炳林，魏文斌主编：《天水麦积山石窟研究文集》，兰州：甘肃文化出版社，2007

麦积山石窟艺术研究所·麦积山石窟研究 [M].北京：文物出版社，2010

费泳，著.中国佛教艺术中的佛衣样式研究 [M].中华书局，2012

花平宁、魏文斌.中国石窟艺术·麦积山 [M].江苏：江苏美术出版社，2013

星云大师总监修；如常主编·世界佛教美术图说大辞典 8 石窟 4 中文版 [M].台湾：佛光山宗委会，2013

中国美术全集编纂委员会·中国美术全集·雕塑篇 8·麦积山雕塑 [M].北京：人民美术出版社，2015

中国美术全集编纂委员会·中国美术全集·绘画编 17·麦积山等石窟壁画 [M].北京：人民美术出版社，2015

孙晓峰.天水麦积山第 127 窟研究 [M].甘肃：甘肃教育出版社，2016

何鸿.麦积山佛影 [M].北京：中国美术学院出版社，2018

麦积山石窟艺术研究所.麦积山石窟文物工作七十年 [M].北京：文物出版社，2018

敦煌研究院麦积山石窟研究所编，项一峰主编：《麦积山石窟内容总录》，文物出版社，2023 年

报纸、期刊论文：

[1] 辛其一.麦积山石窟及窟檐纪略 [J].文物参考资料，1951

[2] 西北麦积山石窟勘察工作完成 [J].科学通报，1953

[3] 西北文化部完成麦积山石窟勘察工作——发现具有民族风格和高度艺术价值的雕像和壁画 [J].文物参考资料，1953

[4] 中央文化部组织麦积山考察团赴甘肃天水麦积山调查 [J].文物参考资料，1953

[5] 麦积山考察团考察完毕返京 [J].文物参考资料，1953

[6] 吴作人.麦积山勘察团工作报告 [J].文物参考资料，1954

[7] 麦积山石窟内容总录 [J].文物参考资料，1954

[8] 麦积山勘察团工作日记（摘要）[J].文物参考资料，1954

[9] 冯国瑞.麦积山石窟大事年表 [J].文物参考资料，1954

[10] 麦积山石窟内容总录（二）[J].文物参考资料，1954

[11] 麦积山石窟内容总录（三）[J].文物参考资料，1954

[12] 麦积山石窟内容总录（四）[J].文物参考资料，1954

[13] 麦积山石窟内容总录（五）[J].文物参考资料，1954

[14] 何汉南.看"麦积山石窟"的意见 [J].文物参考资料，1956

[15] 史岩.麦积山石窟北朝雕塑的两大风格体系及其流布情况 [J].美术研究，1957

[16] 周石.从麦积山石窟谈古代雕塑的继承问题 [J].美术，1962

[17] 张学荣.麦积山石窟的新通洞窟 [J].文物，1972

[18] 李泽厚.神的世间风貌 [J].文物，1978

[19] 余尧.甘肃的石窟艺术 [J].西北大学报（社会科学版），1980

[20] 周鹏程.麦积山石窟测绘 [J].工程勘察，1981

[21] 初师宾.石窟外貌与石窟研究之关系——以麦积山石窟为例略谈石窟寺艺术断代的一种辅助方法 [J].西北师大学报（社会科学版），1983

[22] 张学荣.麦积山石窟的创建年代 [J].文物，1983

[23] 董玉祥.麦积山石窟的分期 [J].文物，1983

[24] 刘大有.从麦积山北宋摩崖题记看元祐两党的斗争 [J].社会科学，1983

[25] 丁梆.冯国瑞先生与其《麦积山石窟志》[J].天水师专学报，1985

[26] 李最雄.炳灵寺、麦积山和庆阳北石窟寺石窟风化研究 [J].文博，1985

[27] 顾森.交脚佛及有关问题 [J].敦煌研究，1985

[28] 秦佩珩.从《麦积山开除常住地粮碑》看明清之际边疆寺院庄园土地问题 [J].许昌学院学报，1985

[29] 刘珙.麦积山——丝路上的一颗明珠 [J].开发研究，1986

[30] 卢焕英.麦积山 [J].化石，1987

[31] 张学荣、何静珍.麦积山石窟创凿年代考 [J].天水师专学报，1988

[32] 黄文昆.麦积山的历史与石窟 [J].文物，1989

[33] 张怀礼，县瑄.麦积山石窟艺术中的古代体育 [J].体育文史，1989

[34] 周国信.麦积山石窟壁画、彩塑无机颜料的 X 射线衍射分析 [J].考古，1991

[35] 徐人伯.麦积山佛像雕塑艺术研究 [J].西北美术，1991

[36] 王锷.冯国瑞与麦积山石窟 [J].社科纵横，1992

[37] 卢秀文.麦积山石窟国内研究概述 [J].敦煌研究，1992

[38] 张锦秀.石窟维修史上的新篇章——麦积山石窟维修加固工程的回顾 [J].丝绸之路，1995

[39] 张锦秀.早期的两对姊妹龛——麦积山石窟第 74、78 龛和第 70、71 龛简介 [J].丝绸之路，1996

[40] 王进玉.敦煌、麦积山、炳灵寺石窟青金石颜料的研究 [J].考古，1996

[41] 张锦秀.麦积山石窟第 115 窟简介 [J].丝绸之路，1997

[42] 李之勤.天水麦积山石窟的题记、碑刻与宋金利州路、凤翔路间的分界线 [J].中国历史地理论丛，1997

[43] 魏文斌.七佛、七佛龛与七佛信仰 [J].丝绸之路，1997

[44] 项一峰.十六国北朝时期麦积山石窟三佛考析 [J].佛学研究，1997

[45] 白云明.麦积山石窟小资料 [J].中国邮政，1997

[46] 孙晓峰.麦积山收藏的两件宋代瓷器 [J].丝绸之路，1997

[47] 张锦秀.麦积山第 142 窟简介 [J].丝绸之路，1997

[48] 董广强.从麦积山石窟看北朝木构建筑的发展 [J].丝绸之路，1997

[49] 张学荣、何静珍.再论麦积山石窟的创建时代及最初开凿的洞窟——兼与张宝玺先生商榷 [J].敦煌研究，1997

[50] 项一峰.麦积山石窟内容总录（东崖部分）[J].敦煌学辑刊，1997

[51] 项一峰.麦积山石窟 10 号造像碑 [J].丝绸之路，1998

[52] 董广强.麦积山石窟崖阁建筑初探 [J].敦煌研究，1998

[53] 项一峰.《维摩诘经》与维摩诘经变——麦积山 127 窟维摩诘经变壁画

试探 [J]. 敦煌学辑刊 ,1998

[54] 侯顺子 , 徐叶彤 , 黄桂花 . 麦积山石窟雕塑与壁画中古兵器拾撷 [J]. 甘肃高师学报 ,1999

[55] 冯力 . 二十世纪中期麦积山石窟研究概观 [J]. 南通大学学报 (哲学社会科学版),1999

[56] 胡承祖 . 麦积山石窟雕塑艺术论略 [J]. 丝绸之路 ,1999

[57] 张锦秀 . 麦积山重点魏窟述评 [J]. 丝绸之路 ,1999

[58] 谢成 . 对麦积山 165 窟两尊菩萨像雕塑意的理解 [J]. 丝绸之路 ,1999

[59] 项一峰 . 麦积山石窟"六国共修"与历代赐名小考 [J]. 丝绸之路 ,1999

[60] 漆姝静 . 麦积山石窟北朝雕塑的风格 [J]. 丝绸之路 ,1999

[61] 董广强 . 麦积山石窟"碑洞"释疑 [J]. 丝绸之路 ,1999

[62] 孙琦 . 从麦积山看魏塑"秀骨清像"的文化底蕴 [J]. 东南文化 ,2000

[63] 谢成 . 通向自由和生命的天窗——解读麦积山 121 窟一组雕塑 [J]. 丝绸之路 ,2000

[64] 王旭 .《麦积山石窟渗水治理研究》通过验收 [N]. 中国文物报 ,2001-04-18

[65] 项一峰 . 麦积山石窟内容总录西崖东中下三区部分 [J]. 敦煌学辑刊 ,2001

[66] 刘俊琪 . 麦积山北魏壁画《睒子本生》图的内容和艺术特色 [J]. 天水行政学院学报 ,2001

[67] 董广强 . 宋代麦积山石窟发展的社会背景 [J]. 敦煌学辑刊 ,2001

[68] 张锦秀 . 麦积山隋代重点石窟述评 [J]. 丝绸之路 ,2001

[69] 麦积山石窟第 127 窟北魏壁画《睒子本生》(局部)[J]. 美术研究 ,2002

[70] 王宁宇 . 孝子变相·畋猎图·山水平远麦积山壁画《睒子本生》对中国早期山水画史的里程碑意义 [J]. 美术研究 ,2002

[71] 刘俊琪 . 麦积山北魏壁画《睒子本生》述评 [J]. 美术研究 ,2002

[72] 陈清香 . 麦积山 10 号造像碑的图像源流与宗教内涵 [C]// 兰州大学敦煌学研究所 , 麦积山石窟艺术研究所 . 麦积山石窟艺术文化论文集 (上)——2002 年麦积山石窟艺术与丝绸之路佛教文化国际学术研讨会论文集 . 中国文化大学 ,2002.

[73] 吴荭 , 魏文斌 . 甘肃中东部石窟早期经变及佛教故事题材的考察 [C]// 兰州大学敦煌学研究所 , 麦积山石窟艺术研究所 . 麦积山石窟艺术文化论文集 (下)——2002 年麦积山石窟艺术与丝绸之路佛教文化国际学术研讨会论文集 . 甘肃省文物考古研究所 ; 麦积山石窟艺术研究所 ,2002

[74] 张乃翥 , 韩玉玲 . 秦地石窟与中原佛教文化初探 [C]// 兰州大学敦煌学研究所 , 麦积山石窟艺术研究所 . 麦积山石窟艺术文化论文集 (下)——2002 年麦积山石窟艺术与丝绸之路佛教文化国际学术研讨会论文集 . 龙门石窟研究院 ,2002

[75] 郑炳林 , 沙武田 . 麦积山与乙弗后有关之洞窟 [C]// 兰州大学敦煌学研究所 , 麦积山石窟艺术研究所 . 麦积山石窟艺术文化论文集 (上)——2002 年麦积山石窟艺术与丝绸之路佛教文化国际学术研讨会论文集 . 兰州大学敦煌学研究所 ,2002

[76] 郑炳林 , 花平宁 . 麦积山石窟第 76 窟建窟时代考 [C]// 兰州大学敦煌学研究所 , 麦积山石窟艺术研究所 . 麦积山石窟艺术文化论文集 (上)——2002 年麦积山石窟艺术与丝绸之路佛教文化国际学术研讨会论文集 . 兰州大学敦煌学研究所 ; 麦积山石窟艺术研究所 ,2002

[77] 吴景欣 . 麦积山石窟第 48 窟四臂观音造像初探 [C]// 兰州大学敦煌学研究所 , 麦积山石窟艺术研究所 . 麦积山石窟艺术文化论文集 (上)——2002 年麦积山石窟艺术与丝绸之路佛教文化国际学术研讨会论文集 . 台北故宫博物院 ,2002

[78] 陈娟珠 . 由麦积山第 127 窟的经变浅谈台湾清凉艺展 [C]// 兰州大学敦煌学研究所 , 麦积山石窟艺术研究所 . 麦积山石窟艺术文化论文集 (上)——2002 年麦积山石窟艺术与丝绸之路佛教文化国际学术研讨会论文集 . 华梵大学 ,2002

[79] 项一峰 . 麦积山第 127 窟研究 [C]// 兰州大学敦煌学研究所 , 麦积山石窟艺术研究所 . 麦积山石窟艺术文化论文集 (上)——2002 年麦积山

石窟艺术与丝绸之路佛教文化国际学术研讨会论文集 . 麦积山石窟艺术研究所 ,2002

[80] 王纪月 . 麦积山 16 号造像碑内容风格辨析 [C]// 兰州大学敦煌学研究所 , 麦积山石窟艺术研究所 . 麦积山石窟艺术文化论文集 (上)——2002 年麦积山石窟艺术与丝绸之路佛教文化国际学术研讨会论文集 . 麦积山石窟艺术研究所 ,2002

[81] 林梅 . 麦积山万佛洞 (第 133 窟) 千佛碑探究 [C]// 兰州大学敦煌学研究所 , 麦积山石窟艺术研究所 . 麦积山石窟艺术文化论文集 (上)——2002 年麦积山石窟艺术与丝绸之路佛教文化国际学术研讨会论文集 . 麦积山石窟艺术研究所 ,2002

[82] 谢生保 , 陈玉英 . 麦积山第 133 窟石刻造像碑研究概述 [C]// 兰州大学敦煌学研究所 , 麦积山石窟艺术研究所 . 麦积山石窟艺术文化论文集 (上)——2002 年麦积山石窟艺术与丝绸之路佛教文化国际学术研讨会论文集 . 敦煌研究院 ; 麦积山石窟艺术研究所 ,2002

[83] 李西民 . 麦积山十六国时期的佛教造像 [C]// 兰州大学敦煌学研究所 , 麦积山石窟艺术研究所 . 麦积山石窟艺术文化论文集 (上)——2002 年麦积山石窟艺术与丝绸之路佛教文化国际学术研讨会论文集 . 麦积山石窟艺术研究所 ,2002

[84] 赖鹏举 . 麦积山石窟造像由"涅槃"到"卢舍那"的转变 [C]// 兰州大学敦煌学研究所 , 麦积山石窟艺术研究所 . 麦积山石窟艺术文化论文集 (上)——2002 年麦积山石窟艺术与丝绸之路佛教文化国际学术研讨会论文集 . 圆光佛学研究所 ,2002

[85] 胡同庆 , 宋琪 . 试探麦积山石窟摩崖龛的功能和意义 [C]// 兰州大学敦煌学研究所 , 麦积山石窟艺术研究所 . 麦积山石窟艺术文化论文集 (上)——2002 年麦积山石窟艺术与丝绸之路佛教文化国际学术研讨会论文集 . 敦煌研究院 ; 甘肃省博物馆 ,2002

[86] 董广强 . 麦积山石窟窟形二题 [C]// 兰州大学敦煌学研究所 , 麦积山石窟艺术研究所 . 麦积山石窟艺术文化论文集 (上)——2002 年麦积山石窟艺术与丝绸之路佛教文化国际学术研讨会论文集 . 麦积山石窟艺术研究所 ,2002

[87] 孙晓峰 . 谈麦积山石窟的北周窟龛 [C]// 兰州大学敦煌学研究所 , 麦积山石窟艺术研究所 . 麦积山石窟艺术文化论文集 (上)——2002 年麦积山石窟艺术与丝绸之路佛教文化国际学术研讨会论文集 . 麦积山石窟艺术研究所 ,2002

[88] 张锦秀 . 麦积山石窟的保护与研究 [C]// 兰州大学敦煌学研究所 , 麦积山石窟艺术研究所 . 麦积山石窟艺术文化论文集 (上)——2002 年麦积山石窟艺术与丝绸之路佛教文化国际学术研讨会论文集 . 麦积山石窟艺术研究所 ,2002

[89] 罗明 . 麦积山石窟保护及特殊病variety的治理研究 [C]// 兰州大学敦煌学研究所 , 麦积山石窟艺术研究所 . 麦积山石窟艺术文化论文集 (上)——2002 年麦积山石窟艺术与丝绸之路佛教文化国际学术研讨会论文集 . 天水师范学院 ,2002

[90] 屈涛 . 麦积山宋僧秀铁壁考 [C]// 兰州大学敦煌学研究所 , 麦积山石窟艺术研究所 . 麦积山石窟艺术文化论文集 (上)——2002 年麦积山石窟艺术与丝绸之路佛教文化国际学术研讨会论文集 . 麦积山石窟艺术研究所 ,2002

[91] 刘俊琪 . 麦积山第 4 窟北周飞天壁画浅议 [C]// 兰州大学敦煌学研究所 , 麦积山石窟艺术研究所 . 麦积山石窟艺术文化论文集 (上)——2002 年麦积山石窟艺术与丝绸之路佛教文化国际学术研讨会论文集 . 麦积山石窟艺术研究所 ,2002

[92] 刘惠萍 . 麦积山石窟伏羲女娲塑像试释 [C]// 兰州大学敦煌学研究所 , 麦积山石窟艺术研究所 . 麦积山石窟艺术文化论文集 (上)——2002 年麦积山石窟艺术与丝绸之路佛教文化国际学术研讨会论文集 . 中正大学 ,2002

[93] 夏朗云 , 王纪月 . 炳灵寺第 1 窟对麦积山西崖摩崖大立佛断代的启示 [C]// 甘肃省敦煌研究会 . 炳灵寺石窟学术研讨会论文集 .[出版者不

[94] 孙晓峰.麦积山石窟与炳灵寺北朝窟龛的异同 [C]// 甘肃省敦煌研究会.炳灵寺石窟学术研讨会论文集.[出版者不详],2003

[95] 李清凌.麦积山石窟的开凿背景与价值 [J].丝绸之路,2003

[96] 岳邦湖.麦积山石窟勘察惊险一幕 [J].丝绸之路,2003

[97] 项一峰.麦积山"碑洞"发现始末 [J].丝绸之路,2003

[98] 张锦秀.麦积山石窟维修加固回顾 [J].丝绸之路,2003

[99] 花平宁,马玉蕻.东方雕塑馆——麦积山石窟 [J].丝绸之路,2003

[100] 路志峻,李重申.麦积山石窟体育文化考析 [J].敦煌学辑刊,2003

[101] 魏文斌.麦积山石窟几个问题的思考和认识 [J].敦煌研究,2003

[102] 谢生保,陈玉英.麦积山石窟第133窟造像碑研究综述 [J].敦煌研究,2003

[103] 董广强.麦积山王子洞窟区调查简报 [J].敦煌研究,2003

[104] 董广强.麦积山北朝帐形窟洞浅议 [J].敦煌研究,2003

[105] 孙晓峰.麦积山北朝窟龛形制的演变规律 [J].敦煌研究,2003

[106] 项一峰.麦积山第43窟研究 [J].敦煌研究,2003

[107] 八木春生,何红岩,魏文斌.关于麦积山石窟第74、78窟的建造年代[J].敦煌研究,2003

[108] 东山健吾,官秀芳.麦积山石窟的创建与佛像的源流 [J].敦煌研究,2003

[109] 王锡臻.麦积山石窟北魏造像风格探析 [J].敦煌研究,2003

[110] 蒲小珊.麦积山第93窟考察 [J].敦煌学辑刊,2003

[111] 孙晓峰.麦积山石窟 155窟初探 [J].丝绸之路,2003

[112] 张晓君.麦积山第165号龛艺术风格评析 [J].丝绸之路,2003

[113] 杨晓东.麦积山4号窟"薄肉塑"飞天艺术赏析 [J].丝绸之路,2003

[114] 金维诺.麦积山的北朝造像 [J].雕塑,2004

[115] 李辉,罗明.北周时期麦积山石窟造像研究 [J].天水师范学院学报,2004

[116] 项一峰.麦积山北魏115窟造像壁画内容考释 [J].敦煌学辑刊,2004

[117] 沈浩.麦积山保护中的涂料问题 [J].中国涂料,2004

[118] 夏朗云.麦积山早期大龛下层焚烧痕迹的考察——麦积山后秦开窟新证 [J].敦煌研究,2004

[119] 柳太吉.麦积山石窟历年文物修复概述 [J].丝绸之路,2004

[120] 刘莉.浅议麦积山石窟北朝造像的审美趋向 [J].丝绸之路,2004

[121] 郑国穆.麦积山第76窟考察 [C]// 云冈石窟研究院.2005年云冈国际学术研讨会论文集(研究卷).麦积山石窟艺术研究所,2005

[122] 董广强.云冈和麦积山早期洞窟的简单比较 [C]// 云冈石窟研究院.2005年云冈国际学术研讨会论文集(研究卷).麦积山石窟艺术研究所,2005

[123] 孙晓峰.从云冈和麦积山看中国北方早期石窟寺的营建与分布 [C]// 云冈石窟研究院.2005年云冈国际学术研讨会论文集(研究卷).麦积山石窟艺术研究所,2005

[124] 郑国穆.麦积山第76窟考察 [J].敦煌学辑刊,2005

[125] 王锡臻.麦积山石窟北周造像风格刍议 [J].雕塑,2005

[126] 崔玲.麦积山与庾信铭文 [J].社科纵横,2005

[127] 郑炳林,沙武田.麦积山第127窟为乙弗皇后功德窟试论 [J].考古与文物,2006

[128] 魏文斌,蒲小珊.麦积山第11窟造像题材考释 [J].考古与文物,2006

[129] 陈玉英.麦积山第123窟"童男童女"造像解析 [J].敦煌学辑刊,2006

[130] 张萍.麦积山石窟馆藏浮雕造像砖 [J].收藏界,2007

[131] 杜斗城.麦积山早期三佛窟与姚兴的《通三世论》[J].敦煌学辑刊,2007

[132] 牛耕田.炳灵寺和麦积山石窟壁画色彩与造型艺术研究 [D].西北民族大学,2007.

[133] 董书兵.北朝时期麦积山雕塑造型研究 [D].中央美术学院,2007.

[134] 魏文斌.麦积山石窟初期洞窟三佛造像考释 [J].敦煌学辑刊,2008

[135] 魏文斌,白凡.麦积山石窟历次编号及新编窟龛的说明 [J].敦煌研究,2008

[136] 郑怡楠.天水麦积山第120窟开凿时代考 [J].天水师范学院学报,2009

[137] 王一潮,张慧,杨皓.麦积山第44窟西魏佛的"女相化"[J].装饰,2009

[138] 魏文斌.麦积山石窟初期洞窟调查与研究 [D].兰州大学,2009.

[139] 魏华.浅析麦积山石窟泥塑造像的时代美 [J].新西部(下半月),2009

[140] 董广强.对麦积山石窟第133窟碑刻入藏年代的再认识 [J].敦煌学辑刊,2009

[141] 项一峰,刘莉.麦积山石窟《法华经》变相及其弘法思想 [J].敦煌学辑刊,2009

[142] 董书兵.北朝时期麦积山雕塑造型研究 [J].雕塑,2010

[143] 王裕昌,魏文斌.麦积山早期洞窟的弥勒造像与信仰 [J].敦煌研究,2010

[144] 魏文斌,张铭.麦积山第100窟调查与年代研究 [J].中原文物,2011

[145] 吴亮.麦积山石窟北朝时期造像的服饰艺术特征 [D].西安美术学院,2011.

[146] 段一鸣.浅议麦积山石窟雕塑艺术 [D].中央美术学院,2011.

[147] 张增伟.中国石窟造像之美 [D].河北师范大学,2011.

[148] 魏海霞.天水麦积山石窟研究综述 [D].西北师范大学,2011.

[149] 达微佳.麦积山石窟北朝洞窟分期研究 [J].石窟寺研究,2011

[150] 八木春生,李梅.天水麦积山石窟编年论 [J].石窟寺研究,2011

[151] 闫佳梅.魏晋南北朝时期麦积山石窟造像艺术探究 [J].大众文艺,2012

[152] 王一如.北朝时期甘肃石窟造像艺术研究 [D].西北师范大学,2012.

[153] 孙晓峰.麦积山第127窟七佛图像研究 [J].敦煌学辑刊,2012

[154] 陈明.麦积山石窟乐伎图像研究 [D].陕西师范大学,2013.

[155] 董广强,魏文斌.陵墓与佛窟——麦积山第43窟洞窟形制若干问题研究 [C]// 上海大学美术学院美术考古工作坊课题组.十院校美术考古研究文集.天水麦积山石窟艺术研究所;兰州大学考古与博物馆学研究所,2013

[156] 孙永刚,屈涛.麦积山石窟第127号窟经变壁画中6世纪中国北方城市图像解读 [J].丝绸之路,2014

[157] 刘珣.北魏时期麦积山与青州龙兴寺佛像造型艺术表现的比较 [D].西安美术学院,2014.

[158] 李姗姗,高阳.浅析麦积山石窟中北朝时期的莲花图案 [J].艺术教育,2014

[159] 董广强.再议麦积山133窟石刻造像入藏年代问题 [J].天水师范学院学报,2014

[160] 董广强,魏文斌.陵墓与佛窟——麦积山第43窟洞窟形制若干问题研究 [J].敦煌学辑刊,2014

[161] 杨筱平,董忠,刘勍,等.麦积山石窟壁画修复方法初探 [J].天水师范学院学报,2014

[162] 孙晓峰.麦积山石窟第127窟研究 [D].兰州大学,2014

[163] 李梅.麦积山石窟第5窟西方净土变 [J].敦煌研究,2014

[164] 项一峰.麦积山舍利塔发掘造像探析 [J].石窟寺研究,2014

[165] 曹小玲,孙晓峰.麦积山石窟北朝时期世俗人物服饰调查与研究 [J].陕西历史博物馆刊,2014

[166] 王亦慧,陈平.北朝时期麦积山石窟雕像艺术研究 [J].雕塑,2015

[167] 王一潮.麦积山西魏石窟形制分析 [J].大众文艺,2015

[168] 项一峰.麦积山石窟第127窟造像壁画思想研究 [J].敦煌学辑刊,2015

[169] 曹小玲,孙晓峰.麦积山石窟第123窟造像服饰研究 [J].天水师范学院学报,2015

[170] 何洪珍.麦积山石窟北周造像特点及演变脉络——以第62窟为例 [J].天水师范学院学报,2015

[171] 魏文斌.麦积山石窟的分期、造像题材与佛教思想 [J].中国文化遗产,2016

[172] 张萍.隐藏在麦积山石窟佛像中的珍贵文物 [J].中国文化遗产,2016

[173] 马千.麦积山石窟文物保护历程回顾与思考 [J].中国文化遗产,2016

[174] 岳永强，王通玲，付文伟.麦积山石窟空鼓壁画的修复 [J].中国文化遗产，2016
[175] 张少昀.麦积山石窟保存现状调查 [J].丝绸之路，2016
[176] 臧全红.浅谈麦积山石窟力士造像的演变 [J].艺术品鉴，2016
[177] 丁薇.砂岩类文物的盐破坏及保护研究 [D].云南大学，2016.
[178] 韩燕.麦积山第四窟"薄肉塑"壁画的形象特征与表现特色 [J].芙蓉，2016
[179] 孙晓峰.麦积山石窟双窟研究 [J].敦煌学辑刊，2016
[180] 白秀玲.麦积山石窟北朝菩萨造像的宝冠 [J].中国民族博览，2016
[181] 杨雷，马李妮，杨晓飞.麦积山石窟北朝时期造像中服饰艺术特征浅析 [J].散文百家（新语文活页），2016
[182] 孙晓峰.麦积山石窟北朝晚期胡人图像及相关问题研究 [J].形象史学研究，2016
[183] 董广强，魏文斌.以洞窟开凿及壁画工艺论麦积山120窟开凿年代——麦积山127窟开凿年代研究系列论文之二 [J].石窟寺研究，2017
[184] 张铭.麦积山石窟第4窟研究 [D].兰州大学，2017.
[185] 张铭.两宋时期麦积山与南方佛教交流——从第43窟宋代题记谈起 [J].敦煌学辑刊，2017
[186] 龙忠.麦积山石窟133窟10号造像碑研究 [J].文博，2017
[187] 段一鸣.麦积山石窟泥塑造像源流——从犍陀罗谈起 [J].雕塑，2017
[188] 伏蓉.麦积山石窟隋唐造像服饰分析及特征初探 [J].甘肃教育，2017
[189] 李梅.跨文化视域下的北魏"褒衣博带式"佛衣设计意涵——以麦积山147窟主佛造像为例 [J].装饰，2017
[190] 高海燕.试析舍身饲虎本生与睒子本生图像的对应组合关系——兼论麦积山第127窟功德主 [J].敦煌研究，2017
[191] 李晓红.麦积山瑞应寺藏道场诸圣牌及牌竿小考 [J].丝绸之路，2017
[192] 张彩繁.麦积山石窟133窟10号造像碑讲解释析 [J].艺术品鉴，2017
[193] 夏朋云，白凡.麦积山石窟第4窟散花楼外檐下仿木构件再勘察——附新发现的散花楼中龛北周壁画建筑 [J].文物，2017
[194] 杨文博.麦积山石窟第78窟研究 [J].天水师范学院学报，2018
[195] 高原，卢娜，李沁.麦积山石窟冯国瑞窟编号考对 [J].敦煌研究，2018
[196] 杨文博.麦积山石窟第133窟10号造像碑降魔图辨识 [J].兰州文理学院学报（社会科学版），2018
[197] 孙晓峰.麦积山石窟西魏时期维摩诘图像研究 [J].丝绸之路研究集刊，2018
[198] 段一鸣.麦积山石窟北朝浮雕艺术浅析 [J].雕塑，2018
[199] 冯维伟.麦积山石窟第四窟研究综述 [J].兰州文理学院学报（社会科学版），2018
[200] 曹小玲，孙晓峰.麦积山石窟第23窟供养人图像年代蠡测 [J].敦煌研究，2018
[201] 董广强.以烘烤工艺论麦积山第78窟的开凿年代 [J].敦煌研究，2018
[202] 杨文博.麦积山石窟第133窟16号造像碑研究 [J].碑林论丛，2018
[203] 杨文博.麦积山石窟螺髻像研究 [J].西部考古，2019
[204] 贾漉.麦积山石窟的二佛并坐像研究 [J].文化创新比较研究，2019
[205] 麦积山北魏壁画 [J].音乐天地，2019
[206] 岳永强.麦积山石窟壁画病害现状调查及研究 [J].遗产与保护研究，2019
[207] 刘丹.麦积山石窟残损洞窟的复原研究 [D].兰州大学，2019.
[208] 周娇娇.麦积山石窟窟檐建筑的复原设计研究 [D].西安建筑科技大学，2019
[209] 张铭.麦积山石窟第133窟维摩变考 [J].中国美术，2020
[210] 张铭.麦积山石窟第12窟窟顶壁画释读 [J].敦煌研究，2020
[211] 王通玲.麦积山石窟北朝造像艺术的风格流变 [J].文物鉴定与鉴赏，2020
[212] 杨文博.麦积山石窟第142窟"猴头""象头"造像研究 [J].敦煌学辑刊，2020

[213] 陈悦新.麦积山石窟宋代佛像着衣类型 [J].文物，2021
[214] 袁莉，曾佩瑶.论麦积山石窟壁画飞天舞蹈造型的艺术特征 [J].青春岁月，2021
[215] 陈月莹，魏文斌.利用BIM技术对麦积山第44窟虚拟复原初探 [J].华夏考古，2021
[216] 惠露佳.麦积山石窟艺术的展览表达 [J].中国博物馆，2021
[217] 李翎.传统与时尚："罗睺罗授记"造像辨 [J].宗教学研究，2021
[218] 孙晓峰.关于北朝时期"乘象入胎"图像的辨析——以麦积山第133窟10号造像碑为例 [J].丝路文化研究，2021
[219] 张铭.墓葬结合，善恶有报——麦积山石窟第127窟净土世界的空间营造 [J].中国美术研究，2021
[220] 化雷，孙常吉.试论麦积山石窟塑像中沥粉堆金审美特征 [J].雕塑，2022
[221] 贺东鹏，武发思，胡军舰，等.麦积山石窟第127窟赋存环境特征及对壁画病害的影响 [J].西北大学学报（自然科学版），2022-04-015.
[222] 何暾.麦积山石窟早期洞窟中不同区域文化的融合——以第74、78窟为例 [J].文物鉴定与鉴赏，2022.09.034.
[223] 刘永增.再登麦积山"上七佛阁"断想 [J].美成在久，2022.03.02.
[224] 董广强.麦积山石窟第4窟开凿时间再考察：以现场勘察为中心 [J].美成在久，2022.03.03.
[225] 达微佳.试探麦积山石窟的开凿和现存最早石窟的年代 [J].美成在久，2022.03.06.
[226] 张铭.麦积山石窟第4窟博山炉供养壁画识读 [J].美成在久，2022.03.01.
[227] 王敏庆.麦积山石窟第62窟正壁菩萨形象探源 [J].美成在久，2022.03.04.
[228] 孙晓峰.芥子纳须弥：麦积山石窟的影塑造像 [J].美成在久，2022.03.05.
[229] 杨雅洁，王去非著《麦积山题记》整理与研究 [D].西北师范大学，2022
[230] 黄俊俊.李浴著《麦积山石窟调查报告》研究 [D].西北师范大学，2022
[231] 张扬.麦积山石窟第127窟《睒子本生》经变画相关细节的再讨论 [J].中国美术，2022
[232] 杨骁东.麦积山4号窟《车马出行图》中"转马"视觉现象解析 [J].美术，2022
[233] 徐博凯，文娟，孙满利，等.石窟壁画地仗修复用土选择研究——以麦积山石窟第80窟为例 [J].石窟与土遗址保护研究，2023
[234] 万佳.多模态话语分析视角下《麦积山石窟133窟》英译实践报告 [D].兰州大学，2023
[235] 张铭.麦积山第140窟天人佛塔图考析 [J].敦煌研究，2023
[236] 吕昂.麦积山石窟第142窟正壁上部悬塑考 [J].天津美术学院学报，2023
[237] 孙晓峰.麦积山石窟第126窟调查与研究 [J].丝绸之路研究集刊，2023
[238] 王涛.天水麦积山石窟始建年代考略 [J].文物鉴定与鉴赏，2023
[239] 白凡.麦积山石窟北朝时期文殊菩萨图像研究 [J].五台山研究，2024

结　语
Epilogue

行经千折水，
来看六朝山。

Sailing through thousands of twists and turns, we encountered Maijishan,
a mountain with a profound and legendary history.

图书在版编目（CIP）数据

行经千折水：丝绸之路上的麦积奇观 / 中国大运河
博物馆编 . -- 上海：上海书画出版社，2024.11.
ISBN 978-7-5479-3455-5

Ⅰ . K879.242

中国国家版本馆 CIP 数据核字第 2024DP7593 号

行经千折水：丝绸之路上的麦积奇观

中国大运河博物馆 编

责任编辑	黄坤峰　王聪荟
装帧设计	王　梓
技术编辑	顾　杰　吴　金

出版发行	上 海 世 纪 出 版 集 团 ⑤ 上海书画出版社
地址	上海市闵行区号景路159弄A座4楼
邮政编码	201101
网址	www.shshuhua.com
E-mail	shuhua@shshuhua.com
制版	上海雅昌艺术印刷有限公司
印刷	上海雅昌艺术印刷有限公司
经销	各地新华书店
开本	889×1194　1/16
印张	22.25
版次	2024年11月第1版　2024年11月第1次印刷

书号	ISBN 978-7-5479-3455-5
定价	368.00元

若有印刷、装订质量问题，请与承印厂联系